FROM THE CORE

A SPIRITUAL JOURNEY OF LOSING EVERYTHING AND FINDING HOPE

CORDILA JOCHIM

CORHOUSE

Published in the United States by CORHOUSE, Inc. / corhouse.com

From the Core: A Spiritual Journey of Losing Everything and Finding Hope / Cordila Jochim.

Library of Congress Control Number: 2019920376

ISBN:(Hardcover) 978-1-7343825-0-1

ISBN:(Paperback) 978-1-7343825-3-2

ISBN:(eBook) 978-1-7343825-6-3

All Scriptures quotations are taken from the Holy Bible, New International Version®, NIV®. Copyright © 1973, 1978, 1984, 2011 by Biblica, Inc. ™. Used by permission of Zondervan. All rights reserved worldwide. zondervan.com. The "NIV" and "New International Version" are trademarks registered in the United States Patent and Trademark Office by Biblica, Inc. ™

Cover design: Dissect Designs

Cover photography: Dana Kae Photography

Printed in the United States of America.

For those in need of God's powerful healing:
He is faithful. It will come.

CONTENTS

INTRODUCTION

I drove from Seattle to San Francisco on a whim. I was in the middle of my healing journey and frequently jumped in the car primarily in search of fun and adventure, but also because, after almost a decade bed bound, I could.

While in San Francisco, I got my haircut at Code Salon after my friend Yuliya told me I had "lady hair." I was not completely clear what that meant other than I was one hundred percent sure it wasn't a compliment. At the cashout, while paying for the haircut, I picked up a small postcard for a local gallery in Noe Valley and decided to find the obscure little gallery and pay it a visit on my way out of town.

The gallery was tucked inside the middle of a residential block in a sleepy section of San Francisco populated by moms with strollers. It was the suburbs in the city and a surprising place to find life-size nudes hanging in the windows. They were whimsical and childlike and completely compelling. I walked in to learn more.

"Those are the Chocolate, Strawberry and Vanilla people," a woman said, coming up from behind me as I stood in front of smaller versions of the nudes that hung in the window. Clever, I thought, one figure was black, one was white, and one had red hair. People as flavors, each tasty and delicious in their own right. In this world, I was a Strawberry person.

"I love your gallery," I said, turning toward her and in doing so, caught a glimpse of a back room filled with people. My eyes hung on them. "Who are they?" I asked, my eyes never leaving the back room.

"Those are the artists," she said, and explained the business model.

The gallery, Creativity Explored, worked with adult artists with developmental disabilities, and this studio was a place where they could gather to create, share, and celebrate their work. Antonio Benjamin, the artist of the nudes, saw people as flavors, she explained. From Antonio's perspective, all the "flavors" think differently. Chocolate people think one way. Vanilla people think another way. And Strawberry people yet another. I wondered if having red hair colored how I thought about the world or the experiences I'd had as a result. Probably, I conceded.

"Would you like to go back?" she asked, motioning to the room.

"Can I?" my answer evident in my question.

"Yes, go right ahead," she said and walked me to the mouth of the room and from there I ventured in on my own.

Immediately an artist was upon me, glued right to my side. He snowed me under a million data points about the gallery, his work, and the artists in the workshop and took it upon himself to personally warn me of a few who might want to sell me their art. Ignoring the irony, he took me straight to his and tried to get me to buy it. What he didn't know, and couldn't know, was that I wanted to own every piece in the entire gallery. I was enthralled.

"That's a dinosaur," he said as I held his painting of a T-Rex in my hand, admiring it. He put his finger on the paper and traced the outline of the dinosaur with his hand.

"Right here. Do you see it?" he asked.

"I do," I said, acknowledging the presence of one very large T-Rex.

"I love the colors you used," I said, and he beamed.

"What's his name?" I asked.

"Dinosaur," he said, marveling at his stroke of creative genius.

"Good one," I validated.

Suddenly, his eyes narrowed, and he looked at me intently. He seemed to have awakened to the idea that I, too, might have a name and asked suspiciously, "What's yours?"

I could see how non-meta named people could be cause for suspicion. Identity should be blatant. In a world where dinosaurs are named Dinosaur, people should be named Person. Or maybe Human. Our identity was clear, until we humans mucked it up by giving ourselves names outside of the obvious. We were dubious and shifty right from the start.

"Cor. My name's Cor," I said.

He jumped back what seemed like ten feet and then came rushing back toward me with velocity and intent. It startled me as much as saying my name appeared to have startled him.

"Are you serious?!" he shouted all the way up in my face, his intense curiosity breaking all personal space and social graces rules. The other artists looked up at the noise and commotion but just as quickly looked right back down, realizing the difference between distraction and alarm.

"Yes," I said, smiling and laughing and still a little apprehensive.

"That is the coolest thing ever," he said to me admiringly, his breath was quick and fierce and laced with awe and wonder. My value had somehow ten-x'ed in his eyes. I breathed out a little.

"You're from the core," he said, shaking his head and stepping back to take me in fully. "I've never met anyone from Middle-earth before."

A hot rush came over me and I choked up instantly. I stumbled through a goodbye to Dinosaur's artist-creator and the gallery attendant, fought my way out the door, got behind the wheel of my Jeep and gripped onto the leather steering wheel. I was completely overwhelmed. I slid my hands to nine and three and rested my forehead between them, trying to find ground.

Heat washed over me again. It was hot and liquid and unformed, just like me. He was right. I may have been in San Francisco in the middle of an adorable little gallery in Noe Valley, but the truth was I was from Middle-earth. Over the course of several years my entire life had burned to the ground. I had lost a relationship, a job, a home, a future, a life. I had lost my health, my wealth, two babies and my chance at motherhood. I had lost the notion of who I was and wasn't yet clear on who I would become. I was gripping onto the steering wheel for dear life because as far as possessions went, it was one of the last remaining things I owned.

"God, hold on to me," I whispered. It was a small but frequent prayer spoken in those moments life threatened to open up and pull me under.

After losing all that I thought contained my identity, it was still obvious in my name. My name is Cordila, but people call me Cor. I am a Strawberry person with hair the color of lava and God was remaking me from the core.

The core is the ground state, from which everything in your life emerges.

God is in the business of full-scale transformation. He covers brokenness with his enveloping grace in a way that is immediate and astounding. Then he drills down to the very core of a person and creates newness from the inside out. His finished work will be a life solid, built on rock. His outcome holds this promise. But the process of how God heals, restores, and transforms a life from the core, well, that's a story of its own.

When I was seven years old, I fell out of a two-story window, hit my head, and was never the same. I limped along for most of my life dealing with crippling neurological symptoms, hiding them from the world until my 30s when I was in a massive car accident and hit my head again. A few months after the accident, I was home and bed bound. I would stay that way for almost a decade. With my seven-year-old mind I had begun telling myself I was "fifty cents on the dollar." Less-than. Broken. Not worthy. Not enough. I spent forty years in the wilderness believing that lie and living it out until I was met by God who brought me out.

The irony is, I thought my problem was physical. I thought if there was a God, his work in my life was to heal me physically, which he did, but it turns out that was only a gateway to healing me spiritually. That I didn't see coming. I was not a woman of faith. I did not go looking for God as my answer. I went looking for healing. I went looking for life. I went looking for truth and encountered God.

It hasn't been easy, God's process of recovery. It has been the fight of my life and in many ways I'm still fighting. But I learned something new about myself along the way: I am whole. And that changed everything.

As I began to slowly recover, both physically and emotionally, and gingerly work my way back out into the world, I also began, very slowly, to tell my story. First to one new friend on a walk around Green Lake in Seattle. Then at a dinner party. Then on stage. And then more stages. And now, I'll shamelessly tell the story of how God resurrected my life to anyone, anywhere, at any time because people need to hear it. People need to hear they can heal. People need to hear they can become whole. When you're sick with the belief that you are unworthy, your entire life experience becomes about you and shoring up your perceived personal deficits. The first thing that changed in my life was a lifting of that veil and an understanding that **seeing oneself as less-than is practically universal.**

It has been the surprise of my life learning I am not the only one who has felt like fifty cents on the dollar. I know this because at the end of every speech, the line of those waiting to speak to me is full of people from all levels of status, wealth, background, and achievement, who, in one way or another, feel unworthy, too. Brain injury isn't the only path to perceived brokenness. It just happened to be mine.

It has been five years since God showed me my true identity, and I'm still learning to live in this new truth. As I've walked this journey of getting to know and understand myself better by getting to know and understand God, the war inside me has only gotten more intense. To downplay this reality is to diminish the very purpose of this book and violate my agreement with myself to tell it like it is. These last five years have been replete with lessons in contrasts: my fifty-cent beliefs and behaviors contrasted with God's view of me and the behaviors that grow out of knowing my true identity. God's process is one of continual refinement, a burning off of all the responses that aren't serving me. And refinement hurts. I am still very much in the battle. Still filthy from the dirt of having fallen. Still weary and wounded but somehow loving it all because I know my life is in God's hands. And I've learned to trust him with it.

If I know one thing in this life, it's that you can be made whole. God can, and will, do it. In this you can both take heart and be warned. Truthfully, God's restoration process isn't easy. It's full-on. It's whole and complete. He leaves nothing left undone. God is a transformationist, pure and simple. And reconstruction always comes with the noise and violence of demolition. That is how God resurrects a life. He starts from the inside and works his way out. He reclaims the person he originally made you to be and rebuilds everything from the core. And while I am often deafened by the sound of demolition and bewildered by what God is doing in my life, I have never felt more aligned.

The best thing about God is he's highly strategic. He has a plan. There is a process. We have a purpose. He's got it handled. Maybe it's because I'm German, or maybe it's because I lived in New York twice, but I needed God to come at me directly with process, efficiencies and intention or I would have burned his approach right to the ground. And that's exactly what he did. He came at me, full-frontal, and radically replaced who I believed myself to be with who he says I am. It all started with understanding my true identity. God gave me my identity. He gave it to me. And yet it has been the challenge of my life to see - let alone be - who God created me to be.

When I was young, my father called me Schatz. It's a German term of endearment (yes, Germans have those, too), and it means treasure. From a very young age, identity alignment was spoken over my life by my father, but who I am to my earthly father is first and foremost who I am to my Father in heaven. I am my Father's treasure, but for me the ability to see that came after forty years in a wilderness of fifty-cent thinking that almost cost me my life.

The moment I was finally able to see who I actually was, whole and complete and perfect in the eyes of God, it changed me fundamentally at the core of my being, and consequently everything in my life needed to change to accommodate this new truth. There is distance between healing and wholeness. There is distance between seeing your identity as whole and receiving it in your core. God takes a person to the epicenter of their being and reconciles a person to wholeness by putting himself at the very center of a life and rebuilds everything from there. **This is what it means to be rebuilt from the core.**

My coach Theresa once asked me, "How do you expect the story of what God is trying to teach about you who you are, and who he is, to be relevant to others who are also searching for healing and hope?" She had been my therapist, coach, spiritual mentor and guide, helping me navigate the tectonic movement that had occurred deep inside.

For the past five years, I have been on a journey of healing physically while healing spiritually and have felt, at times, swept away by a velocity beyond my control. God has a capacity and rigor I have a hard time staying in front of. Sitting in this Jeep, overcome with emotion, is just one example. But for the millionth time, I'm reminded perfection isn't a requirement by God to be used by him. Jesus surrounded himself with real individuals all the time. Raw and human, broken and broken open. I'm in good company because I am nothing if not mid-flow through a resurrected life. Still healing. Still transforming. But also deliciously and inexplicably whole. God specifically uses people like you and people like me. Broken people. Broken open people. Ultimately, that's what we're here to do: share our story. We're his message delivery system to share what he's done in our life and get the word out to a hurting and broken world. And we can only do that because we know what it's like.

So that's what I'm going to do. Share my story. It is not the cleaned-up, sanitized version because it's important to me that I start this journey with you from a place of truth, void of both fanfare or sanitation. The truth is: a life of fifty cent thinking is filled with so much pain from damaging choices it can almost, and sometimes quite actually, end a life. The weight and reality of this truth has changed me, I suspect much in the way your journey has changed you. If you're reading this, I suspect it's because you're under pressure. I suspect it's possible your life has burned to the ground. I suspect you are trying to find life after almost losing it and I suspect you have been to the edge of agony and there is still dirt under your nails from clawing at the ground. So, I don't want to shy away from hard conversations or the brutally honest truth of my life in the hopes that in my story, you will see yours.

I have never felt more clear about my purpose and less sure of my final destination, but I believe that if I share my story of how God met me, pulled me out of my mistaken identity, showed me who I am and how he intends to rebuild me from the core, you might also see that God is doing the same with you. In the end, I believe my personal story will fall away and the book will ultimately be a journey where the God of the universe will meet you where you are and will begin to heal and transform you in the same way he has been healing and transforming me. Your journey has a purpose. Nothing will be wasted; everything will be used.

I want us to be overcomers. The Bible is full of uncomfortable stories and the grimy, real-life battles of those who overcome. As long as life continues to stretch before us, there will be more battles to overcome. We have to fight these battles from a place of wholeness with God's power in our core or life will break us down and that is not an option. It's not an option for you to live broken. Not when I know you are whole. I believe God has more waiting for me and I believe God has more waiting for you.

My friend Dinah jokes that since I can't stop talking about all God has done in my life, I should become a preacher. The only sermon I have up my sleeve is what God did in my life and if I have to preach it to you from the front seat of this Jeep, that's exactly what I'll do.

I

RECKONING

1

BROKEN CANVAS

SEATTLE, 2013

AT SOME POINT, out of my sight, Kevin would have driven up the street and down the block. He would have pulled up to the far side of our one-way street, popping the right side of his truck up onto the low curb, as he often did, to make sure other cars were able to pass through easily while he was at my door. It was July so he would have been wearing brown shorts and low brown boots, uniform issue, and would have climbed into the back to find the canvas. He would have picked it up, probably with his hands given its size, and, holding it around eye level, he would have carried it the ten to twenty steps from the back of the truck to my front door and rang the bell. And when I didn't answer he would have, cool as ice, set that canvas down, and leaned it up against my front door. With the package successfully delivered, he would have gotten back into his truck and driven away, leaving me to open the door, retrieve the box, and notice the giant hole.

While I would spend years coming to terms with what was

and what wasn't in my relationship, I did have companionship during the eight years I was home and bed bound. However, that created problems of its own. My partner was my everything. My day would rise and set with his presence. Days, weeks, and sometimes months would go by when my partner would be the only person I would see. Him and Kevin.

Kevin, my UPS driver, brought packages in droves. I knew if I ordered something online, Kevin would have to drive up, would have to ring my bell, would have to say hello. He was a man of few words and on a tight schedule, so our conversations were never much more than that, but it was human connection and for a woman who had very little human connection, a hello was everything.

I would track my packages closely, so I would be by the door when Kevin rang. There was nothing worse than arriving downstairs and seeing a box by the door, but no Kevin. Worse yet when I could hear the unmistakable rumble of the UPS truck in the distance and open the door to see Kevin in the wind. Under my breath but out loud and out of principle, I would still say hello. Receiving a package from Kevin with a giant hole in it with no Kevin in sight, that was a double whammy.

Online shopping had become a way for me to connect with both the outside world and my inside world that had all but gone underground. My purchases were completely out of synch with the life I was living, which was entirely the point. An ice blue Gwen Stefani blazer; a cool Mackage coordinating outfit with sheer sleeves, sequined shoulders, frog buckles and cigarette pants; leather upon leather jackets, pants, skirts, dresses, all wholly useless to a woman who lived life in doors in the drizzly Seattle landscape. The purchases would transport me to a world in my mind where I was healthy and successful and in need of fancy outfits and work clothes. I lived in pajamas and, on a good day, yoga pants. I called my purchases "real people clothes" and I had a closet full of them.

Furnishing the home also fell to me, which I suppose was appropriate since I was the one in it all the time. We both came to our four-floor palace with the contents from small studios. Together we had two beds, two sofas, two dining tables and not much else. Turning our house into a home was a big task. And an expensive one. And now we would be adding new furniture once again. I was pregnant.

The painting had spoken to me instantly. It was large with layers of white, textured and tactile. Streaks of crimson and charcoal were spread intimately and unexpectedly throughout in a way that felt secret and made me flush. It was visceral and primal and forbidden and unapologetically human. In the middle of the painting was the phrase "I am made of shattered stars." I knew something about the shattering and the often-unexpected beauty released by the crushing. This picture was a reminder.

I had already decided the painting would live in the nursery and awaited its arrival. We had chosen a name for the baby mutually and quickly - Lumen. Choosing a name with light in its etymology and definition, like his name, carried meaning for him. To me, the name just felt right. And as for the painting, if Lumen's name meant light, I wanted the baby to sleep under stardust. But I was staring at a black hole.

On cop shows, when a bullet goes in one side and out the other, it's called a through-and-through. So it was with this work of art. A giant javelin had apparently gone through one side of the box and out the other. It was impossible for the canvas to escape damage. I hadn't seen Kevin when he dropped it off or I would have said something to him. Instead, I called the vendor who connected me to Kent, the artist, who immediately offered to paint another one and send it out that day.

My full and instant attachment to the canvas was impenetrable. For all the damage done, I only saw the beauty. I ran my hands along the wooden frame, sliding easily over each staple that held the canvas in place.

"I don't want another one," I said to Kent. "I'd like to keep this one. Could you help me fix it?"

Kent's wholehearted response felt like connective tissue, weaving us together.

"I think we can fix that!" Kent said conspiratorially. "I will pull a little kit together. Call me when you get it and I'll talk you through it." And just like that, I went from a woman with a broken canvas to a woman with an artist partner-in-crime.

From North Carolina, Kent would pull together items for a patch kit and send it to me in the mail as well as email a video of himself in his studio, patching a similar hole. Once the kit arrived and I was ready, I contacted him as instructed, and he walked me through patching the hole over the phone. The painting was created by him, damaged by life, and co-created by the original artist and a woman carrying a child. It was a special creation made more special by its re-creation through co-creation. Kent and his painting gave me a way to connect to my child by preparing a way for her to see herself. Chosen. Imperfect. Adored. Repairable. I began to wonder if I was repairable, too.

On my birthday, Kevin dropped off another canvas. Also from Kent. I had shared with Kent a little bit about my situation and he had heard my heartbreak and addressed it head-on. The surprise birthday painting he created was white and gold and full of shimmer and sparkle. In black pen and fervent writing, Kent had written the words "sick, disabled, lazy," stacking them on top of each other, one right after the other, dark and black in their shame. They were words I had heard from doctors and those who looked at my life from the outside, not understanding or comprehending how my seemingly in-tact physical exterior could belie a battle that raged within. With a deft stroke of the pen, he had slashed each word out.

Underneath the stack of words Kent had written the phrase "good in bed" and circled it. It was something a colleague had said about my ability to work while bed bound. "Cor can't ever come to the office but at least she's good in bed." I had laughed at the comment then, and laughed again to see it in writing.

I lost Lumen only a few weeks later and left my relationship a few months after that.

My father, a pilot, says it's rarely just one thing that brings down an airplane. When a life comes crashing down, the same holds true.

2

THE FALL AND THE FUNK

Minneapolis, 1979

I WAS seven years old when I fell out of the two-story window with my baby brother. My family lived in a Tudor house in Minneapolis and my father was renovating the attic to make more room for our family's new addition. There was a cut-out window above the steep attic stairs. It had a ledge wide enough for a vase or flower but that day, there was nothing there. I was holding my brother on my hip and had his bum resting on the window ledge so I could hear my mom better. She called up from the kitchen and asked us to come downstairs. Which we did. Just not in the way any of us had imagined. Somehow, my brother and I went over that window ledge and fell down onto the steep attic stairs below. I landed on my back, slamming the back of my head on the stairs. My brother landed on my stomach and, after a bounce, he waddled into the kitchen, totally fine.

My mom heard the thud and came racing around the corner quick enough to see me on my back. The sound had knocked the wind out of her, and the fall had knocked the wind out of me. I spent the night in the hospital because I had blood in my urine but was discharged in the morning and pronounced healthy and whole. Everyone called it a miracle.

We know so much more about brain injury now than we did then thanks, in large part, to football players and soldiers. I also think we are now more accustomed to the notion of advocating for ourselves as patients. But at the time, there was still a deep reverence for the white coat so when the doctor said I was fine, I had to be, even though I wasn't.

Neurological symptoms expressed themselves immediately. I would wake up in my new bedroom in the attic with a start and bolt straight up in bed from a dead sleep, nauseated to the point I thought I would vomit right there in my bed. I would race into my mom's room and she and I would race into the bathroom where we would sometimes stay for hours. In the throes of panic off the charts I would hover over the bowl, ready to vomit but never actually doing so. I became envious of my neighbor, Kim, who was robust and healthy and saw vomiting as funny. In the middle of the night when I would be wracked with symptoms and white-hot with panic, I would close my eyes tight and say, "I am Kim, I am Kim," assuming her identity as my own. That's how it started.

My parents took me to more doctors but the moment I named nausea as my predominant symptom I was shunted to the gastroenterologist, who found nothing wrong. In all the years that followed, and all the doctors I saw, not one made the connection between The Funk I was experiencing and The Fall I had sustained. Unable to find a diagnosis, the adults in the room decided I was jealous of my brother. At some point, after multiple visits to many doctors and countless nights of me running into my parents' room white-hot with panic and sure I would get sick, they tired. Or reached the end of their ropes. Or made the parental decision in favor of tough love. Or maybe they just needed sleep. Because one night I raced toward their room and encountered a closed door. I tried the handle. It wouldn't open. I don't know how long I cried on the other side of that door. Or if they, on their side, cried too. But I do remember the feeling of my heart in my chest. There was this caving-in sensation of feeling so alone. I resolved to do whatever it would take to never feel that way again.

In doctor's offices, on patient intake questionnaires, you are only asked to provide the surgeries you've undergone as evidence of trauma sustained. Since I had what was called a closed head injury, as opposed to an open head injury where your brains become visible or come out of your skull, my brain and the entire nervous system that runs out of the brain and enervates the entire body through the spinal cord, was never investigated. The doctor's circuit had run dry with no definitive outcome. With no explanation for my crippling symptoms, questions began to fly around our house and my brain:

"What's really wrong with you?"

"What kind of child needs this much attention?"

"What kind of person is jealous of her brother?"

"Why would you cause pain to the people who love you the most?"

Although I always knew something was wrong with me buried deep in my intuition, I got stuck on the questions. In the end, we all came to our own conclusions about the effects of The Fall - the doctors, my parents, and me - and they took root.

At seven, I was learning the value of money. My dad had given me a sleeve of minted coins: a silver dollar, a fifty-cent piece, a shiny quarter and a penny, all neatly tucked away and sealed for preservation. Although I couldn't reconcile the life-altering physical symptoms with the adult determination that it was all in my head, I did know something was very wrong with me. The malfunction, whether in my physicality or my character, was a flaw and that flaw diminished my value. To that end, I decided I was fifty cents on the dollar. Everyone else was a full dollar and, because I was broken, I was fifty cents. That was the real impact of The Fall and The Funk it created. It broke something in me physically. It broke something in me emotionally. And it broke something in my family, too. It created a schism between my perceived identity and the truth of who I was. It was a shared illusion.

"Cordila's crazy" had become a common refrain around my house. It was meant to be a joke, but of course, it really wasn't. Hypochondriac. Drama Queen. High maintenance. Just so sensitive (delivered with an eye roll). These were all words and phrases meant to correct what was seen as abhorrent behavior or at the very least call me out for being different. Sometimes all I had to do was show up on the scene to trigger such a response.

In Minneapolis, my mom's best friend was Ann, who provided adult mental health services for Hennepin County. Ann had a son a few years younger than my brother and I would head over after school to help her with him. But mostly I came for the videos. Ann loved her job and told fascinating stories about the different cultural communities that surrounded our very white neighborhood. She told me about the various traditions of Asian countries, the intricacies of castes in the Indian culture and, of course, we talked about the symptoms, effects, and impact of mental illness. It was the hallmark of her work and she would show me videos of those with mental illness. I was riveted.

Ann's home became a refuge. It smelled of her husband's sweet pipe tobacco and musty scholarly books. An Ansel Adams hung on the wall. I felt erudite and learned, soaked in culture and fascinated by Ann's appetite for curiosity. At Ann's I felt seen and accepted and useful and decidedly not crazy. Or at the very least I knew I was in a place where crazy was appreciated. Though I wasn't convinced that was the situation with me, I found the battle against the label, from doctors, my parents and even within myself, already exhausting and I secretly wondered how much longer it would be before I would inevitably end up on the crazy couch.

For my birthday one year, Ann got me a t-shirt that read "People with mental illness enrich our lives." Below it was a list of names: Vincent Van Gogh, Abraham Lincoln, Beethoven, Isaac Newton and more. I wore it until all the names disappeared. Thus began my protest against messages of unworthiness. A t-shirt. A personal billboard. An advertisement for crazy to distance the wearer from craziness. Crazy is as crazy does. Not those who wear the t-shirt.

In the years after The Fall, the nausea broadened from the middle of the night to the daytime, too. To call it nausea is to undersell the severity of the feeling. In an instant, an engulfing rush of near-vomiting would come out of nowhere. Internal alarms would fire off surges of adrenalin which would litter my skin with goosebumps and shoot electric pulses down my limbs and out each digit. Hot waves of urgency would flood through my spine and push me to the edge of terror and keep me there as wave after wave surged through my system, pulling me under into a sea of gasping breathlessness. It was all-encompassing and unrelenting and would rip me from wherever I was, and whatever I was doing, and call me to run. I would run to the toilet, or hang over a lined trash can, awaiting vomiting that never came. Minute after minute I would sit and wait, each second a lifetime in hell. And as quickly as it would arrive, it would dissipate, leaving me trembling, raw, rung out and terrified, knowing that at any moment, at any time, it could come again.

These waves of unrelenting nausea would strike during a field trip to the IMAX theater in grade school, during slumber parties, while sitting on a chairlift on the top of a ski hill - there wasn't a place in the world where I felt safe. But when visits to doctors ended in dismissiveness and dead ends, and in some cases anger and contempt, I learned to keep all of it to myself, driving the symptoms deeper into my body and pushing forward the fallacy that everything was cool and copacetic and above all, normal. I called it "nothing to see here." It was a shared family trait.

One day, while out doing errands with my dad during a college break, we came across the scene of an accident. A white sheet was draped over a body that lay still in the crosswalk.

"Dad, I think that person is dead," I said quietly as our car crept by, waved forward by the police officers who had arrived on scene.

"No. They're probably just trying to keep the dust off her," dad said. Nothing to see here. Keep moving along.

I was a corpse hiding in plain sight.

Physically, I developed excellent skills in coping, escaping, ignoring, and numbing out against any physical assault, internal or external. Emotionally, I became a response mechanism, defending myself against any form of dismissiveness or rejection and validating my right to exist by trying desperately to convince people to love and accept me who had demonstrated they were least likely to do so. I took all the blows head-on, perfecting the art of withstanding physical and emotional torture bordering on masochism, covering onslaughts with, "Nothing to see here, moving on." Living inside the hell trap of my body and the confines of my mind was tedious, terrifying, and unrelenting. And every day I had to make the decision to get up and go again. The tunnel vision of always trying to manage a world so completely out of my control kept my focus on the immediate step in front of me, not vision casting a life. And when all of it got too much to handle, I would run.

Once I hit adulthood there was no place I wouldn't run. Lost, sick, and longing for firm ground, I cycled through two cities in Germany as well as Connecticut, DC, Chicago, and San Diego before moving to Los Angeles.

That which drives us into the wilderness explodes in our life like a bomb. Wandering in the thereafter is to wander through life without sound. In action films when a bomb goes off, after the initial blast, the character subjected to the blast comes to, slowly gets up, looks around dazed and detached, and stumbles forward as if on autopilot, wandering, staring, surrounded by chaos but experientially alone. Outside of an overwhelming ringing in their ears, they are void of feeling, immune to pain, unfazed by mayhem, and without sound. In medical terms, downregulation is the process of reducing or suppressing a response to a stimulus, specifically a decrease in the number of receptors on a cell's surface. Wilderness-inducing blasts do that, they obliterate receptors to stimulus that would normally cause a response and render us numb. I'd like to say I was observant to my circumstances, those that were and those that were to come, but the truth is, after The Fall, I was without sound. By the time the SUV slammed into my car, I was already physically broken, emotionally numb, and too deaf from my own pain to be awake to anything at all.

THE DAY of The Accident was a typically beautiful day in Los Angeles. Crisp and blue. I had woken early, but yoga class wasn't for another two hours, so I threw myself into my Acura Integra and headed toward the beach. I was singing in the car with the window down when from the left - like a shot - came the grill of an SUV. It tagged the Acura's frame between the driver's door and the back seats, spinning me counterclockwise. The force propelled me, in a circular motion, into a fire hydrant, a cement planter and a lamp post before coming to rest, releasing hydrant water in full splendor. I had severed it from its base.

I came to, soaked, and like a pilot in an emergency ran through a systems checklist:

Could I see blood?

Could I taste blood?

Could I move?

Was I alive?

When I asked myself "was I alive?" I remember thinking "it wouldn't matter if I wasn't." It was completely without self-pity but in response to a new, crystal clear version of reality. Death lay on me like mist. I could feel it. Lean into it. Become it. If I was to place the palms of my hands together, pressing the soft flesh of the inner knuckles in one direction and then the other, such was the transition of life to death. As if by choice, the energy could be absorbed and resorbed, back and forth, without effort. So thin the veil between heaven and earth.

I exited the car and walked down the quiet street. The metal and grind had come to rest but the shock of the impact had made a critical shift in my awareness of the world. I walked down the center of the road in stilettos, looking up in profound admiration at the blue of the sky. Such beauty, I thought. Such stunning beauty.

The details of my mid-street rescue would be told to me later by the policeman who said, without filter as I sat in the back of the ambulance, "you should be dead." The police report, as dictated by pedestrian witnesses and evidence at the scene, would recount that two Hispanic landscapers, their flatbed truck filled with grass clippings and lawn mowers, partnered with an Australian motorcyclist to gather me gently out of the street. They then formed a gracious dignity circle around me and removed my clothing, saving me from the shock that was setting in from the force of the impact compounded by the fact that I had been hydranted and was soaking wet. The motorcyclist stripped off his shirt and put it over my nakedness. He was gone before my consciousness returned but his Qantas Henley shirt remained, covering my scratchless body. It would be the second time in my life I would endure excessive physical trauma without a scratch. And the second time my brain would rico-chet against my skull, altering my world with a deafening blow.

"You should be dead," the policeman said again as I sat in the back of the ambulance. I said nothing. If he had been looking for an appropriate emotional response, there wasn't one. I was without sound.

3

DOWNREGULATION

Los Angeles, 2000

I HAD MOVED to LA to pursue a career in acting. That's what I told everyone. In reality, I was on the run. My jumps from city to city were not accidental. My fifty-cent thinking brought all manner of mayhem into my life. The belief of unworthiness created a soft underbelly that would consistently draw strikes and when it did, I would leave. In the question of fight or flight, I was a runner.

A runner will follow the smallest notion of what might offer safety or direction. While I had no contact with Kim after childhood once my family moved away from Minnesota, I heard a rumor she had become an actor. When the pressure in Chicago got too great, and the strikes too many, having no vision for my own life, I moved with lightning speed to Los Angeles to pursue acting, having never set foot on stage.

Hollywood is in the business of leveraging identity intelligence. Using the constructs of myth and archetype, writers craft stories that allow people to relate to characters quickly and fully

by using universal stories embedded in the collective uncon-
scious. Every actor in Hollywood is slotted into an archetype to
facilitate ease of selection during the casting process. It's called
type casting.

When I arrived in LA, I did the things aspiring actors do: I
got headshots, I went to class, and I got an agent. The Actor's
Toolkit trifecta. Through the help of a friend, I landed an
appointment with an agent who sat me down to discuss headshots. She took one look at my red curly hair, freckles and blue
eyes and said, "You're the Girl Next Door."

For years I went out on audition after audition, selected off
of a photo where I represented a slice of Americana in a denim
shirt, a white tank top, blue jeans, and a megawatt smile. When I
walked through the door, however, the reality of me didn't
match the projected image of me and I was sent right back out
the door. I was horribly unsuccessful as the Girl Next Door.

During the days, I worked gigs that allowed for flexibility
while auditioning. I opened doors as a doorman at the L'Er-
mitage Hotel, rotated through temp jobs, and finally landed
more permanently in the admin pit of Donovan Consulting. I
was assigned to Bruce Shane, Donovan Consulting's attorney.

Bruce Shane had a walk that shook the earth and a presence
that shook all stereotypes of a lawyer. He was six-foot-huge and
equally robust. His wispy salt-and-pepper hair fell, open and
cascading, more than mid-way down his back. He fidgeted,
giggled, smoothed the edges of his mustache incessantly, leaned
way too far back in his chair, and spoke faster than his brain
could get words out of his mouth. I adored him.

He let me go to auditions and I let him boss me around.
Although I bossed him right back. If I had been getting mixed
signals about my identity all my life, I had been giving them,
too. I had been a cheerleader in high school and had long honed
a confident, assertive, and exuberant exterior to protect the
vulnerability within.

"Cord!" Bruce shouted, using a name that no one up to that point had ever called me. "Get in here!"

"I'm coming!" I overemphasized and pretended to storm in.

When the casting call for the Wilbur Weiner commercial came in, I told Bruce, who let me pack up and get to it.

Usually when a casting call would come in, it wouldn't contain much information. They would tell you where to show up and when, and provide a brief typecast of the role. That was pretty much it. But on the Wilbur Weiner call sheet, they also mentioned what to wear. I considered this a game-changer because I had been swinging and missing across the board. I was studying. I had coaches. I had headshots. I got calls. But I booked nothing. Being told what to wear was important because I thought if, out of all the variables, what I chose to wear to casting calls was the problem, at least my competition and I would be wearing essentially the same thing and I could eliminate that from the equation.

I showed up to the Wilbur Weiner audition as the quintessential Girl Next Door, as ordered. The room was filled with women who looked pretty much just like me: red curly hair, freckles, blue eyes and the same outfit. My heart seized with hope as I thought "YES! I am so booking this audition!"

I was booking the audition because I was tired of rejection. I was booking the audition because I needed to prove I was valuable and could be of use. After years of not booking auditions, I was booking the audition because I was booking the audition and there wasn't anything anyone could do to stop me. And on that adrenaline-induced tsunami, I walked into the casting office.

Casting offices are rigged for intimidation, of this I'm certain. There is often quite a distance between the entrance to the room and the casting director so when you walk in, you embark on crossing a great divide before you arrive at your destination. A camera is pointed in your direction and often several other people populate the room, some looking at you, many not, all prescriptively unimpressed. It's unnerving by design and nobody in the room that day was invested in changing up the balance of power.

When they called my name, fueled by a magnitude of paper confidence, I ripped open the casting door and was not one foot into the room before the Casting Director wrinkled his nose at me. My hand was still hot on that door handle when I, in a very ill-fated decision, said, "You wrinkled your nose at me," and slammed the door.

The room went dead silent.

"You wrinkled your nose at me," I said again, "and I'm not leaving here until you tell me why."

With velocity I approached the table, closing the divide in mere steps.

The table the Casting Director was sitting behind was filled with grilling instruments: a flipper, a skewer and other instruments generally found grillside. I picked a few things up trying to expend the energy exploding through my cells.

The silence popcorned with uneasy movements from the others in the room but the Casting Director leaned forward in mild amusement. I had challenged him, and he engaged.

"I don't believe that you can grill," he said baitingly.

"I can grill," I said, undaunted, hot-wired to prove. "I'm an actor. That's why you hire me. I can grill things. I grill." I picked up the poker again and thrust it through an imaginary steak and flipped it for effect. I'm grilling now. Watch me grill.

He leaned back in his chair, shook his head and crossed his arms, smiling broadly, adding fuel to the proverbial fire.

"Yeah, I don't buy it," he said, wrinkling his nose again. "And if I don't buy it, it's not happening," he said with finality.

"But I -" he cut me off.

"Answer me this: Have you ever been to a mini-league soccer game? Have you ever thrown a frisbee? Or flown a kite? Have you ever been to Disneyland? Is there anything about you that says Girl Next Door?"

I came officially unhinged; rejection set off all bells in me causing me to escalate. Still grilling the air, I shouted, "I AM the Girl Next Door! I AM the Girl Next Door!"

His face fell and turned white. The desperation and ferocity of my last statement sucked the air out of the room.

"No, you're not," he said quietly. "You're kind of a ball-buster."

In that moment, my orientation flew up to the ceiling and I had an out of body experience. From this perspective I saw myself anew. I was leaned over his table, my poker aimed at his larynx, shouting "I AM The Girl Next Door" right in his face. I immediately stopped, dropped everything, and felt my own face turn white.

"Listen," he said, leaning forward once again now that the threat to his life was gone. "If I need a female CEO to give a presentation in front of an all-male board, I'm hiring you. But you gotta know who you are and who you're not. And you are not the Girl Next Door."

I left the room and stepped out into the blinding California sun. Long after The Fall, I was still disassociated from my identity. My complete inability to see who I was and how I occurred to other people was astounding. It left me feeling naked and exposed. While I could believe I wasn't the Girl Next Door, that never felt like me, I didn't, however, feel like a Ball-Buster CEO either. In my mind, that required a woman less fragile, more confident, and more successful than me. I called my agent and told her I wouldn't be moving forward with acting. Ironically, that is precisely when my one and only acting credit came to me.

"Come back up to set. Your call time is 6 AM," my roommate's voice said on the voice mail I listened to right when I walked in the door.

My roommate was in the wardrobe department on a movie and had invited me to come to set earlier that day. It was shooting out in the valley and although I had hung up my desire for acting, it was still fun to be on set. I had gone up to visit her but spent the day dodging the cameras, on the edge of the action but remaining inconspicuous. The rules on movie sets were similar to casting offices. I knew my place and this time I was determined to stay in it. When the cast and crew were shooting inside the house used in the film, I sat quietly outside. When they were shooting outside, I went inside. Whenever an actor walked by, I shrank back, wanting to remove myself from view. I was inside sitting on a folding chair when Rock Rivera walked by. I recognized him as the notorious womanizer he played on a prime time soap opera that had swept pop-culture. I was sitting in between two crew members who were legitimately supposed to be on set when Rock walked straight up to me and blew my cover.

"Why do I feel like you've seen me naked?" he asked, staring straight at me and genuinely perplexed.

"I don't know," I said and stopped breathing, willing him to go away in my mind.

"Who are you?" he demanded.

"I'm wardrobe's roommate," I offered like it was my formal name, pressing my back all the way into the folding chair. He furrowed his brows, shook his head, and walked back out the door.

In the distance between my leaving set and my roommate's call, the actor set to portray the Rock's love interest in the movie backed out. Collectively, the production team and actors decided I was the perfect person to replace her for the role. The character of Crystal was the ex-girlfriend nobody liked and was dead set against Rock's character getting back together with. So when, while in town for a funeral where Crystal lived, Rock's character caves and reconnects with Crystal for a one-night stand, his friends issue a collective groan. I easily put the character of Crystal on, but when the director yelled cut, I never took her off. The story spoken over Crystal felt like the same one I believed was spoken over me. Our shared resonance of being despised, maligned, dismissed, devalued, and unchosen felt authentically representative of what I had been experiencing in life. I was Crystal. Crystal was me. I locked into that archetype and leaned in.

Shortly after wrapping the movie, Donovan Consulting shuttered its doors. The same day I received the news, a titan in the fashion world, and one of Donovan's clients, called my cell.

"Show up at the office Monday," the Titian said. "You work for me now."

If I had sunk like a stone in acting, I had a meteoric rise in fashion. Within a few short months of starting my job for the Titian, I shot from his Executive Assistant to the Director of International Licensing and as such, needed to spend a few days every month in New York. I was even given a parking spot with my name on it. Well, kind of. The President, who drove the hands-on running of the business, struggled with saying my name correctly. It pained me.

"Just call me Jack," I said one day as he butchered my name mercilessly.

"Ok," he said, his signature slow smile breaking across his face. "Jack what?"

"Just Jack," I said. From that moment on, and as my parking space reflected, whenever he'd call me name from down the hall he'd say, "JJ, get in here!"

The PR Director of the fashion company also had to be in New York frequently and schmoozed his way into a sweet deal with the Bryant Park Hotel bordering Bryant Park in Midtown Manhattan. I was the beneficiary by proxy. I had never stayed anywhere as chic. The hotel was nestled up against the back of the New York Public Library looking out over Bryant Park. The hotel was mid-block with a small, unassuming entrance. Inside, the potent lobby was lined in wall-to-wall red. I signed in and received the keys.

By contrast, the hotel room was all white save for the floor, the bed frame and a small, square table - all made of dark wood. My room was a corner unit, shaped like an L with windows lining two sides. The bedroom had windows on two sides and the bathroom, long and narrow, had one entire wall of windows. Opposite from the windows, running along the long wall, was a deep bathtub, a glass shower and a toilet. With all the lights out I put my bag on the bed, made my way through the bathroom to the toilet and sat down. Exhaling against the dark I noticed the distinct flare of a cigarette pulled by a deep drag on the roof of the building next door. Only then did I make out a man sitting on a bucket. Strangely, for the first time in any city I had visited or lived in, I didn't feel alone.

I was meeting a client for dinner that night but in the wake of what transpired, I've lost contact in my mind with whom. Shortly before the meeting I left my room, rode down in, and exited, the red elevator, and took the stairs down into the cellar below. It was dark and moody but without a moment's delay I was caught by an elegant Indian man dressed in black.

"Are you meeting someone?" he asked.

I nodded.

"Why don't you have a seat right here and I'll get you a drink. What am I fetching?" His inquiry was polite, and action packed.

I sent him bar-bound with my order as I sat down and adjusted myself in the seat, looking for a safe place to put my purse and smoothing the twist in my skirt that had puckered on entry. I wondered if I was dressed right for the occasion or potentially underdressed. My hair and makeup routine consisted of showering and leaving my curls wet to air-dry and applying mascara and lipgloss for emphasis and effect. I thought I looked California cool, but New York played on a whole different level. When I looked up, there, directly across from me but decidedly at my table and furiously typing away on his BlackBerry, was the most handsome Indian man I had ever seen. Possibly hearing my deep inhale, he looked up, too. Right as perplexity was mutually jamming our mental circuitry, the waiter returned with my drink.

"Here you go!" he said triumphantly and slid into the booth next to the man. "I'm Sanjay," he said holding out his hand and, nodding to the handsome man he said, "This is Krish."

I laughed. It was the smoothest maneuver I'd ever encountered.

Krish and I exchanged numbers and met up later that night for a midnight walk. It was electric. We had barely arrived back to the front of the hotel when he turned on me like a light, pressed himself into me, and me into the building, and kissed me with force. He smelled like vanilla, everything about him the right shade of dangerous.

"Let me up," he pressed.

I smiled and turned my head. I caught the doorman's eyes and he quickly looked away. Krish, oblivious, bit hungrily down on my neck.

"Krish this is embarrassing," I said, weakly pushing him away. "I need to go in."

He was on my mouth again, irresistibly.

"Let me up," he said, on repeat. "Don't you trust me?"

"I don't trust me," I said, grabbing him by the hand and leading him inside.

And I was right. We were not to be trusted.

We began a mercurial love affair. When the Titan fired all eight people in the licensing department at the fashion company and made me VP of Licensing, Krish broke up with me. He was a director. When he became president of the company he worked for, he asked me out again. Our coupling was fragile. Anyone who held us, knew.

THE TRAVEL and the tedium with Krish was beginning to wear me down, as was my meteoric ascent. I can't say I came by it honestly, which made it more difficult to metabolize. When the Titan emptied the licensing department, needing someone to fill the seats, he put me in and slid me all the way to the top. It was a huge job that I knew nothing about. In a scramble to learn, and desperate to succeed, I upped my time in New York to two weeks every month. On the weekends, I would come into the office in LA and try to catch up. When the Titan fired the other people he did not replace them. I was doing the work of all eight positions.

It was a Saturday when the PR Director came around the corner of my office. While it was Executive Row, it still was a warehouse, so the walls of our offices went only halfway to the ceiling allowing for conversations to be overheard that should have otherwise been out of earshot. It was because of these low walls that the PR Director heard me come in. When he rounded the corner from his office to mine, he found me staring straight ahead, unable to make eye contact or respond.

"You ok?" he asked slowly. I said nothing.

A short time later, still staring at the wall, I overheard him talking to the President.

"I'm concerned about JJ," he said.

"Oh yeah?" the President asked, through what sounded like his signature slow smile.

"Yeah. I feel like she's breaking," the PR Director said with decided seriousness, his concern audible.

"Good," the President responded. "We're trying to break her."

When I finally broke, upon giving my notice, the Titan got up out of his chair and physically chased me down the hall shouting, like in bad movie, "Do you know who I am? I'll make sure you're never successful again!"

The ending with Krish came equally catastrophically. During my last trip to New York we had gone to Tao for a party. He held my hand as we squeezed in past the rope but once inside, he let it go, and was immediately swallowed by the crushing crowd. I spent the next hour fighting my way to the back of the restaurant, presided over by a two-story gold Buddha statue, looking for him with every step. No sooner had I fought my way all the way to the front again, and was ten feet from the front door, when my cell phone rang.

"I'm at the back by the Buddha!" Krish shouted.

I pressed my cell phone to my ear, backing up to a large planter pot and bending forward, trying to hear him against the din of the crowd.

Before I could respond, an extremely tall man threw an elbow in my general direction and, at five-foot-seven, it connected with my face, the pain of which sent me backward, buckling my body where the back of my knees met the edge of the planter pot, and I fell inside. I was at a glamorous party in New York City inside of a pot. So, that was awesome.

I sat there for a while, resting inside the sheer exhaustion of ignoring the fact that Krish had purposely let go of my hand and lost himself in the crowd. It had not been the first time, nor was it the first time he would plant several women at the same party. I was not a singular sensation; I was just the one in the planter pot. I shimmied myself from left to right until I was able to free my elbows and press myself out, using the rim of the pot for leverage. I left the club.

Outside it was pouring rain. I stood in it until it frizzed, dampened and then soaked my hair. Once soaked, the rain streamed down and wet my face. I blinked mascara out of my eyes and waited for the ringing in my ears to disappear.

"Hey! Hey!" A man in a dark cotton jumpsuit came jogging

toward me carrying a red umbrella, waving at me and calling for my attention. I looked up dazed as he popped it open, stretched it out to me and unwrapped his face in a smile.

"Here," he offered. "I don't want you to get sick."

And with that, he ran back to his Waste Management truck, climbed into the cab and rumbled off. I stood under red cover and looked after him for a moment before turning and walking back to the hotel.

AFTER I LEFT the fashion company, I spun out into the current once again. As the holiday's advanced and I was looking for presents for my family, a friend named Chad was having something made of leather and I, lost at sea, tagged along.

Chad sat on the mattress of the leather craftsman's one room apartment while I rifled through scraps of leather on the floor, pot smoke tangling in my curls. I was entranced by the symphony of swatches: stingray, embossed crocodile, top grain leather, hair on calf, whip stitching, metallic splits. The leather passed through my hands with a silky heft. The smell was heady, the textures intoxicating. It was a new world and I was riveted. I took a piece in my fingers, pressing my thumb upwards into the suede side to test its flexibility. A rich and impenetrable scent, that reminded me of Ann's husband's sweet pipe tobacco, hung in the room as I picked out a cognac colored, embossed croc leather hide and handed it to the craftsman.

"This one," I said.

I designed, and the craftsman made, a beautiful leather portfolio for my brother to take on his modeling go-sees. As it sat in my house in the weeks before Christmas, it gathered a choir of admirers. After Christmas, still not clear on my next step forward, Mom said, "Why don't you do that leather thing?" And just like that, Thickskin was born, a name that, within it, carried the mark of the very thing I wanted to call forward.

Taking what I'd learned in the fashion industry, I booked an appointment and flew to New York to take a meeting with a showroom interested in the image of the Thickskin portfolio I had sent over. At the meeting, with pride and gusto, I removed the leather portfolio and placed it gently on the table. The Showroom Manager's face fell immediately.

"Is this it?" he asked.

"Yes," I said, beaming.

"This is all you brought," he said, obviously irritated. "I can't do anything with this. What is this?" He was already looking at his watch, which wasn't a good sign.

"But I thought -," I stammered.

"You need a *collezione*," he said emphatically, passionately, and with Italian flair. I laughed but swallowed it whole when I realized he wasn't joking.

"I cannot sell one item into a store. You'll need to provide more SKU's."

He pushed his chair back and got up. I immediately jumped to my feet, afraid of the inevitable ending that was quickly coming.

"You need to sell more things," he said.

"Like what?" I asked desperately.

"I don't know. Bags!" he said, turning away from the table. "Lots and lots of bags." He walked off and was immediately absorbed into another discussion.

I left that meeting and New York and began designing bags. Lots and lots of bags.

The year I left the fashion company and started Thickskin wasn't a good year. For anyone. In New York, two planes had slammed into the side of the Twin Towers in a provocative act of terror. Unsure of what to expect, or what might happen next, the Israeli government sent a group of young soldiers to guard the homes, schools and synagogues in the Hasidic Jewish neighborhood in which I lived. I woke up to soldiers guarding my front door. I fell into their group immediately.

The Israeli soldiers, thrown together in a foreign land, expressed, as a unit, something I had never seen before: a sense of belonging I only knew to call tribalism. Everyone appeared to be an accepted and valued member of the group. Parties, Shabbat dinners and weekend hangouts were all excuses for the group to get together. There was a resilience and ease and surprising levity woven into the spirit of every soldier I encountered, even in the face of the unthinkable.

"How do you do it?" I asked a soldier named Yoav one night after his brother received word of the death of a friend. "How do you live among the threat of terror every day?"

"We just do," he said. "Death will not take life from us. When something happens, when a bomb goes off, we call those we love to make sure they are ok. When they are not, we deal with it. Our community helps us grieve. And when they are ok, we hang up the phone, keep drinking our coffee and go about our day."

While the Israeli army protected my front door from terror, terror was alive inside my house. A year after the Towers fell, two men came into my home and slammed themselves into me to devastating effect. One at the beginning of the year, one at the end. I knew them both. I'd let them in. I did not make a sound. Nothing to see here. Moving on.

By the time the SUV drove into the side of my Acura Integra in late 2003, debris was already everywhere. My body was bruised and my ears were once again ringing. Though the rubble had been cleared away and it was no longer smoldering, New York was a city still scarred and yawning. Like a moth to a flame, a city gouged out at its very core seemed like the most obvious place to run.

4

A PLACE TO HIDE

New York, 2004

A WARM WIND swept through the room as I lay on top of the crisp, white sheets. I was back at the Bryant Park hotel with the lights off and the windows open. Musicals greatest hits sung by Broadway talent made their way up from the grassy knoll of Bryant Park and through my window, courtesy of my ringside seats to *Broadway in the Park*. Outside, New York was a collision of humanity, together alone. The movement of the city beat with a rhythm and pulse. Inside the Bryant Park Hotel, it was soft and still, at the center of the world but in the eye of the storm. Taken together, New York offered me a place to be quiet and still, but never alone. A friend called to see how I was doing after The Accident and check in on how the Thickskin handbag show was going.

"I'm moving to New York," I said, a stunning revelation to us both. The decision to move wasn't one I made consciously. I made it viscerally. Once again, I was on the run, exchanging mayhem for refuge.

I didn't own much in LA but sold most of it and took my mattress with me. I showed up in New York before my bed arrived and settled into an empty apartment, recreating what I felt at the Bryant Park. My apartment was a luxurious studio alcove in a renovated warehouse in the Meatpacking District on Horatio Street. I had four doormen: Big John, Jon, Jean and Richard. Outside, the meatpackers threw buckets of blood in the streets. Inside, it was plush, posh and pristine. Between the blood in the streets and the girls on the corner, my apartment in New York provided just the right amount of edge, enough to be entertaining but not scary. I felt at home. I felt safe. I leaned back into the arms of the city hoping to finally find peace.

The acute nausea that had been with me on and off since The Fall had become constant since The Accident. I made my way through New York, from bathroom to bathroom, on secrets and lies. Jumping out of a cab and running into a flower shop screaming I was pregnant and had morning sickness and needed a bathroom. I was directed to one instantly. Finding an abandoned massage room on the lower level of Equinox Gym and spending several hours there, trying to summon enough energy to stop the room from spinning so I could make it home. Ducking into a nail salon and opting for a chair massage because it was stationed by the bathroom. With single dollars I purchased time, minute by minute, until the waves of nausea subsided. It was an expensive afternoon. It never crossed my mind to leave New York or seek help from doctors. A year passed this way.

Thickskin was doing well and was under consideration by the Academy Awards® to be in their 2005 Official Oscar® Presenters Gift Bag, a perk given to those celebrities who presented Oscars to the winners. I had to fly to Los Angeles to present the line to the board. Simultaneously, I was also having to deal with a lawsuit from the accident. Despite all the evidence of fault, the insurance company of the person who hit me didn't want to pay. My lawyer liked to use me as a weapon and insisted I fly out to mediation to show I'd be a sympathetic witness, all while attending tradeshows and showing the Thickskin line. It was still a lot of coast to coast flying and on a flight back to New York, my body broke down.

"Don't move!" I screamed as I slid down onto the floor of the back of the town car. The world was spinning. I couldn't find ground.

"I have to, Cor. It's JFK. I can't stay parked here. They won't let me." Dominic was my driver. I barely knew him.

"Dominic, please don't move. Please," I said, my agony palpable.

My eyes were squeezed shut, my breath quick and urgent. I was trying not to vomit.

The plane ride had been awful. Shortly after takeoff I had felt an overwhelming wave of nausea and ran to the airplane bathroom where I shut myself in, taking the smallest of sips of the 7UP passed to me by the flight attendant, who continued to knock at the door as I drifted in and out of consciousness from sheer exhaustion. Thirty minutes before landing, her knocking became insistent.

It had been a grueling week. I had flown from New York to LA for the law suit. After several hours in mediation, I had won but the cost on me physically and emotionally was incalculable. The person who hit me never showed. From there I went to San Francisco for a trade show for Thickskin and then up to Seattle for my brother's wedding. The morning I left for New York I spoke to my mom on the phone while waiting to board. She'd spent decades on the rescuing end of my body breaking down.

"I don't feel great," I said. The nerves of the week had affected my stomach and I'd had diarrhea.

"Just close your eyes and get some sleep, girlie," she said. "I bet you'll feel better soon."

I wish that had been so.

"You have to return to your seat for landing," the flight attendant said insistently through the bathroom door. She was kind but firm.

I opened the door and slid down the aisle, my hand on each seat back, pulling me forward to my row. The flight attendant followed as a failsafe.

"Let me have a wheelchair meet you at the gate," she urged.

I had been here so many times before, in an airplane, on the subway, at a restaurant, in an interview, in a movie theater, drunk with nausea, incapacitated, miserable. This was nothing new. I shook my head vehemently, dropped into my seat and soon we were on the ground.

I thought in baby steps and rest stops. Baby steps off the plane, rest stop in the first bathroom. Baby steps down the escalator, rest stop on my suitcase at the bottom. Baby steps to the curb, rest stop behind the construction petition as I waited for Dominic. The humidity of the June evening was obscene. Tom Brokaw was curbside, too, and looked at me nervously, my white face not generating much confidence. I smiled weakly. He smiled back, tight and wary, and took a sideways step further away.

Dominic arrived and I slid into his car and onto the floor.

"I really have to move," Dominic said again, his voice soft and sorry. "I live close. Five minutes. I will take you to my house."

The spidey-sense of people everywhere should enact at the thought of an incapacitated woman being taken to the home of an unknown man. If mine did, I didn't care. I was putty, blind with exhaustion, and Dominic was promising rest. I nodded and Dominic drove off, slowly.

We arrived. I hadn't vomited by the sheer grace of God. Dominic opened the back door of his town car and slid me to himself by my ankles until he could grab hold of my wrists. Using my arms as leverage, he peeled me from the car. My head dangled between my shoulders. I was wrung out entirely. There were stairs leading up to the apartment. I can't tell you how we climbed them. I don't actually know.

I entered the apartment first, Dominic guiding me from behind. There were several adults watching TV and a young child at their feet, all sweating in the heat. The apartment offered no relief. They looked at me and Dominic, perplexed. Dominic said something to them in Spanish and continued to guide me through the living space to a small door in the corner. Opened at its widest, the door hit the frame of the single bed. I fell into it, Superman looking back at me from the print of the sheets. The cool from the small, window-unit AC washed over me as did relief to finally be laying still.

I split my time between the only bathroom in the apartment and Dominic's bed. Somewhere in the night, Dominic brought me Gatorade. Slowly, slowly, I found ground. The world grew still. My breathing expanded from quick, short and shallow to slow, methodical, restorative.

With Dominic squeezed in the corner of the room, next to the bed, on a small chair, I sat up and took sips of Gatorade, Dominic's hand on the curve of my upper back. Around 3 AM, I was sitting without assistance. Around 4 AM, I told Dominic I was ready to drive into the city, and we made our way out the front door again. This time I walked on my own power and remember going down the steps.

We drove into this city in silence. I rode in the front seat. The city was quiet and beautiful. The sidewalks were wet from sanitation's wash-down. Curls of steam escaped the pavement. The city lights caught slivers of their ascent. My breathing was easy.

My building was at the end of Horatio Street, cornered up to the West Side Highway, overlooking the Hudson River and New Jersey. I stepped out of the car and took my suitcase from Dominic; his eyes still brimming with worry. There was a new layer of intimacy between us. I met his gaze with confidence, gratitude, and a rinse of embarrassment. What a night.

I walked into the lobby of 110 Horatio, expecting a blast of cold air. There was none. Big John, the building's tall, large Indian doorman, looked wet and wild. His eyes were bloodshot and glassy, and his black hair clung to his forehead. He was a huge man. I worried what would happen if he fell.

"I need water," he said, in my general direction, with the flatness of a death knell. I wondered if he actually saw me or if he spoke out loud simply because he had felt the air change when I had come through the door. Desperation will cause all manner of interesting responses. This much I knew.

I ran toward him and grabbed his thick, hairless arm and pressed firmly. "I'll get you some," I said, leaving my luggage right where it was, and ran up three flights of stairs.

Just moments before, I was being rescued, and now I was rescuing. The heat was claiming victims everywhere. I opened up my apartment, grabbed an oversized blue glass, filled it with water, chased back down the stairs and shoved it into Big John's meaty hands. He grabbed it with both hands and drained it. I watched the liquid go down.

As Big John sat metabolizing the water, I walked over to my mailbox in the lobby, still listening for him in the background. Mail in hand, I walked back over to him and stopped in front of the lobby counter, looking at him intently.

"Feeling better?" I asked.

He nodded.

"Thank you," he said with gratitude.

I nodded.

"How was your trip?" he asked, coming around the counter to walk with me toward the elevator, his booming personality coming back online and life coming back to his eyes.

"Great," I answered with a big smile. Jazz hands. Cheerleader. As if my own torturous hours never happened.

The elevator opened and there was a millisecond pause. A chill of caution blew at the hairs on the back of my neck, standing them on end. Ignoring my intuition, I stepped forward. The doors closed. The elevator lurched upwards. And stuck.

It's unknown how hot it was in the elevator. Outside it was above one hundred degrees and humid. In the lobby, the AC was out. In the elevator, the air was stifling. I was in the elevator for forty-five minutes.

At some point during that time, firemen arrived to crack open the doors with the jaws-of-life. By the time they did, I had been drained of whatever life-force I had left. I crawled my way to my bed that night and lost time. Days passed. Then weeks. Jon, the building doorman who also owned a corner market, hung hot oatmeal on my door every morning. I crawled to it as well as in and out of the bathroom. It was not the first time in my life I had resorted to crawling. Once months passed, Mom arrived. She gave her number to all four doormen in case of emergencies. This was one.

There were, in essence, two kinds of people in my life: those who accepted my illness, whatever it was, and wanted to rescue me from it; and those who held me, and my illness, in contempt, wanting to personally punish me for it, often disbelieving I was sick at all. The audacity of ongoing illness and unrelenting symptoms made people angry, disgusted, dismissive and scared. I would be uninvited from parties, bullied, chastised for perceived weakness, called out as selfish, and left to stand alone and whispered about the rare times I was able to physically show up. If my illness imposed a sense of loneliness, the feedback from others offered a dose of devastation. My defense mechanisms were designed to save others from discomfort and me from ridicule and shame. For those who desired to rescue, my illness was galvanizing and catalytic. They would run at my symptoms like a firefighter to open flame and heroically spirit me through. They offered safety and rest to an inner world gone wild. They were a panacea to the desert of my soul. My mom had been my rescuer on countless occasions.

Needing to be rescued was not a new thing. Mom would fly to wherever I was in the world and stay until I would bounce. A bounce would always come. After any given physical crash, I would struggle for a while, but soon experience an uptick from non-functional to able to get by. After my extraction from the elevator, Mom flew to New York and stayed for a few weeks until I could walk to the corner. And then down the block. And then to the grocery store, where I stood numbly beside her as she shopped; shoving food in my fridge since it wouldn't go down my throat. Truthfully though, I could barely function. We never considered doctors. Not me. Not Mom. They never offered relief or solutions, so we had come to handle this kind of thing in-house.

After several weeks, Mom left, but a true bounce never really came. A few months after she left, I sublet my apartment and followed her home to Liberty Lake, Washington. I stayed there for a few months until I was stable - barely - and then went back to New York City. As one does.

When the Academy Awards Board had selected Thickskin as a participant in the 2005 Academy Awards Official Oscars Gift Bag I remember celebrating when I got the call. While it was an honor to have been selected, it came at a cost.

A coupon for a specially designed Thickskin piece was placed in the bag with the likes of other big name, high-ticket items. My selection was predicated on the quality of the Thickskin product and brand, but also on my willingness to create a custom item that would meet the same bar, with a similar price tag, as name brands like Rolex and Fendi. I designed a leather script book binder and, to up-level the product, wrapped it in stingray. The celebrity presenters would receive a certificate the night of the awards, and would have to personally call me to collect their item. To further ensure it went directly into their hands, it would be engraved with their name. This was the Academy's fail-safe to prevent regifting.

The payoff for such expensive marketing would be an unveiling of the Oscar Gift Bag in a segment on The Oprah Winfrey Show. Thereafter, brands would hope for a sighting of the celebrities in possession of the gifted item at the exact time of a paparazzi photograph, and follow-on placement in a magazine. The Holy Grail was if celebrities became clients and told all their friends. That's what I was hoping for anyway. Maybe for bigger brands, with big marketing budgets, the prestige of the placement was enough. For me, and Thickskin, this was a high-stakes gamble. I calculated the risks based on the numbers I received and decided it was a go.

Functioning under the assumption that celebrities, who were showered with free gifts with regularity, couldn't be bothered placing a personal call to retrieve more loot; the expected, and historical, gift recovery rate was 17-20%. When I decided to take the risk, that was a manageable cash expenditure. A year later, Thickskin had become, to my knowledge, the most redeemed gift in Oscar history, clocking a recovery rate of a jaw-dropping seventy percent. The thought never occurred to me to stop the blood loss. I should be so lucky. When straggler celebrities called to redeem their gift after the one year cut-off mark, I told them they wouldn't be receiving it. I'm fairly certain I wasn't nice.

The one-year mark of the Oscars coincided with the advent of the Manbag Competition. The men of the Oscars had responded in droves and that, coupled with my sales statistics, told me that my line resonated more with men than with women. Not surprisingly. During design, I gravitated toward acid-eaten leather; ballistic material found in bulletproof vests; unbreakable guitar straps to sling bags over shoulders; and heavy, gargoyle zipper pulls the size of an adult index finger. The Wall Street Journal, Variety and Cargo magazine all featured the Manbag and hailed Thickskin as one of the first lines to produce, and encourage, elegant bags for men. Through Krish, who was in the music industry, I had also developed a clientele of famous male musicians and made custom pieces for several of them.

Pulling together some of the male friends I had made in the fashion industry, I plotted a Manbag Competition event to take place at Takashimaya on Fifth Avenue, across from Bergdorf Goodman. It would be judged by DJs, designers, executives, and founders of respected fashion brands. Men from all over sent in their designs. The plan was that several of the designs would be produced and the winning design put up for sale at Takashimaya. The judges were selected. The designs came in. The bags were made. The event never happened. I was too weak to make it go.

When I returned from Liberty Lake, I had made two decisions: get a job and hire a trainer. I needed work and health to sustain life in New York. The grueling schedule of owning a company where everything rested on my shoulders was too much for my body. I reasoned that if I could outsource that pressure by getting a job, I was sure I'd be fine. I'd run into Sam Edelman while repairing some shoes. He and his wife, Libby, invited me to dinner and, during dinner, asked me to join them in Vegas for a shoe show. I knew there was no way my body would handle flying, or a shoe convention in Vegas, so I had to turn it down. In desperation, I called Krish who introduced me to Beyonce's handbag licensee. I met with them excitedly but they manufactured overseas and I would need to travel frequently, so that was also a no. The owner of a boutique I shopped at on Bleecker Street in the West Village asked me to be his buyer and merchandiser. It would require frequent buying trips to Paris, however, so, no. As quickly as unbelievable opportunities were surfacing, they were slipping through my fingers like water. It was all compounding heartbreak.

I began looking for more traditional work where I could stay put in New York, ignoring the fact that I could barely even make it through the interviews without running to the bathroom, or secretly lying down in break rooms.

While I wasn't one for church, Equinox at 97 Greenwich Avenue in New York's West Village was my sanctuary, and stretching, my meditative art form. On good days, when I could walk the few blocks to the gym, I would stretch my legs out in front of me, lock my knees, press my ankles together, bend forward, close my eyes, and hold. And hold. And hold. After the pain of the strain and the muscle spasms, holding the stretch became a place of rest. My breath would flow in and out, blending time. At some point, once fully surrendered to the release, it became easier to stay in than come out.

If nausea had been my predominant symptom since The Fall and The Accident, the bone crushing fatigue that had developed since the night of The Elevator was quickly becoming a close second. I thought maybe, if I hired a trainer, it might replenish my exhausted energy stores.

Hiring a trainer seemed like a great and rational idea. I had recovered to the point of walking the few blocks to the gym and was distressed at the amount of time I had spent in bed. I felt loose and tight in all the wrong places and working out seemed like a way to rectify both. Plus, I had spent a lifetime pushing my body through excruciating pain. Hiring a trainer was my version of, "Thank you sir, may I have another?"

Mike started the workouts slowly and predictably. He put me on the treadmill for a five-minute warm up and then sent me to the mat for lunges and deadlifts. Muscle memory from years of working out created a smooth flow when I squatted down, picked up the weight ball and stood up. What was uncommon was the keeling over. The first time I nearly passed out, it was funny. And then it wasn't so funny. And then it was discouraging to me and concerning to Mike, both for my personal well-being and his ability to attract and retain clients. But when I dropped in front of Jodie Foster, things got real. He gently insisted I get a doctor's note before he would train me again.

Passing out as a symptom was a game-changer. It fired off different alarm bells at doctor's offices and I was sent to a cardiologist for the very first time in my long and storied medical career. Dr. Brian Boatman, of New York Cardiology, put his stethoscope to my heart, listened for five seconds and said, "I know what's wrong with you." Five mother-loving seconds after a lifetime of, "There's nothing wrong with you. It's in your head."

"It's not in your head," Dr. Boatman said firmly, almost fiercely, when I told him my symptoms felt like I was having a panic attack.

I sat stunned and sheepish in the chair in his office.

"Never say that again," he said. "Ever. If what is wrong with you is what I think is wrong with you, you have been physically pretty miserable all of your life. Am I right?"

I nodded. My lip quivered and my eyes crested with tears. I held them back with all of my might.

"I know," he said. "But the minute you say the words panic attack, doctors will not take your physical symptoms seriously. And your symptoms deserve to be taken seriously. They need to be."

Dr. Boatman ordered three tests to confirm his prognosis: an echocardiogram, a Holter monitor test, and a tilt-table test. They would range from innocuous to hilarious to torturous, in that order.

The gel for the echocardiogram slid on quick and cold. The technician turned the screen toward me so I could see the chambers of my heart fill and compress, valves clicking open and closed. He checked and measured while I held and released my breath. The results were normal.

I was then strapped into the Holter monitor test for twenty-four hours. While it measured and recorded my ECG, I walked around the sweltering city wired up nefariously. It was August 2006 in New York City, and I was hot-wired in a post 9/11 world.

New York had a way of colliding people. If I had seen him coming, I would have turned and walked the other direction but he was, at once, upon me.

"Hey!" Krish said excitedly.

I had long since stepped out of being a member of Krish's harem and, though he had been helpful with Thickskin and the interview with Beyonce's people, I hadn't physically been around him in years. Purposely. Loving him had been a painful, dead end street.

"Hey," I said lightly and smiled tightly.

Krish moved in with both arms to cover my awkward silence, wrapping himself around my middle and pressing his lips against my neck. I love-hated how he smelled.

Jumping back, he looked at me quizzically, having encountered hardness beneath my shirt. With eyes wide open, he assessed the red and green wires that jutted out from both sides, visible beneath my billowy black tank top. Sweat ran down my chest.

"This is for - I've been having some problems with my heart lately," I said flatly, addressing the obvious.

He nodded slowly, empathetically, and after a moment said, "I totally get it. I've gotten a few grey hairs recently, too."

Apples-to-apples. Clearly.

I passed the Holter monitor test the same way I did that moment: an unexpected dip in heart rate momentarily but otherwise fine.

The tilt-table looked harmless. It was housed in an unusually small exam room. The lights were dimmed and a small, cozy lamp illuminated a little desk containing a notepad. Dolphin music played calmly in the background. The table itself was flat and padded, like a massage table, with planks for arms stretched out on either side. I laid back and rested my head comfortably on a pillow, while the technician strapped me down: legs, abdomen, chest, arms. It was easy and relaxing. The only warning of danger was the IV shunt installed to push adrenalin and fluids, should the effects of the test stop my heart.

The test would run for five to fifteen minutes as the technician established a baseline blood pressure and pulse. Once achieved, the table would be tilted upright for forty-five minutes, and blood pressure and pulse would be measured in response to standing. If no discernible malfunction was observed, adrenalin would be administered via IV to instigate a malfunction, if one existed. All-in-all, the test would run about two hours. Within four minutes of the initial tilting, I was white as a sheet, sweating profusely, gagging and struggling to not pass out. My blood pressure had plummeted from 106/56 to 79/47 and my pulse shot from 76bpm to 112bpm to keep up. There are simply no words for the horrifying effects the test unleashed throughout my entire system. It was a visceral explosion. The technician brought the table flat and immediately pumped a bolus of saline solution into the shunt, promising I would feel better soon. I didn't.

I rested for a while after the bolus drained. My blood pressure and pulse settled back to baseline and the test was conclusive and complete. The technician smiled and said I was free to go, and that the doctor would be following up with me soon. I smiled back, nothing to see here, walked out the door, hung a left instead of a right, walked down the hall, found an empty room and shut the door. I was unwell.

The room looked, and felt, like a morgue. It was wide and freezing, lined with metal gurneys, metal cabinets and medical supplies. I reached for the nearest gurney, climbed up onto it and laid down. I told no one I was there and stayed in that cold room until the building closed, my coping and survival defense mechanisms running at full tilt. At closing, I took a cab four blocks to a friend's apartment, collapsed on her couch and stayed for several days. When I finally made it the remaining few blocks home, by cab, I didn't leave my home for months. Again.

I received the tilt-table test on August 7th, 2006. I received the official results and diagnosis of dysautonomia, a deregulation of the autonomic nervous system, on August 8th, 2006. For nearly three decades I had been told there was nothing physically wrong with me. I had weathered crippling symptoms that affected nearly every organ in my body. I had summoned a herculean amount of internal fortitude at the advent of every day, knowing the journey that lay ahead. I had lived a life so profoundly isolated and alone because even when I was around people, my mental capacity was nearly totally consumed with running internal defense against a symphony of malfunctioning systems and alarms. I couldn't enjoy the moment. I couldn't concentrate on other people. I couldn't listen to conversations. I couldn't do anything outside of manage an overwhelming urge toward fight or flight. That piece of paper validated the physical trauma and the effect it had on my body. It did nothing to document the emotional devastation the instinct to continually prove, defend, validate and substantiate my very existence had on my sense of identity and self-worth. That would take another decade to adjust and, in the end, would require divine intervention.

There is no cure for dysautonomia. Dr. Boatman began cycling me through various medications. Nothing worked. Most made me feel worse. Remarkably, even after the diagnosis, I continued to believe I could make it in New York on my own. My functional capacity and bank account were near zero, but I pushed on in the illusion. I continued to interview and move through life in a way that cost me dearly on all fronts. In one of my last evenings in New York, I took myself to a Vince Vaughn movie and had walked several blocks through the crisp evening air, dizzy, determined and delusional. I lost equilibrium before the end of the movie and retreated to the theater stairwell, sat down against the cold, hard stairs, and pressed my cheek into the cool of the stairwell wall. I sat there for hours.

It was in that dark stairwell I encountered the moment where I knew, unequivocally, I could no longer go on. I could not move forward. I did not have it in me to take one more single, solitary step. I had used up all of my willpower, exhausted all of my energy, and spent all of my internal fortitude on the fight required to live my life. There was nothing more. I had no more to give. Nothing. In the battle for surviving life, I had to concede loss. And in the quietest of moments, in the dark of a stairwell, the light that had ignited my mind, body, and soul for so long, snuffed out.

It's amazing what I had onboarded over the years in an attempt to find healing. I'd duct taped garlic to my feet. I'd gone to a chiropractor my family called "Woo-Woo," who tapped my head while pushing on my arm to purge my body of parasites. If there had been a shaman who waved bones over my head and danced in circles, while stroking my cheeks with feathers, I would have said, "Yes, absolutely. Let's do it. I'm there." I say this by way of explanation for Paloma, for whom there is no explanation.

Paloma is a psychic, clairvoyant and music teacher. I acquired her from a friend, who used her to make sense of her business. I used her to make sense of my life. A few days before the movie theater stairwell, I had called Paloma from my bed, where I had been immobile for days. Frustrated and looking for celestial answers, I called Paloma. She picked up on the first ring.

"Your soul is longing for a peaceful place," Paloma announced. That was the thing about Paloma. She didn't ask any questions. She didn't fish for information. She'd just start talking.

"My apartment is quiet," I said, issuing my working life-mantra, "Never give up." Paloma lived in Seattle. My New York apartment was magical. How could she know? This was my place. This was my peace.

"By the water," Paloma said, by way of course-correction.

I looked out at the building across the way from my apartment on Horatio Street in New York City, the city of my soul.

"Oh, you mean like Brooklyn?" I asked.

It was a legitimate question. New York and Brooklyn are separated by water. As, I suppose, are New York and New Jersey, but I didn't mention Jersey. It didn't even cross my mind.

That moment in the stairwell was my undoing. I had been holding on, physically and emotionally, for so long, fighting with all of my might. When I let go, the floodgates that held my nervous system malfunction at bay opened, overwhelmed my circuitry and shut my body down. I paid $5,000 to get out of my lease, packed up my belongings and arranged for indefinite storage. Mike rented a car and drove me down to Philly, where an old college friend on a business trip performed an extraction and escorted me home. By the time I got home to my parent's house, I had lost the ability to walk, I often couldn't talk and sometimes my body would forget to breathe.

Only a few days after the stairwell, and shortly after my call with Paloma, my body was, indeed, in a peaceful place by water, my soul in tatters. I had come home to die.

As I lay in bed and looked past my feet out the sliding glass door to the lake just beyond the sand line, I thought about Paloma and wondered when peace for my soul might finally come.

5

THE LURE OF DEATH

Liberty Lake, Washington, 2006

My parents chose to move to Liberty Lake, Washington as a visual, mountainous panacea and refuge after many years in the flats of Minneapolis, Minnesota. Minneapolis was the hub to Northwest Airlines and my parents, the proverbial pilot/flight attendant coupling. Both my parents had left home early - my dad left Yakima, Washington for the Navy in his teens and my mom, her native country - and both took up careers in taking flight. Running was in our DNA. So when I returned home and moved back in with my parents, wings clipped, on December 12, 2006, everyone was uncomfortable.

We had one rough conversation in the living room, where my dad had looked at me quizzically and said, "This isn't normal." And it wasn't. None of it was. And if I had held onto an illusion that I would be fine, my parents held it, too. Especially my dad, for whom self-reliance was a foundational value. My returning to the nest in my mid-thirties was well outside of his plan and he was struggling to comprehend why it was in mine.

Our conversation was not graceful. I was home and sixteen again.

Days after I returned home, my parents left for Germany. My Omi was rapidly aging and when you roll the dice on who's most likely to go first, your child or your eighty-year-old mother, you don't think it's going to be your child. No one ever does.

They left and I was alone in the house. It was bare and cold and dark. And it was Christmas. While driving anywhere seemed ill-advised when I struggled with walking a straight line, I got in the car and, using surface roads, drove to the closest Christmas tree stand, bought a tree, brought it home and decorated it with white lights. I didn't have the energy for more decor. I took a picture of myself and the tree on a timer and sent it to my parents. Merry friggin' Christmas. They sent me back a one-liner: Good for you.

A few days later, my Granddad called from Seattle to say Merry Christmas.

"Wish you were here," he said.

"Me too," I replied, and meant it. The house was lonely and I was alone with my thoughts.

I don't know if I heard something in his voice, or if I simply had become accustomed to moving toward physical risk, or if I thought it would be my last Christmas, but on Christmas Day, 2006 I got back in the car and left Liberty Lake for Seattle, four and a half hours away.

Washington State has incredibly diverse landscape when cut crossways with a car. Outside of Spokane, near the Idaho border, where Liberty Lake sits, the pine trees are tall and green, the ground mostly brown and the seasons, well-rounded. In the middle of the state, things turn bitter and hard. In 2008, NASA prepared prototype robotic vehicles for future lunar travel and road-tested them in Moses Lake, Washington. Its sand dunes, windstorms and extreme temperatures are apparently the closest earthly resemblance to the landscape of the moon.

Just a few clicks down the road past Moses Lake, Interstate 90, formerly called the Sunset Highway, crosses the Columbia River at Vantage, Washington, and marks the official halfway point between Liberty Lake and Seattle. The town, population seventy, feels radically underpopulated given the majesty of the views. The Columbia River Gorge, up to 4,000 feet deep, stretches for over eighty miles and vaults skyward on both sides of the river. Navy fighter jets often twist sideways and scream through the canyon, for practice and pleasure, splattering the rock walls with their trademark roar. It is not the canyon's only acoustic use.

In 1980, Seattle-based neurosurgeon Vincent Bryan II, and his wife Carol, purchased a several-hundred-acre parcel of land high on the cliffs above the Columbia River over-looking the canyon. In the middle of nowhere, the closest town of Quincy and the nearest paved road some six miles away, the Bryans wanted to find land in Washington State with similar latitude to the great wine-growing regions of France, with the soils and microclimates needed to grow premium grapes. They found it near Vantage, Washington and shared it eagerly with friends. On a hike from the top of the cliffs to the bottom, Vince, who stayed behind, noticed he could hear every word the hiking group was saying, some 1,000 feet below. Within short order, the Bryans erected a small stage down near the river and put musician friends on it. Now, music from the Gorge Amphitheater, from the acoustic folk-rock of the Dave Matthews Band to EDM festivals featuring Kascade, also leaves sound on the canyon walls. And Cave B, a beautiful, small winery and boutique hotel, with cliff houses and yurts and a farm-to-table restaurant, cozies up right next to the Amphitheater, perched high above it.

At the halfway mark, I was doing ok, but growing fatigue was pushing a twist of nausea to the surface.

Another hour or so down the road, around Cle Elum, water from the sky begins to water the ground and, ever so slightly, green appears. First pastorally, and then grandly, and at the peak of Snoqualmie Pass you are enveloped in the majesty of the Cascade Mountain Range. Jagged peaks slash the sky on both sides and snow often blankets everything. The range itself is home to the mighty, and sometimes volcanically angry, Mts Rainier, St. Helens and Baker. Interstate-90 on this stretch is often closed for rock, snow or avalanche mishap. By the peak of Snoqualmie Pass, I was not ok.

For the next hour, I pulled off at nearly every exit to stave off nausea and hold back from vomiting in the car. By the time I hit Uncle Dan's and Aunt Nancy's house, I was engulfed in internal torture. I made a quick round of hellos through the living room, pulled along by Uncle Dan, and then retreated to the floor of their master bathroom and wrapped myself around the base of the toilet. After an hour, one of my uncles knocked to check on me. An hour after that, and after I'd crawled to the guest bedroom, my cousins Jax and Jason came and sat on the floor by the bed, keeping me company and telling me jokes.

For the next month, the entire time my parents were in Germany, I lived in that guest bedroom, leaving only for short visits to the hospital where Granddad had landed the day after Christmas and would die a month later. The day he died I had visited him at the hospital, nausea mounting to unmanageable. My last vision of him was when I chased back into his room to grab my purse, having forgotten it, and ran back out. I didn't say anything to him, the nausea was too severe. In his morphine haze he didn't notice. At least that's what I tell myself. I can't bear to think he was conscious as I moved in and quickly out, not even touching his leg, announcing my presence or speaking his name. It would be the last time I saw him alive.

My parents landed from Germany just in time to see him alive before he died. My dad would never see his father conscious again. The first time I saw my mom was when she knocked on the guest bedroom door later that night to see if I wanted to go back to the hospital. They had been at the hospital briefly and left Grandad's side with a promise to return in the morning. He died right after they left and they were going to go back and sit with his body.

I wanted desperately to go but the harsh demands of my own body kept me in bed. I heard the door close and smashed my head back against the pillow, tears pooling in my ears and running over, fists and teeth clenched, hatred of my broken body never more acute. As my Granddad passed from one life to the next, I wondered if it was possible to draft off of a departing soul.

On our drive back home to Liberty Lake, the Funk hit. Hard. I began to shake with convulsions.

"This is not normal," Dad near shouted. It was becoming his refrain.

We had stopped at the Costco gas station in Issaquah, just outside Seattle, having left my aunt and uncle's house a few minutes earlier. I hadn't felt well all morning and had sat in front of the fireplace, eating a banana and a bagel, hoping bland food would make it better. It didn't.

By Costco, I had the shakes.

The Funk was a progression of levels but always started with extreme nausea. Extreme. Then my face would turn white, with a gentle hue of green, and the muscles that held my skin to my skull would loose and droop, sagging my face, eyes, cheeks and chin. Then the tremors would start, rocking my body with rolling trembles. They would originate in my core and spread to my legs, which occasionally would jerk sharply. That was Level 1.

Mom was twisted around in the passenger seat, her soft

hand stroking my arm.

"Oh, girlie. What can I do? What can I do?"

Even with my dysautonomia diagnosis, doctors had struggled with symptom management. A few, shockingly, continued to perpetuate the notion of anxiety. One neurologist sent me to therapy, which I entertained briefly, and then quit.

When The Funk progressed to Level 2, I couldn't reply. The ability to speak would disappear and be replaced by deep moaning. Not from pain, but necessity. The rhythmic moaning pushed old breath out and called new breath in. The moaning helped me keep breathing. Without it, the breath would rest in my lungs on exhale and my system simply wouldn't desire to inhale. At all. Ever again. I could hear my mom and understand everything she was saying. I just couldn't reply.

My mom got out of the front seat, opened the rear passenger door of the SUV, and crawled into the back behind me, wrapping her whole body around me, her right arm holding my head back against her shoulder, her cheek pressed next to mine. She desperately wanted to repress what my body wanted to express. Truthfully, it felt awful.

My dad stood outside the open door, looking at the scene with wild eyes.

"This isn't normal!" he said again. There was an incredibly high value on what was perceived as normal in my family. Everything about my situation was out of bounds. And I had lost the ability to hide any of it. Although my mom had been exposed to my ever-growing list of symptoms and their increasing severity, it was all pretty new to my dad.

"I'm making a command decision," Dad said with finality, his Navy background kicking into gear. "We're going to the hospital."

It was meant to instill confidence. It didn't. It was, however, decisive action. And that, in itself, was good for something.

Someone called Aunt Nancy and Uncle Dan from the car

and let them know we were on our way to the hospital. We would most likely need to stay at their house again. At least my parents would. Who knew what my destination would be? That's the thing about illness. It tends to involve everyone.

We arrived at Overlake Hospital in Bellevue. My dad checked us into the ER as my mom took me to the bathroom in a wheelchair, where I hovered over the toilet as she stood and watched, back pressed to the wall. We were back in the same moment together, just like we had been when I was seven years old. I was nauseated, panicked and trembling. She stood staring at her child, caught in the throes of something she couldn't understand, wondering what in the world was going on. Thirty years had gone by, and a diagnosis had come, and we were still stuck in the same loop; trapped together in terror and confusion, while waves of nausea pulled me under and under and under and under. It left us both gasping for air.

Dr. Gregrey Bennett ordered a brain CT scan and I weathered the test without vomiting. As we all waited for the results of the scan, I had a hard time containing my excitement.

"A brain tumor would be so awesome!" I said to my dad from the gurney. I couldn't see my mom. She was behind me.

My dad's face was devoid of all color, except for the piercing blue of his eyes. Eyebrows, hair, lips - all white. He looked at me completely bewildered as I twisted toward him, extolling the virtues of a brain tumor. In the world of normal, we were no longer even on the planet.

"A brain tumor would be great!" I exclaimed again, conferring with myself. "At least then they would know how to fix it."

Dysautonomia is a syndrome with a precipitating origin. We knew I had dysautonomia, but finding the originating cause, like a brain tumor, would put me squarely on the map of a pathway to care. As for dysautonomia itself, some doctors didn't even know what it was, and I was so very tired of explaining something I was learning about myself. I was so very tired of being an anomaly. I was so very tired of being an outsider. A brain tumor had an inside crew and I wanted in.

My mind was already down the path, fantasizing surgery and chemotherapy and shaving my head bald, so when Dr. Bennett came back in with the news that there was no brain tumor, my composure disintegrated along with my hope. My sobbing surprised everyone. Dr. Bennett didn't interrupt, letting it pass through the entirety of my body and spirit.

"It's not a brain tumor?" I sobbed, with overwhelming disappointment.

"It's not," he said. His eyes were fixed on my face, not moving. He stayed with me, within the moment, as I processed the news.

"Then what is happening? Why am I so nauseous?" I asked, my voice shredded and raw. My eyes red from crying.

"I don't know," he said, looking at me directly, unwaveringly. "I don't know."

I thought about him the whole way home. In all the years I had paid visits to doctors, all of them had something to say, very little of it encouraging and none of it helpful. So the simplicity and honesty of Dr. Bennett's answer gave me hope of a different kind. When we got home I wrote him a note, thanking him. What he gave me that day was bigger than the discovery of a brain tumor. He transferred the power over my own body to me. I would never look to a doctor to heal me again. I would never assume they had all the answers. In the future, I would expect them to either function as my partner, helping me on my quest for health by listening to the wisdom I had as the steward of this body, or they'd be gone. I would fire many doctors after that day, starting with those who said it was "in my head."

Back at home at the lake, I kept deteriorating. I was constantly sheet white. My scalp was peeling, as was my back, as was the weight from my frame. I was in bed twenty-three out of twenty-four hours a day. In the event I got up, I had to drag my hand along the wall to keep oriented and steady. Breathing was mechanical. Swallowing, almost impossible. It was becoming routine to awaken and find my mom sitting on the edge of the bed, her hand hovering over my nose and mouth, to see if I was still breathing. I was continuing to see doctors and trying to find help, if only for my mom.

We found an alternative doctor in Spokane and Mom had taken me to get an IV infusion of power vitamins. She sat across from me on a padded stool. I sat in a big, burgundy lazy boy that swallowed me whole. It was not so much that chair was so big, but rather, at that point, I was so small. The doctor found a vein easily but within minutes of the fluid flowing, the world went dark and I heard Mom say, "I think we're losing her."

I would go down again in another vitamin IV attempt, this time ending up on the bathroom floor, Mom next to me, calling for help.

As I sat on the edge of the bed in the upstairs guest bedroom, I didn't even need to call for her, she was already on her way, sensing something was wrong. I had the blood pressure cuff around my right wrist, holding it up against my heart. The numbers came in: 70/40. The nausea was overwhelming, the edges of consciousness closing in. As Mom rounded the corner, I was sliding from the bedside to the floor.

"I'm going down," I said, against closed eyes.

"Get your legs up," Mom commanded, dragging my body closer to the closet doors, pulling one leg up after another.

My breathing slowed and became audible. In. Out. In. Out. The moaning started. Mom pushed down the legs of my yoga pants. She grabbed one exposed thin, white leg and with both hands squeezed hard, dragging her grasp from ankle to knee. She did the same thing on the other leg and then back again, trying to shove more blood to my head and heart.

"Help me, Mom!" I pleaded, the fear in my voice palpable.

It's extremely scary to stand at the edge of consciousness and stare it down. It's much easier if unconsciousness sneaks up on you and takes you from behind.

She grabbed me by my arms, which were flung above my head, and pulled me from the closet door. My legs fell from door to floor.

"Up!" she ordered, more to herself than me.

Wrapping my arms around her neck she got me standing, and then she put my body over her shoulder and carried me down the stairs. Once downstairs, she slid me off her shoulder and rested me against the coat closet, pulled two ski jackets off their hangers, wrapped me in one and herself in the other, threw me back over her shoulder and headed toward the door. She slid open the sliding glass door to the patio with one hand. It was winter and freezing outside. With me slung over her shoulder, she took quick and heavy steps down the sand to the dock. The ice that had accumulated along the shoreline snapped as she raced down the beach. Stepping surely on the dock, she walked down a few planks before slipping me off her shoulder and sitting me down near the dock's edge. With my yoga pants still bunched up around my thighs, she dragged one bare leg after the other and placed them in the icy water. In solidarity, she sat down beside me and thrust her legs in as well.

Life returned to my body quickly, with a hot rush. My cheeks flushed with circulation.

Mom and I said nothing for a long time. We sat at the edge of the dock, our legs calf deep in ice cold water, and looked out over the still, flat lake at the beauty of the overlapping blues: ice, open water, cold snow, blue green trees, navy mountains, crystal sky.

Later that evening, the three of us sat in the living room and talked about my future. My parents were still assuming I had one. I wasn't. They tossed around words like "assisted living facility" and I countered with "do not resuscitate" and "medical directive," assuming it would all be over soon.

I was crying when Mom came into my room later that evening. Like a child, she would come in every night and tuck me into bed. It didn't matter that I was pretty much always in it. The schedule and cadence of a nighttime tuck in gave her peace when she had none. She needed it and I wanted to give her a tuck in with a smile. I loathed crying in front of her.

"Oh, girlie," she said and sat down on the edge of the bed. I wiped my tears, but they kept coming.

"I don't want to die The Bag Lady, Mom," I cried quietly.

I had liquidated Thickskin, selling the last of the bags at, or below, cost. There were two people interested in buying the company but both wanted me to have continued participation. That wasn't possible. And if by some chance I were to ever recover, I'd need something to go back to. I kept the trademark and the name and got rid of everything else.

"I don't want to die The Bag Lady. I don't want that to be all I did with my life."

She grabbed me by the face with her large, cool hands.

"It won't be," she said with a hollow force, looking me straight in the eyes. "It won't be."

Neither of us could be sure but she held to hope for the both of us. But in her tears, I could see that even her hope was waning. In the dark of night, when all were in bed, I had begun asking death to take me. And soon.

Shortly thereafter, my parents went away for a few days to visit my brother. I had been vomiting and was terribly cold and drew a bath to get warm. I was so thin. I was so cold. The systems that operated my body had down-shifted into hibernation. I was growing a thin layer of hair on my stomach, like a pelt, to protect the vital organs behind my rib cage. I stripped naked and stepped into the tub, bent my body at the elbows, and slid into the water until it surrounded my neck. It felt so good. Warm. Welcoming. Enticing. Magnetic. I slipped under and the water lifted my hair, weightless, away from my head.

How many breaths would it take, I wondered?

The water was still around me, the cold of the tub pressed against my neck and spine. I guessed two. Three, tops. By then my lungs would be filled with water and maybe peace would finally come. That was the hope anyway. I looked at the break of the water above me, eyes burning but clear.

As I lay there, my mind played a fast-forward to the moment of discovery. I saw my dad tear into the bathroom, encountering my naked, bloated, stiff body; the water cold and stale around me. I saw him claw against the air toward the bathtub and yank me out by one arm, his only instinct to get me out of the place where I took my last breath. I felt his desire to stop and rewind time, so that this moment could come undone. I saw his face and felt the velocity of his desperation. It propelled me, in one movement, from laying to standing.

I stood violently in the tub, gasping for air, dripping, shivering and wet. I got out quickly and looked back at the water in sheer terror. What had I almost done? I caught a glimpse of myself in the mirror. My body was a shock of white, electrified with goosebumps. My eyes were wild and fully awake. My ribs stood out in the front and back. I could count every one.

Everything was falling away. Everything I had defined myself by: designer, entrepreneur, athlete, yogi, New Yorker, lover, friend - it was all falling away and there was nothing I could do to stop it. I was so far below the surface of the earth. There was no daylight, not even hope of some. But if the only thing I had command over were my actions, if my actions were to speak for who I was as a person, I didn't want suicide to be my last one. In a world that was seemingly folding in on itself, the only thing I knew was this: when faced with the decision to succumb to the lure of death or stand for life, I would stand. I desperately wanted to die but I knew now it would not be at my own hand. I had made the decision. That moment would not come again.

6

RIVERS IN THE WASTELAND

LIBERTY LAKE, 2008

THE SUN WAS warm on my skin, filling me from the inside. I had survived the winter and with the arrival of the sun, life had returned in many forms, including a little bit of my own. After a particularly hard rough patch, I had been unable to eat for ten days; sick, nauseated, unable to swallow. Weirdly, my mom and I noticed I felt better after the 10-day fast than before, and my blood pressure was better, too. I began experimenting with my diet, cutting out gluten and dairy and, in doing so, regained my ability to walk without assistance and get out of bed for extended periods of time. I walked down to the edge of the water and slipped my feet in up to my ankles. It was much warmer than the last time. Neal and Ava's dock was littered with kids and laughter and I wanted to get a closer look.

Neil and Ava Humphries lived next door to my parents and were the proud grandparents of six grandkids who were all, with the exception of the oldest, under nine: Sean, Michael, Kyle, Matthew, Hayden and Holly, whom I called Sister in solidarity against the all-male crew. The beach stretched outward from my parents' house in both directions. All the homes on the lake oriented their faces lakeside, which was littered with patios, docks, sun umbrellas, and water toys. Most of the properties were without fences, literal or figurative. On the lake, the waterline was the only divide.

Matthew had been on a trip when I had met, and bonded, with the other kids. He was now back and curious about his grandparent's new neighbor.

"You live here?" he asked, pointing to my parent's house. He was incredibly slight, his thick glasses possibly weighing more than his head. He looked at me skeptically on introduction.

"Yes," I said.

"With your parents?" he asked, his eyes narrowed.

"Yes," I said.

"Aren't you a little old for that?"

The openness in his face, and the fact that he was seven years old, padded the delivery. He was quizzical, not critical.

"Yes," I said simply. "I'm sick."

He took in the information, nodded once, and ran to join the other kids.

The winter had passed at the lake in grey days and cold skies. Mom didn't like to turn on lights, or much heat, so the house had been dark and cold as well. In the spring the ducks were born. Mama ducks would lead endless trails of ducklings around the perimeter of the lake, and all would dip their bills in the algae that hung in the shallow water of the shoreline.

Scoot stood out right away when he was yellow and new and fluffy. He was very small, smaller than his siblings, and often trailed behind them, wiggling his little body frantically, struggling to keep up. One day, they passed by and he wasn't with them. We all wondered where he went. By the time we saw Scoot again, he was light brown and totally alone. I felt him in my heart.

Creatures of nature are cruel to outcasts and underdogs. They are often abandoned, cast aside, or killed. Not by us though. The Laker Kids and I loved that little duck and named him Scoot. Every time he swam by, we would run after him. We considered it our job to cheer him on.

Scoot would arrive soundlessly, blending in with the brown sand at the water's edge until somebody would spot him and off we'd go, running alongside him at the shoreline as he swished through the water.

"Hey, little buddy," Hayden offered soothingly.

"Go Scoot!" Kyle shouted.

"We love you, Scoot!" Holly and I cheered, with our arms around each other, her small fist pumping in the air.

If The Laker Kids were gone and I was alone when Scoot swam by, I would walk out on the sand toward the water, where the soft under-churning turned damp and hard, and look at him. I wanted him to feel seen. When you're so alone, sometimes you just need someone to bear witness to your existence. In essence, that is what The Laker Kids did for me.

Every time The Laker Kids would come to visit their grandparents, they would run to my parent's door looking for me. Sometimes I would feel well enough to go outside and Mom and I would sit on our dock while the kids swam in between the Humphries dock and ours. It was always a frenzy of splashing, shouting, shoving off dock ends, faux drowning each other and laughing. A lot of laughing. Other times I wouldn't feel so great and we'd all stay inside. My mom had a big jar of Jelly Bellies and we'd make jelly bean concoctions by mashing together flavors in our mouths. Then we'd open our mouths and blow the scent on each other to see if we could guess the flavor mix. Other times I'd be really sick, unable to move or talk or play at all. I would hear Holly or Hayden come to the door and ask for me and my mom would say, "She's not feeling well today." All the Laker Kids knew what that meant. They would go away on soft bare feet carrying downcast hearts. Usually, even after being turned away, they would come around to the sliding door of my bedroom where the lights were out and I was lying still. I would see them push the flesh of their fists and foreheads against the glass, shielding their eyes from the sun as they looked to make out my frame. Sometimes I'd wave. Mostly I wouldn't.

As time wore on and the Thickskin inventory and opportunities to sell the company disappeared, I began looking for ways to get rid of the Oscar debt. Though my health appeared to have stabilized a little, I was still incredibly low-functioning and had the sense it could all turn on a dime. As the urgency of my situation retreated just a bit, the pressure of the $30,000 Thickskin debt began to way heavily. I didn't want to leave that to my parents on the event of my passing. I began putting out there that I was looking for work.

Someone in the neighborhood introduced me to a man named Brad, who owned his own recruiting agency. I met him at the Starbucks in Liberty Lake. Dad drove me there and sat in the car. Immediately, and despite my circumstances, Brad hired me to place reps and managers as a pharmaceutical and medical recruiter. I never worked harder. I lay in bed and churned calls without stopping. I tacked all my open opportunities to a cork board, moving candidates along like horses in a dead heat. Within a few months, I had placed two reps at $15,000 each for a total of $30,000. The specificity of the outcome to cover my need astounded me.

Working felt good and I began to get hungry for industry. A woman in Seattle who had grown a $5M infant/toddler fashion company on one novel concept - a baby leg warmer - heard about me. She flew from Seattle to Liberty Lake to meet with me on a day I was feeling particularly unwell. Unfazed, she lay on the floor of my parents living room carpet with me and laid out her vision for a new product line. She had landed Target as a client and was selling the same product into Target as she was to her boutique customers. The boutique customers weren't happy so she asked if I would launch a new product line for her, starting with brand development. I knew very little about brand development, outside of what I had done for my own line, but I married that with what I'd learned about myth and archetype while in Hollywood and dove headfirst into creating her new line. The project took me three months to launch at the end of which Nicole issued me a startling challenge: move to Seattle permanently to sit on the BabyLegs Executive Team.

After two years of living with my parents, and possessing the job-limiting inability to sit upright much of the time, I was terrified and pretty perplexed by the proposition. How could she even suggest something like that? I couldn't understand it. I didn't feel like I deserved the opportunity, as non-functional as I was, but was lured by the idea of productivity, a job, a life in a city and the chance at feeling somewhat independent again. Sensing my trepidation, Nicole suggested I come over to Seattle and meet her team. It was relatively lightweight solution, to a normal person. To me, it was a huge expenditure of energy and would require a barf bag. Again.

My parents drove me over the mountains the near five hours from Liberty Lake to Seattle where they waited as I interviewed with the rest of Nicole's team. I couldn't sit upright very long, so it wasn't much of a surprise when I got sick during the interview. Nicole, without missing a beat, drove me to her house and settled me in her bed. While her husband brought me 7Up, she cycled her staff through the room to continue the interview. Stunningly, I got the job.

I found a month-to-month furnished apartment on Craigslist and rented it sight unseen in a building that reminded me very much of New York. It was beautiful and industrial, with exposed brick, wood floors and an open ceiling. Not unexpectedly, there were several others in line ahead of me and the landlord let me know I was third in line. The chances I would get the unit, unlikely. I don't know why my mom pushed me to contact the landlord again or what caused him to Google me in the interim, but those two actions shot my application from third to first. I got the apartment and was on my way to Seattle.

I left everything I brought back with me from New York in storage, not knowing if I'd even be able to make it on my own one single, solitary day. As my parents drove me over the mountains, I lay in the backseat, clutching a barf bag, my functionality unbearably low. Upon arrival, my parents parked the car and, with one on each side of me, walked me to the apartment door. My mom and I had fuzed into a single unit, nested together. Separating from her felt impossible.

"Do you think you'll be okay?" Mom asked, and then immediately said, "You'll be ok," and smoothed a hand over my hair.

The moment the landlord opened the door I knew he was in trouble. I saw it in his face. I watched it happen. He fell in love instantly. His smile was wide, his frame was long, his skin was brown and to a woman who had been locked away under the earth's crust and hadn't kissed a man in years, he was air and I was gasping for it.

He would retell that moment from his side many times over. He would say when he opened the door and saw me, he heard a voice ask, "Will you love this woman?"

And he said, "Yes."

To him, I was love. To me, he was air. The combination left us breathless.

7

BUYING TIME

SEATTLE, 2008

OUR COLLISION WAS cataclysmic and instantaneous. My previous attempts at dating with a profound and severe illness were difficult at best, netting nothing long term. I had been out of practice for several years when the Landlord came along. His pursuit was potent and so intense and although I wanted what was on offer, I also had the extreme urge to take cover. He'd asked me out within days of my moving in, but my resistance was deep and thick.

"Do you want to go out for dinner tonight?" he asked, with a smile I was quickly finding irresistible.

"No," I said flatly, with both hands pressed against my heart's door.

"Tomorrow? Friday? Saturday? Sunday?!" His excitement was escalating. I needed to buy time to relieve the pressure.

"Fine. Sunday." I said, pushing it out as far as I could.

On Sunday he emailed me.

"We still on for tonight?"

In the space between his invitation and his email, the pressure to try and hide and suppress my symptoms again after they had busted open at the seams seemed impossible. I didn't know how to come clean upfront and had no practice in caring for myself or saying no.

"That's up to you," I said, in an attempt to walk the line of flirtation and toughness. He was my landlord after all. I had landed in Seattle and on Day One I was already in a bind.

"I'm in yoga pants and I'm not changing," I emailed. "I'm not cute and I may not even be nice."

When I put my foot down against physically going out, he solved it by suggesting dinner and a movie at the loft. When I said I had no DVD player, he showed up carrying one. When he arrived and I hadn't changed out of my yoga pants, he made me feel beautiful. During dinner I almost vomited up the takeout sushi. I didn't say anything and he never even noticed. By the time we had watched three movies laying on the couch, his body wrapped around mine, I was swimming in bone-crushing fatigue. By the time he went to kiss me goodnight, I was desperate to have him gone.

"I'm crushing on you hard," he wrote the next morning.

I responded by sending him the fourteen-page medical history document I provided every new doctor, and issued a strong warning not to get tangled with me.

"This isn't baggage," I said. "This is freight."

He back-peddled initially, saying he didn't think he could take all that on in a romantic relationship but thought I was cool and wanted to be friends. But the next day, when he arrived to take me for a walk, he kissed me half on the cheek, half on the mouth and within moments he was holding my hand. Our relationship moved forward but fundamentally stayed the exact same. He would spend the next seven years hovering over the same indecisive ground, and I would spend the next seven years trying to be worthy enough to be chosen, in his mind and my own.

The mix was quixotic. Essentially, when I moved in, he never moved out. Instead, we fell headlong into a pool neither of us could get out of. Our connection was deep and magnetic. It was also inescapable and full of an undertow both of us did a good job ignoring. Six weeks into our relationship he lay on his stomach on the bed, giddily looking up at me. I lay on my back, propped up against a pillow, exhausted from the output of working a full-time job and balancing a new live-in relationship, all while shackled to the cement boots of chronic illness that consistently dragged me down. But, as always, his sweet face and broad smile drew me in, tooth by tooth, until I was woozy with love. His eyes sparkled mischievously. He was ripe with thought, so I reached out and plucked it out of his mouth.

"What are you thinking?" I asked, resting one hand on the side of his face, his strong nose elegant and overwhelming.

"I'm wondering what kind of ring you want," he said, and smiled even wider. We were only six weeks into our relationship but the thought of marrying him felt inevitable. Our love felt profound and engulfing. I picked out a ring. But it never came.

Instead, the chips were chiseled bite by bite. Like when he went to his Grandmother's birthday and didn't want me to go. He said it was important his family's support of me come organically and I likely wouldn't be accepted. With rejection yeast to my fifty-cent thinking, I didn't even think to ask why not. My denigration was swollen and whole. Or when he invited his mentor and his wife over for dinner, he said to me, as they knocked at the door, "My mentor means a lot to me and he doesn't want me to date you." With that, he opened the door to greet them and offered a warm hello. That same man's wife later told me I was ruining the Landlord's family simply by dating him. My presence was deemed cancerous, and the more I rooted into his life, the more forces rallied to protect him and excise me out. The less likely he and his family and his culture and friends seemed to accept me, the more I leaned into proving myself worthy. The deeper the rejection, the more I dug in.

"Can you walk?" his mom asked. "I have something I want to show you."

His mom's sister was having a big party at her house and I was thrilled to feel well enough - and had been invited - to attend. I was sitting on the floor between the Landlord's legs as he sat on the edge of the fireplace when his mom extended her hand to me and smiled warmly. This was our second meeting. Our first meeting had been a disaster. Over dinner she had made it clear I wasn't an acceptable choice for her son. Now we were amongst her entire family and I wanted so desperately to belong. Her extended hand was a lifeline. This was acceptance. This was girl-time; a conspiracy in the garden, just the two of us. I looked back at the Landlord with a look of bewildered excitement, grabbed her hand, and followed her outside.

The garden was precious and lush. Her sister, who had no children of her own, spent all of her free time grooming this space to perfection and it showed. His mom led me to the patio under a warming lamp.

"Feel this," she said, reaching her hands up to catch the warmth.

I lifted my hand near the lamp. It felt nice. Warm. I tilted my face toward it, letting her see how much I was truly enjoying it.

"Stay here," she said, still smiling, as she walked back inside and shut the door. I smiled wide and nodded and kept my face turned toward the lamp.

I don't know how long I stood in the garden before I realized she was not coming back. Before I realized I had been actively put outside like a dog. Before I realized this was the

opposite of belonging. At some point, sheepishly, quietly and
heartbroken, I walked back inside.

He said nothing at all.

AFTER A FEW YEARS TOGETHER, we moved out of his loft into a
four-floor palace, which would be our home for five of my
seven years in captivity; caught in the vice-grip of an illness
unrelenting and captive to the notion that incremental steps
sideways in our relationship would lead to meaningful strides
forward. Purposely moving in together felt like we were going
somewhere when, in fact, we were going nowhere at all.

Being homebound does curious things to the mind. Outside
of the constant feedback loop of life, I was regressing. Externally, I was aging, but on the inside, I was on rewind. As the
world advanced beyond me and life moved forward for
everyone I knew, my life forced an uncommon dependency on
the man I loved, causing me to revert emotionally. And in a very
strange way, he got something from caring for me. When I was
at my sickest, we were at our best. He would notice the symptoms before I did. Something would flash across my face, a sag
would take hold at the corners of my eyes, and he would elec-
trify. Slipping his hand in mine, his confident grasp would
signal the onrushing crash and he would move whatever mountain necessary to spirit me to safety. Once there, his fingers
would spin circles on my back, encouraging the movement of
spinal fluid, a touch he had come upon intuitively. My illness
would be the only place in our relationship he would be confident. Or touch me. Cut off from his family and hidden away
from the world, we were a house of many deserts. My illness
was the ocean. It was massive and unfathomable and we would
run to it with our arms wide open. In it, we came together and
were one.

Most days, I would work from bed. I was able to walk (most of the time), and talk (most of the time), and cook up laughter despite the oppressive Seattle skies, which would sometimes make me cry. There was, I suppose, much to cry about: an illness that robbed me of my vitality, my partner's family who despised me for it and broken bonds within my own family of origin. Each a weight of crushing magnitude in its own right. Taken together, almost unbearable, for us both. But we had each other, and as imperfect as our relationship was, we were two halves of a magnet, anchored together and nearly impossible to separate. We clung to each other constantly, desperately, even as our magnetic field threatened to pull us under.

In the seven years we were together and I was home and bed bound, I cannot say I was without love. I was not. I cannot say I was without friends. I wasn't that either. I also can't say I didn't have industry. I did. The most extraordinary people found their way to me and gave me high-visibility, high-responsibility work, which I executed from bed. But if I had always had trouble seeing myself for who I was, during my time with him I became unrecognizable. My voice became higher, my personality lost all heft and my mannerism turned childlike in his presence. Trapped inside all day, my entire nervous system would orient to the sound of his car in the garage, his key turning in the door. On the "good days," I would run to the door to meet him, screaming his name and throwing my arms around his neck before a single foot fell across the threshold. On "bad days," I would listen as his feet would carry him to me, step by step. He would enter the master bedroom, fall onto the bed and into my arms, and push his nose into my neck as I pushed mine into his. We would inhale deeply, pulling in each other's scent through long and desperate inhales. In this space, we belonged to each other in the most profound way. But in all the ways that mattered, we held no tether.

As I was regressing and we were stagnating, time was

marching on. Year after year, I was various shades of severely incapacitated, disabled and unwell. I continually tried everything possible to find healing, and in the course of exploration came across a strict diet developed by a neurologist in London called the GAPS diet. Adhering to it religiously was allowing for some headway. As I marched forward through the arduous regime, a crack of light entered and hope for a better day slowly made its way through the door.

During the course of our relationship, I had turned forty. With the advent of some physical improvement, questions about children and family surfaced in a way that was inconceivable before. I was torn. On the one hand, I could think of nothing more beautiful than to have a baby with him. I loved him. He was the whole of my heart. On the other hand, I felt selfish. How could I think of bringing a child into the world in my condition? How could I care for it properly?

The thought took up a good deal of my mind as he pressed me forward toward a yes. He was hungry for family and saw a baby as a way to build a bridge between me and his family of origin. I can't say I didn't want children. It wasn't that deliberate. Somewhere deep inside, I thought a child deserved better.

With the new diet, I was having more and more good days and even the notion of what a good day meant was expanding. I was now able to ride in the car for extended periods of time without a barf bag and take short, small walks around the block. As we sat at a traffic light one day, I looked out the window at an unlikely couple on the corner. The man was in a wheelchair. He had no apparent ability to move much of his body outside of driving his chair with the hand-lever. A young girl of eight or nine stood beside him. As the light turned green, he advanced his chair across the street. He must have said something to her because she laughed in sheer delight. The wind carried the sound of her laughter through my open window along with what she said next. After she laughed, she climbed up on his chair and called him "Daddy."

The indecision that kept me bound, unlocked and ran down my face. At once, I could see that his disability was a delivery vehicle for empathy, compassion, awareness and understanding in a way nothing else could be. It was undeniable. Someone even more debilitated than I had a child and I did not think him selfish. In fact, I had the overwhelming sense that his disability would be the fertile ground in which her young mind would form differently than her friends from able-bodied parents. I wanted to see her in her 20s, her 30s. Who would she be in her 40s, like me? I saw the crack in his humanity as a point of reference that would flood over her and undoubtedly color her life. If this man brought a child into the world, despite all of his physical brokenness, maybe, I thought, I could, too. We began trying for a family.

I got pregnant quickly after our first try, but miscarried at only six weeks. Less than a month later, I was pregnant again. With Lumen. When I first got pregnant, he said, "It doesn't make sense not to get married." I agreed. It didn't. Marriage had become a huge battle between us. After his inquiry of what kind of ring I wanted at our relationship's six week mark, a ring never came. He had a million reasons why he couldn't, shouldn't and wouldn't marry me; most of them having to do with my illness and his family's rejection of me over it. Every time I asked about our future, he would buy time. And even after the first and second pregnancy and his pseudo-proposal, a ring still didn't come. Getting better and becoming pregnant wasn't bringing us closer together. It was driving us farther apart.

We stopped sleeping in the same bed. Saying my body was emanating too much heat for him to sleep next to me comfortably, he would get up and go downstairs to the guest bedroom in the middle of the night. Eventually, he stopped coming upstairs altogether.

In the quiet of night, I would look up at the ceiling and spread my hands across my belly. With space to breathe and the ability to actually think without physical symptoms warring for my attention, I found myself facing the most terrifying question I had ever encountered: what was it that I truly wanted? Three simple words came to me instantly: *Committed. Connected. Convicted.* I whispered them out loud. And then again. And then again. Once they came out of my mouth, they locked in my mind and I took a stand within myself for a committed, connected, convicted relationship. And for the first time in my life, I believed it could be mine.

It was such a foreign concept to me, believing I could take a stand for something. Most of my life had been lived with the outflow going the other direction. How could I make others happy so that they would love me? How could I prove I was worthy so that I could get to belong? For years I had been trying to get love from the most unlikely of sources, attaching my kite to an unfurling string. In creating the mantra, it wasn't that I suddenly no longer needed or wanted love, but that a break occurred between my wanting love and my needing him to provide it. And the only way I knew to sustain that break was to call what I actually wanted by name: a committed, connected, convicted relationship. I was going to start with the hope that this desired relationship would be with him, but at the same time, I committed to being okay if it wasn't.

The purpose of the mantra was to anchor me to my own internal commitment. I didn't want to leave him. I loved him deeply. But my feelings were confusing. How I felt about him was wrapped in layers of love that also sometimes felt like pain and hurt and anger and resentment, but also gratitude and thankfulness. I couldn't anchor into my feelings for him because my feelings were a moving target and too convoluted to achieve the clarity I was looking for. In truth, I wasn't looking for an answer to my relationship: should I stay, or should I go. I was looking for the answer to life. Was it possible to have less heartache and fewer tears? Could there be an existence where I would feel safe in the world around me; less burdened with the constant need to prove, prove, defend, defend, defend? Could it be possible to live a life where I wasn't giving all of myself away in order to simply get love?

In my notebook, I wrote down this simple sentence: *I am taking a stand for a relationship that is committed, connected and convicted.*

So if, after seven years, two pregnancies and two throw-away proposals, he still wasn't convicted about being with me or wanting to commit to a life with me and our child, I would have to leave. Upon that realization, I stopped breathing.

He may have been my Landlord but I had been the one renting out my body and time.

∾

WE SAT in our family room upstairs on the third floor. I was on the couch and he was at the desk. We were doing our 401K planning.

"Ok," I said walking over to him with my laptop. "This is what I'm doing."

I put the laptop on the desk so he could see my plan on how I would assign my assets upon my death, with him listed as the beneficiary. It wasn't a decision as much as it was an opening to a conversation. He was the father of my child and I wanted to make these decisions together. I ran my hand over my stomach, enamored with it's very slight but palpable swell, and leaned in to kiss his neck. I loved how he smelled. As I was inhaling his scent, he turned his computer screen away from me slightly. I froze. Ice licked up my neck and ran across my shoulders, stiffening me. I leaned over his shoulder and looked at the screen.

"What are you doing?" I asked, thick with double meaning. There came no answer.

I looked at the line that said beneficiary. I was not listed. Neither was our unborn child.

"You don't need it," he said, by way of explanation.

The value attached to my life, and the life of the baby I was carrying, was worth nothing. We had made the decision together to create a child. He made the decision alone not to cover it. Or me. I was improving but I was still horrifyingly fragile. With no covering, I was at risk. The baby and I both were. And I had allowed it to happen. I may have struggled with my sense of self-worth but I knew one thing very clearly: this baby was not worth nothing.

I began actively edging toward the idea of ending our relationship. He did, too.

"How was Ricky?" I asked, when he walked up the steps into the kitchen. He had gone to see his best friend Ricky for dinner and regardless of how things were fraying, I still loved seeing his face come through the door.

He turned through the kitchen as if he was headed upstairs. I came around the island to intercept him and give him a hug.

"He's ok," the Landlord said. "I told him I don't know if I can be happy in this relationship," he said, in passing.

I can't say what happened immediately thereafter. I've lost it from memory and don't actually know.

That night, I lay in bed in the room above him, crying softly. The master bedroom was dark and still when he came up the stairs and got into bed with me. He hadn't done so in a very long time.

"Let me fix this," he said, nuzzling my ear. "I'm going to fix this."

The next morning, he left the house. I didn't ask him where he was going. I didn't care. A few hours later he came back with a roasted chicken and a ring. He handed me the chicken first, and then the box.

"Don't leave," he said.

I opened the box. It held a thin band of diamonds encased in platinum. It was exactly the ring I had told him I'd wanted a very long time ago. I started at it. How was it possible to get something you so desperately wanted and feel sad? He looked at me and waited for the answer to the question he never actually asked.

"Well?" he asked.

"Maybe," I said. "I don't know."

"We should call your parents," he said. "They're waiting for our call."

Weeks after he had proposed and we had told my parents, he still hadn't told his. When he finally told his parents, his mom almost had a heart attack. Or so he said. I wouldn't know. He went to tell them solo. I was not welcome in their home.

I lost Lumen a few weeks after that.

I KNEW it was gone because my body went quiet. The hum of pregnancy, the manufacturing of human life, the constant hot and mechanical strumming that vibrated my body from the inside out, fell silent. I knew the feeling because it had happened once before, months earlier. We sat in the waiting room of the Special Care Pregnancy Clinic, both of us looking straight ahead.

"It's gone," I said.

"We don't know that," he countered.

But I did.

We walked into the dark room and I laid down to receive the gel on my belly. The med tech slid it around silently. We could see the baby. We could hear the heartbeat. It was slow.

I was offered a D&C but the baby wasn't gone yet and I

wanted to carry it as long as I could, until it left on its own. The miscarriage I'd had at six weeks was painful, but it wasn't unmanageable. I expected this one, early in the second trimester, to be the same. It wasn't.

Early in the evening, two days before he was set to leave on a business trip, the contractions started. The pain escalated quickly and I moved into the guest bedroom to be closer to a bathroom. The previous miscarriage I had walked out; pacing, moaning quietly to myself that quiet moan that to the listening ear could be either pleasure or pain and rubbing my lower back. My movements and sounds had been rhythmic, methodical and predictable. This was chaotic and pulsing and not at all in my control.

"Can I call 911?" he asked. He stood with his back pressed against the window, facing the bed. I shook my head fiercely, my curly hair stuck to my wet brow.

I moaned and rocked and gripped the bed frame as blood left my body in copious amounts. I would do this on my own. Millions of women did this all the time, I reasoned. I had done this before. I would do it again. While tragic, it was a natural process of life. That, and I wanted to feel the pain. If I couldn't feel the life inside me anymore, I wanted to feel all of it as it left.

Another wave rocked through me, pushing downwards from behind. I slammed my face in the mattress to muffle my moan, gripping the bedsheet and crushing it in each fist.

Nine hours passed before the pain subsided. It was early morning. I had labored through the night and he had stood by, watching. Now he was finally asleep and I went downstairs, pulled together some breakfast and called my mom.

"I think it's over," I said. I was exhausted; rung out by the loss but relieved it was over. I could breathe again.

"Good, sweet girl. Now get some sleep."

We talked a little more as I ate my breakfast until there was another twisting inside.

"Mom, I'm not feeling so well again. I think I need to go upstairs to lie down." In the world of labor and delivery, that had been the calm before the storm.

The pain that rained down next cracked open my body and brain in a way I was completely unprepared for. My friend Julia had accidentally put her hand through a window while closing it, severing veins in her wrist. Recounting the story to me while she was sleeping in the same guest bed I was laboring in, said, "I had this thought that I had done something I couldn't undo." She suddenly became aware that the damage done could potentially end her life. I don't know where that line is exactly, but the feeling is unmistakable. I had crossed it.

"Call 911," I directed on the next contraction, without hesitation. He actioned it immediately.

Five men, in gear and getup, filled our guest bedroom. Their sea of uniforms created a wall. One paramedic stepped forward in my general direction. I was on my hands and knees on the bed, rocking back and forth, moaning loudly, white-hot with pain. I felt like an animal and so exposed.

"Is this how you're most comfortable?" he probed gently.

"I am not comfortable," I said viciously. "*At all.*"

While the one paramedic guided me onto my back and took my vitals, the others looked on. All men. I wondered what they thought. They saw trauma on the regular and yet they seemed rigid with fear.

The first shot of morphine brought no relief and another shockwave ripped through my body.

"Please help me," I whispered.

"Your blood pressure is really low. I can't give you anything more, it could stop your heart."

The paramedic and I looked at each other in the eyes, communicating nothing and everything without words.

"Ok, guys," he said. "We're going in."

They strapped me onto a stretcher and took me down the

stairs to the waiting ambulance and loaded me in. While the Landlord stripped the bed and packed a bag, I rode in the ambulance to the nearest hospital, an uncapped adrenalin shot aimed at my heart.

I arrived at the ER and was quickly connected to a saline drip, which would be the delivery vehicle for any additional medication needed. Several liters of water went in over eight hours. None came out.

The room was dark. When the Landlord arrived, he sat in a chair in the corner on his phone, while I managed waves of nausea and consciousness. We didn't speak.

A doctor entered, with several staff, and sat down in between my legs. With a very long probe, he entered to explore the situation. I winced at the pressure.

"Can you push?" he asked gently.

I shook my head. If it was an option, the answer was no. I had very little left to give, and whatever I did have left I was using trying to stay conscious.

Over the next few hours, doctors would come in to discuss, amongst themselves, if I was in kidney failure or organ shut down; as they couldn't not understand why my body was not expelling the water they had been pounding in me through IV. In the end, I was sent out the door with a prescription to purge the remaining "fetal tissue" from my uterus and a prompt to follow up with my neurologist; the water issue a greater concern than the miscarriage. To them.

The Landlord left for a business trip the next day, as scheduled. My parents arrived and slept in the guest bedroom, not wanting me to be alone. In the middle of the night, I awoke to slight pressure in between my legs. Something was wanting out. I ran to the bathroom awkwardly, one hand between my legs to catch whatever was leaving. I made it to the toilet, hand still in place, as the remaining "fetal tissue" slipped into my hand. It was the baby.

I looked at it intently. It fit neatly into the palm of my hand. Dark eyes sat behind stretched skin in an oversized head. The spine curved gracefully, but tightly, in a wide C. The fingers delicately alighted the end of small limbs, separated and perceptible. I didn't know what to do. The house was dark. My parents were asleep. I was neither frantic nor entirely coherent when I made the decision to wrap the body and put it in the freezer, but that decision kept me up all night long wondering if the action would be considered criminal. No matter the size, it was, after all, a body in the freezer. I lay awake until morning.

When I heard motion downstairs, I went into the guest bedroom. It was morning. Dad was in bed and Mom was in the bathroom. I went over to Dad's side of the bed. Mom came out and I told them what had happened. It would be yet another time I would watch my dad cry on account of me.

We went downstairs to the freezer and Mom slowly unwrapped the body. It had fuzed to the tissue I had wrapped it in and the pulling at it tore apart my heart. We called a friend of the family who had been a neonatologist and he told us placing the fetus in a saline bath would have been the preferred choice to the freezer, and cautioned against holding out hope that cause of death could be deduced.

The fetal tissue, and our relationship, was too far gone.

LOSING Lumen triggered a relapse into *nothing to see here, moving on.* I did not mourn the loss. I shoved it down. Though my mantra was still embedded in my consciousness, I shifted from powerfully taking a stand to whispering against the dark of night while I still lay in bed upstairs alone, "Please don't take him from me. I can't lose him, too."

By the time I got around to calling my neurologist, and successfully getting in to see her, we had passed through the holiday season and had begun another year. When I told her of the miscarriage, and that the doctors had administered three liters of fluid but none had come out over the eight hours I had been in the ER, she seemed non-plussed.

"Yes. That's how we treat dysautonomia," she said flatly.

I was completely baffled as to why she had never mentioned it before. She agreed to a month-long, weekly trial of IV saline solution. I began the treatments with the same weary and wary hope with which I approached all new treatments: hopeful they would produce their desired outcome but nervous my hopes for true recovery would yet again be dashed. If recovery was an island, I put my heart into a small boat offshore, beyond the crash of the shoreline.

After the month-long trial, I was a new woman. I had been improving ever so slightly with the diet, and it had helped me turn the corner, but this level of improvement was astounding. My excitement was off the charts!

Back when I was very ill, one doctor I had seen along the way had sat the Landlord and me down in his office and asked, "What will you two do if she gets well? What are you looking forward to?"

We looked at each other. Was he serious?

"Everything!" we shouted in unison.

There was a long list of things we lamented not being able to do together. Simple things. Easy things. Driving in the car. Going on road trips. Going out for dinner. Going to the movies. Going to the grocery store. Playing tennis. Traveling. Our list was never-ending.

The IV treatments were opening up the possibility to live in a world we had only dreamed of. But as I began rapidly improving and was able to leave the house, we became trapped together inside it.

It was early evening when I ran downstairs into the kitchen where he was standing, looking into the fridge.

"Let's go to Mt. Rainier!" I shouted.

Mt. Rainier lay just a few short hours south of Seattle and is considered one of the most dangerous volcanoes in the world. Its stunning presence in Seattle's backyard was a constant reminder of the sheer force of nature. I thought we could find a cute little hotel at the base and in the morning wake up to the mountain looming before us. He closed the fridge. He did not share my excitement.

"We'd have to pack," he said.

"I know," I said smiling and excited, jumping up and down like a kid.

"You're just so tough," he said, shaking his head.

"What do you mean?" I asked, my excitement draining slowly.

"We'd have to figure out what food to bring for you, and make sure you have your weighted vest, and take your barf bag just in case," he said. "You're just so much work."

We stood there in silence. All excitement gone. A heaviness remained.

That was the second time he'd said that phrase in a few days. Earlier he'd told me he had to be with his friends to have fun. That being with me felt like work. I couldn't disagree. Dealing with my body was tedious, and even though I was getting better, I understood why he was bringing up everything we'd need to do and what could go wrong.

Regardless, I could not contain my excitement at my improvement. I bounded into the neurologist's office a month later with all the fanfare of, "Ta-da!" It was working. Big time. She agreed, but then said she wasn't going to continue the treatments any longer. My chin hit the floor and an explosion of panic went off in my chest.

"I don't want your body to get used to it," was her explanation.

People received ongoing medication all the time, I thought,

and this was water. *Water.* I fired her immediately and received a standing order from my primary care physician for weekly infusions of saline. I was improving. I felt my body healing and expanding, soaking up water like dry, parched land, and there was no way I was going to stop now. No. Way.

As I was soaking, expanding and growing, we were grinding forward, neither of us really knowing what to do. We were on incredibly shaky ground but I was convinced that my physical improvement would give us new life. I wanted to pay him back for all the times he lay on the bathroom floor with me, all the times he drew circles on my back, all the times he held my hand like he meant it when I was going down, all the times he chose to stay with me instead of going out with his friends. I felt, by being with me, he had taken it in the teeth and I was finally in the position to show him, and his friends and family if they were watching, that I was a woman worthy of investment. For the first time in my life, I actually began to feel like one.

Sometimes he'd call me his fiancé. Sometimes he wouldn't. Sometimes I'd wear my ring. Sometimes I wouldn't. When I was pregnant, he wanted to get married but when I lost the first pregnancy he backed away, only to renew his tepid proposal during the second pregnancy. When I lost the second pregnancy, he decided not to try for another. As a choice for a wife or mother, I was seemingly an optional one.

We had just come back from looking at yet another wedding venue we couldn't agree on. We were three months away from our supposed wedding date and nothing had been locked down. He was following me up the stairs to the den when he said it.

"If we get married, we should just do it at Town Hall," he said.

I stopped cold.

If.

And that one word brought it all down.

~

"CAN'T we just go back to being us again?" he begged, half-heartedly. We stood on opposite sides of the bed we no longer slept in together.

Committed. Connected. Convicted. Those were the words I'd used.

"I would love that," I said. And deeply meant it. "Do you feel convinced you want to be with me?"

He opened his mouth. I knew him well enough to know not to wait for words. None would come. It was a smoke screen.

"Listen, I would love nothing more than to stay with you. To be 'us' again. But I am taking a stand in my life that after seven years together, the person I am engaged to, the person I got pregnant by, would know, beyond a shadow of a doubt, that he wanted to be with me. If that's you, great. But if that's not...if you can't...I can't take less than that. I can't."

The sickness of the situation turned my stomach. My body had violently emptied my womb of the two babies we deliberately created together, the second of whose remains I still had to bury. I knew if I walked out the door, it would be the end to so many things, my chance at motherhood just one.

We stood in silence. There was nothing more to say. No other reason to stay. I walked out of the master bedroom, down the never-ending flight of stairs to the garage, got in the car and drove away. I walked by Kent's "sick, disabled, lazy, good in bed" painting on my way out the door.

As I drove away from the house, I called my parents from the car to see if I could stay at their condo in Seattle for a few days, while the dust settled and the road ahead took more certain shape. Saying it out loud, telling my mom I'd left him, brought reality to the situation. Of course I could stay. As long as I needed. No one was surprised.

On arrival at the condo I stepped into the shower to ground

myself in something visceral. I felt at odds with space and time. The liquid slid over my body, weighing me down. I got out of the shower and roped my hair back into a tight ponytail, punishingly. It pulled at my temples. Although this moment had been coming for so long, I was unprepared for its uprising. I walked into my parent's bedroom, naked, and pulled open the dresser drawers looking for something loose and unencumbered. I grabbed my dad's big white v-neck undershirt and slid it over my head. It fit like a dress.

I walked into the guest bedroom and sat on the floor in front of the closet mirrors and looked at my reflection. My eyes were blank. Not empty. Just blank. As if I knew nothing about the person staring back at me; my reflection ignited no recognition.

Committed. Connected. Convicted. I had suppressed it after losing Lumen but it had flooded back with a vengeance. The mantra had started small but grew within me, irrevocably, in the dark of night. It came slowly, slowly, avalanche. And that avalanche moved me out the door.

As I sat on the floor in front of the mirrors and leaned forward into them, my breath lit up the glass. Looking closer into my eyes I saw something I had not seen in a long time. A spark. A flicker. A sign of irrepressible life-force. I would do whatever it would take to fan it into flame.

8

MESSENGERS OF LIGHT

Summer, Seattle, 2014

After I left him for everything we were, and everything we weren't, the things he used to do for us, I had to do on my own. The Big Mac was broken. I lumbered into Apple, carrying it with both hands. The Big Mac was our communal computer but really more his.

As an IRS mechanism to accept the BabyLegs work, I set up CORHOUSE, Inc., and called it a brand strategy agency. Loving the work, I continued to take consulting projects and introduced the Landlord to the world of brand and identity creation. When we did projects together, I was the strategist and he was the designer and, as such, he needed a big and powerful computer to run all the design programs. The Big Mac also housed the company's financial bookkeeping software, which we used to reconcile accounts every month. Possibly for this and other reasons, he left the Big Mac when he packed up his stuff and moved out. However, as the main user, all of his logins were saved and the Big Mac had become my personal torture device. Specifically through notifications.

Gmail: Notifying me his mom sent another women for his review mere days after our ended engagement. Not unexpected for his culture. Or his mom.

Spotify: Notifying me his brand new girlfriend sent him a Dave Matthews song that reminded her of their blossoming love, just weeks after we separated. I did judge her taste in music and it felt good, but not good enough.

After several failed attempts at logging him off, I employed a friend who wiped the whole computer clean; all except for the Apple iOS itself, which popped up an unhelpful notification every time I booted up the computer. It said, "The Big Mac would like you to remember the Landlord." This, when I was doing everything I could to forget.

When it began choking and dying, I finally took the Big Mac into the Apple store, and while the Apple Genius was working on it I asked him to remove - for the love of all things holy - that notification. He logged me in, asked me to push a few buttons, which I gladly did, and it was magically gone.

Nevertheless, the Big Mac would ultimately die on the Genius Bar. I felt so free walking out of that store without that computer; like I had cut yet another cord that tied me down. The unleashing expanded my heart and pushed it forward in my chest. As I opened the door of the Apple Store and walked out into the uncommon Seattle sunshine, I dialed my mom back. She had called as we were wrapping up and I told her I'd call her right back. When I walked outside I selected "Mom" from my recent calls but a strange man answered the phone. I stopped walking.

"Mom?" I asked, confused.

"Wrong number," a man's voice said quickly and hung up.

Weird. I went to my favorites and found her name. With purpose, and very carefully, I pressed "Mom."

Him again.

"I don't get this," I said. "I'm calling Mom and I'm getting you. And you're not my mom."

He laughed.

"I don't know what to tell you," he said. "Wrong number."

This time he didn't hang up. We sat in silence for a moment.

"Ok," I said, still totally perplexed but now a bit suspicious. What had this man done with my mom? Did he steal her phone? Did he steal *her*?

"Well….I guess I'll say goodbye again, then?" I said, drawing it out, just in case he needed more time to make a confession.

"I guess," he said, and hung up again.

The moment, I mean the red-hot second dead air came on the line, I recognized the voice. It wasn't my mom. It was the Landlord's dad.

Somewhere in the process of logging me in to log him out, the Big Mac, in its final act of defiance, had merged all of our contacts together. My Mom contact now contained both his mom and my mom's contact information, using his mom's cell phone, inexplicably, as default.

The next day I went right back to the Apple Store and, over the course of five hours, had to manually remove each of his contacts from my phone, one by one.

By the time I left Apple, I was starving and decided to chase into Whole Foods and pick up a few things. No big deal. Except that it was a huge deal. In the previous eight years, Whole Foods, or any big box retailer with fluorescent lights, was decidedly off the menu. The expansive space, the flickering lights, the flooding inputs of smells and sounds were all too much to handle. The few times I had made it into the store with the Landlord, we took a selfie by the eggs. Eggs were at the very back of the store. Eggs meant I went the distance. Generally, thereafter I would hightail it right back out but I had made it to the eggs. So, it was astounding that with months of IV saline solution coursing through my veins, I was able to chase into Whole Foods without giving it much thought.

While I had taken to wearing "real people clothes," stepping out of what had been a near decade in yoga pants, I was back in them. The trip to Apple had been rough. My eyes were thick from crying and my face glistened from the moisture I heartily applied to keep my skin from drying out under the onslaught of tears. I was a hot mess.

On my way into Whole Foods, a man restocking apples while wearing a cowboy hat greeted me with a sly smile and tilt of his brim. That was nice, I thought. Taking pity on the puffy lady. Sweet. I made my way through fruits and veggies to the fish counter where a fishmonger delivered a big smile and friendly commentary as I picked out a delicious salmon filet. On my way back toward cash out, I stopped by to get rice snaps where a man was perusing the shelves.

"Hi," he said simply, his giant grin confusing me.

"Hi?" I asked, more as a question than a statement. Was it me or was it Friendly Man Day at Whole Foods? In the decade I'd been under, had the earth warmed into a welcome palooza? I want to reiterate that I was not looking good. In the slightest. There was obvious carnage on my face, and I may have cried again between the fish counter and the rice snaps. I was the person others would run from or at the very least avert their eyes. This was wonky.

I got out of there as fast as possible and went to the butcher shop hoping it would offer more sanity.

"Can I tell you something?" the butcher shouted at me. I was still at the front door, not two steps inside, and he was behind the counter, clear on the other side. I approached the counter. I was not in the mood to yell. Or speak at all, for that matter. I just wanted to get my bones and be gone. I nodded at him to go ahead. Let it out, I thought. He clearly wouldn't be able to focus on my order until he got whatever it was off his chest.

"My girlfriend and I got back together," he said, his eyes glistening.

"Did you break up?" I asked. Here was something I understood.

"Yes. We were apart for two years. She my Baby Mama but it don't matter. We were apart, apart," he said with verbal and physical emphasis. "And now, we not. We back togetha'. Like togetha', togetha'."

He threw both arms up in the air champion-style, a victorious fist at the end of each arm. A whoop followed. His enthusiasm caught me and shook me hard.

You can't know the outcome.

I crawled back into the driver's side of my Jeep, shut the door, and sat still in silence. I felt like I had physically walked through a land of possibilities: I could stay single forever; I could meet someone new at, say, Whole Foods; or we could find our way back to each other. I couldn't know the outcome. And if I couldn't know the outcome, how could I justify the tears?

The tears proclaimed the situation as decidedly bad. A dead end. Closed. Finished. Walled up. I'd had my one chance at love and it was gone, and I was the one, in the end, who pulled the pin and threw the grenade. A good or bad assignation allowed the situation to be brought to a conclusion. Embracing an unknown future required, at its very core, an open heart. Was I willing to open my heart to the myriad of possibilities? Or did I need to know? Did I need to be in control? Did I need to decide my future based on my present circumstances, or was I willing to leave room for a little mystery and magic?

There is an ancient Taoist parable of The Farmer who has one horse and one son. One day the farmer's horse runs away, and his neighbor comes over and says, "I'm so sorry about your horse! What bad luck!"

And the farmer says, "Good or bad, who can know?" The neighbor is confused because this is clearly terrible news. A horse is incredibly valuable and for the poor farmer, likely the most valuable thing he owned.

But at dawn the next morning the horse returns, and brings with it a dozen wild horses. The neighbor returns to celebrate. "Congratulations! What great luck!" he shouts in jubilation. The cool-cat farmer looks at him and simply says, "Good or bad, who can know?" The neighbor shakes his head, confused at the farmer who is unwilling to celebrate.

Later that afternoon, the farmer's son is breaking the horses when he is bucked off a stallion and suffers a break of his own. The friendly neighbor comes over again and says, "I'm so sorry about your son. What bad luck." To which our farmer once again replies, "Good or bad, who can know?"

The next day, war breaks out in the land and all of the able-bodied men are called into battle, except the farmer's son, who has a broken leg and cannot fight.

There was a lot of conviction to be had in calling something good or bad. Conviction around something's intrinsic value seemed important. Or was it? What if healing from this present hurt was less about knowing and more about waiting? It lengthened the thread that was wound tightly inside me and put more runway before me.

My Aunt Siggy and cousin Tobias had come from Germany for my wedding, even though it had been cancelled. We were weathering storms, boats thrown together, and the lake had pulled us all there, a healing respite once again.

I was looking up at the ceiling in the dark from my mattress on the floor when Siggy turned on the bedside light. I knew what she was reaching for. My Uncle Manfred had died of a massive heart attack while watching soccer in his easy chair at the end of an active day. Siggy was still reeling from the loss, looking for something to hold onto, since she could no longer hold on to him. I knew the feeling. I closed my eyes and listened to the sounds: the crack of the spine as she opened the book, the slide of his photo as she pulled it her direction, the soft unfolding of his letter to her the day of their son's birth, her tears on the page as she read the poetry she had memorized and knew by heart. The book was her touchstone. And I needed one.

The Landlord had sent me an email with the subject line "love letter" from his hotel room a few nights after we had broken up. In it he said he knew from the very beginning we would never work out; like a rocket willing to leave scorched earth behind as it boosted itself away from the planet. If he had been air to me, he was quickly turning to vapor. I began to wonder if he had even been there, or had I?

"What do you want from life?" I had asked him once as we stood in this very room. We had been looking at wedding venues in Liberty Lake and our tether was fraying irrevocably. I was desperately trying to understand him and find a way to his heart. I was also trying to provoke him into speaking to me about our future to get clear if there even was one.

"I want a sense of family," he answered. "And I want to travel. And I want to run or bike or kayak every day."

I nodded, knowing I could never be someone through whom he could fulfill those needs.

"What do you want?" he asked me in return, compulsorily.

"I want mystery and adventure," I said, looking out at the hill of green pine trees on the other side of the lake. "I want to live with a sense of awe and wonder every day."

He nodded. We brushed each other with our words but our minds were miles apart.

I left my non-wedding weekend, bought a journal, and sat with the blank pages before me. I would not be folding up his love letter in my book. There would be no photo of him. There would be no poetry, lamenting over love lost or freedom found.

I felt under the earth's crust. As if a crack had opened and I had been pulled under. But this was different than the schism I had experienced as a child, when my worth split in two and I was left aces down. This was different than being dragged under, in a suffocating manner, into a world where illness ruled. This was a secret place. A sacred place. There was something holding me. In its force, I felt a sense of awe and wonder.

The journal lay open on my lap when a text came in from Bart, my boss in New York, whom I loved dearly and had asked to be my best man. His text read:

> *I want to tell you something. There is a beauty and energy and intelligence and sheer life-force about you that is so extraordinary. And everybody sees it. I love you. - Bart*

I uncapped a black pen and wrote that down. It was my first journal entry. It was a touchstone. I would spend the next five years filling up over fifty journals, none with words of my own.

9

ROCK BOTTOM

Fall, Seattle, 2014

Landing in New York after almost a decade was an indescribable rush. I cried on take off when I felt the plane achieve lift. After so long fighting against gravity, achieving lift was an extraordinary feeling. Bart's text had galvanized something in me. I had booked the flight to New York to try and chase that feeling down.

Agio, the company I worked for, was headquartered in New York. After five years working for the company, I would be meeting some of my coworkers for the very first time. If New York had been home, it certainly wasn't any longer, but Bart was letting me stay in his apartment in TriBeCa, which wooed me into a sense of residence. New York was the last place I had been before I fell off the face of the earth and I was in the inquiry if I wanted to come back. Because Agio was there, it would have been incredibly easy for me, and helpful for the company, to have me move back. But Bart, in another display of acceptance and understanding, wasn't applying any pressure.

Just an open door. Only I wasn't sure I could walk through it, if I had the stamina for the city again. I felt fragile and raw in a way I never had before. My toughened exterior had long-since shattered and I was easing my way back into society, one small step at a time.

I had also been invited to speak to women on Wall Street about brand strategy, on my birthday no less. I could think of no better way to spend my birthday than on stage in New York.

I awoke the morning after my arrival to the phone ringing.

"Is there something you need to tell me?" Jen asked.

I stretched out like a cat inside the covers and looked lazily out at the water tower on the building of the rooftop next door.

"Not that I can think of," I said, and yawned and pushed my head back into the pillow. New York City. I felt deliciously triumphant.

"*Really*," Jen said, sounding incredulous. It was more of a statement than a question. Jen and I had gone to college together in Germany and had moved to New York at the same time. Our friendship had weathered several men and the accompanying stories. But she was extra protective this time.

"Yes, really," I laughed, and stuck one leg out of the sheet onto the covers and stretched it all the way out through the toes. "Why? What's going on?" I asked, as my leg and entire body relaxed again.

"He just checked into SeaTac Airport on Facebook. He's coming to New York."

I froze.

I felt the heat rise up from my gut to my face. It had only been a few short months since we had separated and I hadn't spoken to him, or seen him since, and had no plans of doing so. After I assured Jen of this and we hung up the phone, I stepped out onto Bart's balcony overlooking the Hudson River. New Jersey looked industrial and weathered. I knew New York well, as did Jen. It collided people. Especially me and men. But my choices were to stay locked up inside, a stow-away princess in yet another castle, or step out into the city I had finally made it back to, and reclaim lost ground. I bit down into the latter. If I ran into him, so be it. His presence in the city would not keep me inside. After finally achieving lift, this would not keep me down.

The Fall sun felt good against my skin as I walked up toward my old neighborhood. TriBeCa, where it flanks the Westside, has a strange feeling of emptiness. The distance between the streets feels much greater because far fewer people populate the landscape. Warehouse buildings take up entire city blocks and while the same often holds true in midtown, where office buildings occupy large footprints, those buildings are often made of glass, their bustling lobbies pouring a crush of people out onto pulsing sidewalks. Down in TriBeCa, people were more or less out of sight.

I wandered up Washington, past Horatio Street, my old block, and into the heart of the Meatpacking District. The High Line, that had been in discussion when I lived here, was now the centerpiece of the neighborhood; a crowning take-back-the-landscape monument to a new and sanitized New York. The meatpacking shops had been replaced by high-end retailers and while it all looked nice, I missed the blood.

On my way back down to TriBeCa, I slipped into a massage studio, lay on the table, and let my skin be kneaded into dough. The day spent walking the city had been thankfully uneventful and invigorating, but also enlightening. When I lived in New York before, I had come as if pulled by some magnetic force. If New York was pulling me now, it was a one-sided magnet. For me, the charge was out.

After several weeks in New York, I left, knowing I wouldn't return as a resident. Not now. Not this time around. That was clear though little else was. My home had sold. So on September 18, 2014, on my birthday, while I was speaking to the Women's

Leadership Action Forum on Wall Street in New York, the contents of the home I had shared with the Landlord and was still living in alone, were moved from one palatial, four-floor home, to another a few doors down. When I finally returned home, I drove back to the same neighborhood, walked down the same block but opened up a different door. That's how life felt after returning from New York: the same, but different.

Now what, I wondered?

Recognize that something has begun. You've already changed.
You've already reset how life is going to go.
Theresa, Journal #3

~

AFTER STEPPING off the plane from New York, I stepped into an interview cycle with a huge tech company in San Francisco. I wanted change. Big change. A new beginning. I was itching to run.

After three months and thirteen interviews, the company extended an offer. On offer the internal recruiter said, "Oh, by the way. This position is seventy percent travel. That's okay, right?"

Seven. Zero.

While I had successfully traveled to New York and back, it had required a month's rest on either side and a lot of recovery IV's before I could travel again. Seventy percent travel was not an option, nor had it been mentioned anywhere in the interview process. When I said I couldn't physically handle that much travel, they retorted I wasn't a culture fit and rescinded the offer.

Whatever buoyancy I had manufactured, whatever you-can't-know-the-outcome peace I was trying to embrace, whatever happiness I had been swimming in from reclaiming some of my health again, when the company rescinded the offer, the roof came down.

Red and blue lights strobed across my face as I stood on the other side of the glass door with my arms crossed, shaking my head. No way was I letting them in. But they were insistent, and they were cops. I opened the door angrily and marched back up the marble stairs with them in tow and slammed myself into a dining room chair. My eyes were swollen from crying, my face unrecognizable.

"We're here to check on how you are," she said gently. "Your neighbors are worried about you. They said they heard screaming. Were you screaming?"

I sat there and glared at her. Seriously? It was November. The windows were closed.

"Is anyone else in the house?" the male cop asked, with one hand on the butt of his gun, looking around corners and up the stairs.

I shook my head with a deep eye roll. My scowl deepened. This was perfect. Just perfect.

"I understand that you don't want to talk to us. We can sit here with you for a while, but at some point you are going to need to tell us what's going on so we can help you."

A sharp laugh cut through my throat. The pressure inside me was building. I stood up and went to get myself a glass of water. I threw the water down my throat and the glass in the sink and spun around, knocking into her. She had followed me.

My whole body yelled, "Back up!" And she did. But only a little.

"You want to know what's going on?" I asked, my words coming out like shrapnel. "I'll tell you what's going on. I was bed-bound for almost a decade because I have a neurological condition that jacks up my brain. I got pregnant twice by a man I was engaged to but lost both babies, and then him. And he's already with someone new after only a few months, while I still sit here feeling like I can't even breathe! And then, after thirteen interviews over three months I got my dream job offer, but without mentioning travel once - *once!* - during the interview cycle, on offer they tell me the job is seventy percent travel, which I can't do because of my jacked up brain, but when I tell them that, they rescinded the offer! Oh, and after I already told my boss I was leaving. So you want to know what's going on? That's what's going on." I said, and then realized - I'm not done.

"I'm having a moment!" I shouted in the direction of the neighbors. *"Is that not allowed?"*

I walked back over to the chair, slammed myself down again, and crossed my arms.

"I'm sorry," she said sincerely, after taking a little bit of time to let what I'd said settle in the room. "That's rough."

Tears crested over the bottom of my eyes, the dam broke once again.

"It sucks," I said quietly, covering my face and curling forward on myself. "It really sucks."

I cried for a minute more, then stilled myself and sat up, my anger interlaced with something sour and biting. Exacerbation.

"So this is what rock bottom looks like," I laughed acerbically. "The cops showing up for a well-person check."

"People care about you and just want to make sure you're ok," the male cop said.

They shared a look.

"You know," the woman cop approached me gently, coming into my space. I steeled myself and met her eyes, hard and unflinching. "In ninety-nine percent of these cases we show up at a house and take the person with us for a seventy-two-hour hold."

My eyes narrowed and my blood ran ice cold.

"My sense is, if we do that we'll only piss you off."

She smiled. I smiled back. And laughed once, hard.

"You seem like a really strong woman who's had a lot to deal with. We just need you to tell us you're not going to hurt your-self," she said.

The gravity of the situation fell over the room. It left me breathless and ashamed.

"I'm not going to hurt myself," I said quietly and meant it.

She nodded and we met each other gently in silence.

"We're happy to sit here with you for a while if you like," she said.

I nodded and we sat and, after a time, I stood. They stood, too. I motioned to the stairs and followed them back down, their guns and gear shifting loudly in their belts. I unlocked the front door and let them out into the night. The woman cop stepped over the threshold and turned back around.

"Take care of yourself," she said as goodbye, looking me in the eye. I saw something in her. I recognized it. Pain. It was deep, but it was there.

I pressed the glass door closed with my hand, turned the lock, and was alone in the house once more.

You are VERY strong. It will be hard for a while, but it will get stable. You have lots of people praying for your strength.
Mom, Journal #3

INTERCESSION

Winter, Seattle, 2014

Agio's management offsite was that same month. I was eager to see everyone's faces again, if only patched in over video. Bart had known about the interview and the offer. He had been my most winning recommendation. When it all fell through, we both moved forward as if I had never planned on leaving. After the flurry of possibility kicked up by New York and the potential of San Francisco, things had settled into status quo.

Mid-way through Day One of the offsite, I began to develop a little cough. Hours later, I was coughing so hard I could taste blood. I made an emergency appointment with my doctor and walked the two blocks from my front door to their office. The doctor looked into my throat and up my nose and, after exiting briefly, returned wearing hazmat. Washington State was in the middle of a whooping cough epidemic and people were dying. Until we knew the results of my test, I would be quarantined. Once again, I was on lockdown. And I was so relieved.

Life in the outside world was disorienting. I was that cryogenically frozen person, the girl under the stairs, removed from life and its feedback loop and reinjected anew; stuck in time but also fresh and undone. Being around people was new and exhausting. I had always felt so cut off from other people; stuck inside myself and far back from the surface, beholden to the belief the only one suffering in the world was me. My growing awareness of other people also awakened me to their pain. I began to see others as the walking wounded. They carried burdens I knew nothing about but the effects were obvious: a heaviness in the shoulders, a sadness in the eyes, tension around the mouth. I could suddenly see it all. I came out of my illusionary world where I was the only one in pain into a world of people suffering all around me. It was shocking and draining, magnetic and repelling, all at the same time. I wanted to open myself to the world and really see it and feel it, but my boundaries were porous and I would absorb others pain right along with mine. The weightiness compounded.

I was grateful for quarantine. Whatever the reason, I was requiring a lot of sleep. Although sleep was no longer restful. It was dynamic.

The Landlord had taken the master bedroom set and I was in a new room, in a new house, but the orientation was still the same. While he had never inhabited this space, I carried the ghost of him with me. I had long stopped searching for him in the middle of the day but in the night, I was reaching still. I would search for him, unthinking, in the dark of night; my hand slipping into the space between the sheets; my mind, expecting his warmth, awakening at the shock of the cold. The emptiness was a pit that pulled me in and under. Paloma had told me that rose quartz would open my heart to healing, and prepare it to love again, so I bought a small heart made of rose quartz and slipped it in the spot where my mind wanted him. It was small and smooth, manageable and cool with stillness. It resembled my present state: small, pulled tight, chilled but not frozen. It was a piece of me, externally, that reclaimed his space as mine. When my hand continued to reach for him, it would encounter the heart. I would pull it to me, place it in the small divot between my breasts directly over my heart, or over my eyes, or at the base of my throat, and I would wait for sleep to come again; the coolness of the rock anchoring me in this new reality.

My dreams had become a communication hotline between me and another dimension. The minute I had been cut loose from the gravitational pull of my profound illness, my feet could not find ground. My mind would dance between deep, overflowing gratitude and strange suicidal thoughts, not of taking my life, but giving it over.

I was so grateful for the healing I was experiencing, yet I was also so weary and spent. I had used all of my energy fighting my physical battle but once relief in that area finally came, an emotional journey began. I wasn't certain I had the strength for it.

I lay on my back, ankles crossed, arms spread wide open, rose quartz heart on my throat, and opened my voice to the heavens.

"I want to let go," I whispered against the night. "I am glad I was here. I learned things. I loved. I left a legacy in the hearts of those I touched, but I don't want to be here anymore. I want my road to end."

Quiet tears formed in the corners of my eyes and crept slowly toward the pillow below.

"If there is a God and you are here, if there is a way to send that request to you and have it answered, I would do it tonight. I guess this is me doing it. I want to do it. Go peacefully. Be done. Let others fulfill themselves with living. It can be a beautiful thing, I just don't want to do it anymore. There is nothing more for me. I loved. I was loved in return. So deeply and desperately. But I am complete. Please let my journey be over. Please. My soul just wants to come home."

Peace hung in the room and I received a response in words soaked up by my cells.

"You have asked to come home and I have brought you home. You will be in this world but not of it. You will sit here with me and see the world in a way that is detached and present. There is no judgement. He was my gift to you and was exactly who you needed him to be. I asked him to love you and he said yes. He committed to being with you but he did sacrifice something to do it but he did it because he loved you like he had never loved before and he misses you, too. But as you got better and started asking things of him he could not deliver, he had to say no. You would have parted anyway but your pressure made it happen sooner. It was always coming, from the very beginning. He just knew it much sooner than you. His destiny is not your destiny. He will be happy and I will take good care of him because he is mine and that is my commitment to him. Just as it is my commitment to you. I know your life has been hard and full of disappointments. That was necessary for your journey and the reason can't be revealed to you just now. But please trust me. What I have for you is just as beautiful as what I have for him. This is his reward. He listened to me when I asked him to love you. He said yes. Your heart is hurting and what comes next will be a slow unfolding that will require patience. Stay with me. Stay close. I will wipe away any tears you need to shed and take them back to me because they are mine and I put them in you with love. They are healing you and you have many tears yet to cry. You have to shed them so you can find joy. You will have other people who will carry you, it just won't be him. You will feel more detached and this, too, is necessary, as it will help you see the world as it is. And only then will you understand the place I have for you. That will be your place of peace. I have a different path for you, Cordila. That is enough for now."

I felt the words fill me as I slipped under again into sleep. While sleeping, I dreamed of the Landlord. He was happy. I wasn't. I wondered if I would be alone forever. I don't know if I surfaced into consciousness again, but the words found me wherever I was.

"Why do you assume what's ahead will not bring you joy? Didn't he make you joyful? Didn't I put happiness in your heart? You can see it unfolding all around you, layers of happiness and learning. I have prepared them for all. No one is immune and no one path is the same. Look how much love is around you, including from him. They all love you because of who you are, and how much they feel you love them in return. That is who you are, and who you will be: a great lover of all. Even his mother felt your love after she lashed out at you from her fear. She felt your love and loves you, too. Even she wants your happiness, just as she wants happiness for her son. If you let yourself, know that you can feel him. You can feel anyone you choose, past, present or future. So, when you need to, as you wait, close your eyes and feel what it will feel like to be loved by the new man I am sending. He wants to come to you right now but I am asking him to wait. It all will wait for you now. You have everything you need. You are surrounded by love. You can take your time. I know this is hard. No one is rushing you. Nothing needs to be done. I have hit pause so you can heal because I need you. I need all of you; the Cordila I created. I will use you because that is what you asked of me. I heard you then and I hear you now. Nothing in your journey will be wasted. Everything will be used. And whether you see him again, or not, is your choice. He will always receive you with love in his heart but he will never again be yours. He never was. I planted uncommon love in his heart for you to get him through what he needed to get through. He will never love like that again. He will love more quietly. More peacefully. Because that is what he has asked of me and that is what he desires. So now this time is for you. Heal as you must. I will be patient. Nothing will pass you by. Soon enough, it will be you who will want to emerge. Soon enough you will come to me, laughing, asking 'what's next!' And I will be waiting."

After all that, an old lover came to me in a dream and told me to get back into my body. Because when you get spoken to by what feels like a voice from another dimension, it's apparently ok to follow that with an ex-lover chaser. I didn't know what to make of it, any of it. It was all so weird but weird had been my norm. Regardless, I took all of it to Theresa, my therapist, who was helping me process the severing of my relationship and the coming back to life. She was my verbal sounding board, making sense of what felt so profoundly nonsensical.

"This is intercession," Theresa said, and encouraged me to keep listening.

Wait on recovery. It will come.
Theresa, Journal #4

∾

NEW YEAR'S EVE 2014 was the line of demarcation between my years spent with him and a future without him. It was a line I was eager to cross.

I didn't know my cousin Jax well. We hadn't grown up together and he was male and seven years younger. Not the makings for early childhood connection. But Jax always rallied in trauma, wherever the need. He had the ability to fill cracks like water. When I asked if he would ring in New Year's Eve with me at an art gallery where we would wear white and paint on strangers, he didn't hesitate before saying yes. He arrived with his car enshrined in dry cleaner's bags and we rode to the event serial-killer style.

It was early morning by the time we returned. I made myself a cognac with sugar cubes and hot water, the German remedy for a cough. Mine was still lingering. The living room was warmed by the fire and 2014 was behind us. Jax was sprawled out on the white leather couch and I was lying in front of the fireplace, soaking up the warmth from the wood floor. I was a few cognac's in when I said it. Quietly.

"Jax, I don't know what to do next."

Jax had slid so far down on the low-profile couch he was almost laying flat. His head was back, his throat open toward the ceiling.

"You don't do anything," he said. "You be the dot."

The air sparked electric. I sat up and grabbed my ever-present journal, pen in hand. Jax sat up, too.

"What's the dot?" I asked.

"The dot is a point and from that point, everything exists in all directions, the possibilities are endless. The entire universe can collapse into one point. It can all collapse into nearly nothing and then explode into everything," he said, exploding his fingers for emphasis.

"The point isn't acting out on its potential but you, as the point, know there is infinite potential within you. With infinite possibilities in your point, you can never know everything, so in that way, you can't know what path to choose. So, you have to reach out to that fourth dimension. That's where God is. God is infinite and can create everything from nothing. And if you lived in that fourth dimension, you would still exist in the third dimension, but you'd have a different perspective on what you're going through. A godly perspective."

God was such a convoluted concept to me. I had been raised in church as a child, very loosely, and had returned once or twice over the years. The notion of God was there but never took hold, not in a way that was meaningful, impactful or ever-lasting. It was one thing to call on God's name at night when you were tired and sad and alone. It was another to actually believe in him. I knew Jax to be a Christian, but I wasn't expecting a conversation about God to include the universe and multiple dimensions. There was just enough intrigue to open me up further. The cognac helped, too.

"How do you be the dot?" he asked, rhetorically. "It's not about you. It never was. God calls us to service. He calls us to serve others. And sometimes, he calls us to just be still, to sit by the babbling brook. You'll think of nothing. Or you'll think of something. But if you sit and wait, something extraordinary is going to happen. Just be. Being the dot is acknowledging that none of this is up to you. If you believe in God, you believe you still have purpose. If he was through with you, you'd be done."

If I believed in God. I liked that. It was an opening. An invitation. A question to answer, if not now, then soon. Jax paused and I looked up at him, eyes wide, pen still warm from writing feverishly. His mouth slid into a smile. Me, taking notes at 3 AM, several cognacs in. It was so Type A. He laughed, full and loud.

"Sitting still is not something that comes naturally to you, cousin, and that's great because you'll have to pay attention to it. I think you think getting out there and doing things will fix you, and that may not actually be right. You need to learn to respond versus react. When two things come into contact with each other, the inherentness of their being changes in reaction. When that car hit you, your car reacted. As humans, we react to everything. Our bodies react. Our emotions react. But as humans, we're different. We have the choice to choose to respond. You have the ability to choose to respond to whatever is happening."

You don't have to react right away. Think. Give yourself time
to think.
Michael, Journal #5

"Yes! That's how I feel," I said. "Like I just react and respond all the time. I shouldn't let things get to me so easily. I gotta keep people out."

I had been a reactionary machine. A visceral reaction mechanism. I was desperate to change that. I had also made some mistakes when I first left the Landlord by befriending a few people who saw my vulnerability and my deep need for engagement. I'd let some people in I shouldn't have in a mix of naivety and excitement, and in reaction to loneliness and fear.

"I need to do a better job guarding my heart," I said. "What's that saying about guarding your heart?"

"Above all else guard your heart, for it is the wellspring of life. Proverbs 4:23," Jax recalled easily. "But you're actually missing the point."

"The wellspring bubbles up and spills over onto the ground around it and runs down and joins the creek. But the water has to come from somewhere. It's not coming from you. If the heart is the wellspring, it's coming *through* you. It's up to you to decide where that wellspring is coming from. If you believe in God, you believe life is coming from God, flowing through you, to others. To guard your heart is to connect your heart to the wellspring and guard it with your life. 'Guard your heart' is not to close people out. 'Guard your heart' is to protect the connection, so that what flows out of you is good. Guarding your heart is not about you, it's about allowing yourself to be a conduit between yourself and the people you interact with, so they can also experience God through you."

I felt something still inside me. I was so tired, so profoundly tired. I may have received relief from the intensity of the symptoms of my illness, but my survival mechanism of constantly battling against life was still alive and going strong. What Jax was proposing was a new way of living, a life of stillness. How could I get there from here? How do you sit still to move forward? It seemed like an absurd equation.

"How are you going to just be?" Jax asked, reading my mind.

"You just do it, because that is how you're going to bring you back. The head is so tied to the heart. The mind is so connected to what's going on in the body. Everything you're going through makes you so infinitely relatable to a whole cadre of people because you have no control!"

I snorted. No kidding.

"When you flip a coin and you have no control over anything, you have no one to blame. You can't even blame the coin."

I didn't like that. I wanted to blame. There were so many people to blame, starting with blaming myself, my favorite target.

"There are a lot of people who lay blame on themselves or lay blame at the feet of others. You will be able to effect change in people's lives, not fix them, by explaining what you believe about destiny, fate and chance, because you can relate. How do you be the dot? You chill. You relax. You acknowledge the day-to-day and you set it aside. You think beyond this dimension and beyond this time. You let yourself be open to what you have to say to yourself, and what God has to say to you, and sometimes they're indistinguishable. That's how you be the point: you just sit. And you wait. And you get better. And the answer to the question of, 'How long?' is, 'As long as it takes.' How long do you have to be the dot? Until all of you - physical, mental, emotional, spiritual - all of you is ready to explode with potential.

Your path can be, for the moment, unknown. I don't believe it's unclear. I believe it's unknown and yet it sits right before you. But as the point, the point doesn't move. Things pass through it. Things go around it. But the point waits in its infinite potential. Your path is unknown and clear, and it is not one you can physically travel. Your path is internal. It will be alternately and simultaneously smooth and bumpy. But along that journey, and at the end of that journey, you will become well and you will help others. When you're well enough inside, centered, everyone knows it, can see it, and is drawn to it.

People will know it and will listen. And it has nothing to do with actions you take on the outside."

That idea of helping others felt ludicrous. I could barely help myself. But something about what Jax said made me think about Tiesto.

While living in Los Angeles, I met international DJ Tiesto three times. The first time it shocked me. The second time it surprised him. The third time it planted a seed in me from which I had never shaken free.

I had been introduced to electronic dance music (EDM) while living in Germany and in the EDM world, Tiesto was King.

If I could live in a dance club, I would. My friend Dinah, who's an interior designer, told me designers specifically create spaces where people can be "together alone." That's what it's called. The reality is, people like being around other people. We find peace in each other's presence, even when we don't speak. When I was living and going to college in Germany my body was in a battle with chaos, so a dance club seemed an unlikely place for me to find peace. Yet that's exactly where I found it. The inside of my body was discordant but engulfing it in the rhythm of an external pulse seemed to bring it into harmonious alignment with my surroundings, if only for a little while.

So years later, when I was living in LA and working out at Crunch Gym on Sunset, I was still using Tiesto's music to bring my body into alignment when he manifested in the flesh. I knew he was in town. The guy I had been dating, Dov, had gotten passes from work, but when I had broken up with him, I left the notion of seeing Tiesto in person behind. The concert was sold out.

I walked out of Crunch sweaty and satisfied and took the outdoor escalator down from the third level to the second. Coming off the escalator I noticed a line outside Tower

Records. Fueled by intrigue, I walked forward to get a closer look. Tiesto.

I called Billie from inside and issued an urgent request for her to buy a disposable camera and come up to Tower Records at the speed of light. There are friends who honor and respect your personal desires and those who get into action around them. Billie was the latter. She got there in time for us to capture a few pictures of Tiesto, arched over his turntables, earphones held up to one ear, manipulating the sound. Billie opted to stand outside while I waited in the long line for Tiesto's autograph. His long arms bent out to each side while he signed CD cover after CD cover. When I approached the table and spoke to him, he had not yet looked up from his flow.

"Tiesto, your music makes people really happy." I said, the reverence in my voice not hidden.

He stopped and looked up, quizzically at first. The line was comprised of mostly young Asian men so hearing the voice of a mid-thirties woman was probably not what he expected. His eyes were spread far apart on his broad face. One eye looked at me and the other slightly to the side. It threw me off a little, as did what he said next.

"Really?" he asked sincerely. "That's all I want."

When you watch someone's face softened, the structure of it changes. The planes rise and spread. Where they were previously stretched across bone, they fill with fluid and become spongy and flush. His eyes watered. Both of them. His words held us together in their truth.

"Are you coming tonight?" he asked.

"Yes," I said simply, without missing a beat.

He nodded and we smiled, the moment broken by his handler who moved me along.

I stepped out into the sunlight where Billie waited and told her what had happened.

"Cor!" she wailed. "Why didn't you ask him for a ticket?"

I had no words for her, or me. That had been my obvious opportunity and I'd let it slip by. Yet I was so certain I was going to see him that night. So, when Dov called later and said, "This is stupid. We're still dating. And we're going to Tiesto tonight." I accepted.

Dov and I stood outside and waited. And waited some more. The line going into the club began to thin. Suddenly, a metal door off to the left popped open and a woman called Dov"s name. We followed her down a long hallway, down some stairs, and down another long, dark hallway until we came to a small door. The second time I met Tiesto, he was facing the green room mirrors when we entered, being interviewed on camera. He stopped when he saw me come in the room in the mirror's reflection. I was stunned to be in that room and utterly shocked to be in Tiesto's presence twice in one day. He seemed equally surprised. After the interview was over, he came over and we all talked. Nothing of consequence was said but I'll never forget his look of surprise. It was a nice reminder that making a human connection with someone matters, and that life surprises us all.

The third time I met Tiesto it was intentional. A year after our first and second meetings, I sat in the lobby of the Mondrian Hotel, vibrating in excitement waiting for him, wondering if he'd remember me. When he came out of the elevator, it was clear he did not.

In the space between our meetings, I had married my passion for EDM music with my newfound love of leather and created a Thickskin DJ bag with Tiesto in mind. Glossy black stingray. Ballistic canvas. Gunmetal clips. Indestructible straps. It was a thing of beauty and this was my chance to give a bag to him personally. Well, actually, theft brought us together.

I had carefully wrapped the DJ bag in absorbent paper and delicate cloth and addressed it to his management offices in care of him, envisioning the moment he'd unwrap it. I had attached a card and sent it on its way. When I followed up on the gift a few weeks later, his management office told me, nonchalantly, that they received the bag and someone else had commandeered it and thought it was great.

"No worries," they said. "Just send another one. We'll make sure it gets to him."

That bag cost hundreds of dollars to create and the only way I'd give him another one is if it went directly from my hands into his. I made that known.

"He's staying at the Mondrian next week," the receptionist said, and made the arrangements.

"This is the bag?" Tiesto asked, turning it over in his hands in obviously amazement. I have never been more grateful for an inanimate object in my life. In an attempt to connect to him, I had greeted him in German. He's Dutch. It's not the same. As he turned the bag over and over in his hands, I surrendered my need to always be the cheerleader, always connecting, always reaching out verbally, and just let it all go.

He looked up at me, meeting my eyes. I nodded with a small, soft smile.

"It's beautiful," he said. And I could tell he meant it.

He left me there for a moment and ran back up to his hotel room. The extravagance of the gift had overwhelmed him, and he wanted to give me something in return. He came back down with his new CD in hand, with a personal message written on it, along with an invitation to spend New Year's Eve with him that year. Truthfully, neither of those things was the gift.

I left the Mondrian, drove home in silence, and sat in the car in front of my apartment building in a daze. There is a fullness surrounding a person, a roundness of aura, that stretches out beyond their being and calls them forward into who they could be and who they might become. Tiesto filled that space entirely and I'd never encountered that before. It called to me.

I sat in the Acura with both hands on the wheel, the engine off and silent. My life felt purposeless. Aimless. Void. I was spinning in circles but taking no ground. I was self-driven, self-propelled, self-oriented and sometimes self-sabotaging. I didn't know what I wanted but I knew I wanted less of myself and yet so much more.

Before my car would be totaled, before my life would be irreparably altered, I would sit behind the wheel of that very same car, with eyes closed and heart open, and whisper, "Here I am, God. Use me."

Sitting by the fire with Jax brought that moment back to mind.

"God, use me."

What had I even meant by that? I was not in the habit of calling on God. I held no expectation that a force, or source, beyond my awareness or comprehension held the responsibility, or ability, to use my life in such a way as to bring the peace and fullness I was looking for. Also, I reminded myself, clearly nothing had come of it. Only a few months after giving Tiesto the bag, I would have The Accident. I almost didn't make it to Tiesto's New Year's Eve celebration. I was reeling from the crash and nailed down by its effects. I showed up moments before midnight, watched from the VIP lounge, and left seconds after midnight. Tiesto and I never connected.

If God was going to use me, breaking me down as ruthlessly as he had seemed like a strange way to use a person. I was the definition of useless. You don't use someone bed bound. You don't use someone who moved through life as fifty cents on the dollar. You don't use someone who couldn't successfully bring a new life into the world. My idea of God using me included an establishment of elevated position. Everything about me and my life had gone in the absolute opposite direction. I couldn't get much lower down. I hadn't thought about that prayer (was it even called that?) for a very long time. And now, over a decade later, the notion resurfaced in my mind.

The sky was taking on a hint of morning light as 2015

cracked the dawn. It was the first day of a new year. It was time for Jax to go home and I walked him downstairs to the front door. He wrapped both of his arms around me in an engulfing hug.

"Say yes to what God is offering you, Cor," he said, while still holding onto me. "Be the dot."

He turned and put a hand on the door handle and turned to me, smiling mischievously, his eyebrows dancing.

"It takes a ridiculous amount of effort to just sit still. It's a lot of waiting around. But rest is recuperation, so let it happen and don't be in a rush."

I let Jax out into the cold and walked the three flights of stairs up to the master bedroom, turned on the fireplace and crawled into bed, eyes glazed against the dancing flame. In the coming months, I would move out of this house, too, and take another step toward building a new life. But in the warmth of the moment, I gave myself over to idea of rest and recuperation, and the stunningly beautiful thought that if I let it happen, healing - true healing - would come.

II

HEALING

BEGINNING TO CRAVE

SPRING, SEATTLE, 2015

DAMMIT! I hammered the steering wheel. I had purchased a Jeep because it was a symbol of freedom and adventure but I felt paralyzed. I was out looking for a new place to live and realized I had just driven in a circle. How can you live in a city for eight years and not even know your way around? I sat at an intersection, somewhere North of downtown Seattle, and couldn't move. There is a difference between choosing to be still and recognizing when you're stuck. I was stuck in scared. The house I had been living in had sold. I had thirty days to find a place, buy it, and move in.

At the end of 2014, Jax and I had agreed to each embrace a mantra for the new year. Mine was to "allow for mistakes and learning." If I was going to be the dot and stay open to a world of possibilities, I had to open my heart to the reality that I had no idea how this was all going to go, and I had to give myself a little grace as I tried to live in the unknown. I pulled over to the side of the road and called Lynn, my financial advisor.

"What neighborhoods do you like?" Lynn asked.

"I don't know," I said. I didn't know Seattle. I didn't even know myself.

I had been saving money assuming the Landlord and I would buy something together. Buying something alone felt totally overwhelming.

"Ok," Lynn said, breathing out slowly as a cue for me to follow suit. "Let's take a beat. Do you want to stay in Seattle?"

"I don't know," I said, breathing out. I closed my eyes and tipped my head against the seat rest.

"Do you want to stay here for a year?"

I turned my head and looked out the driver's door window at the beauty of Seattle, awash in greens and blues. "I don't know," I said again, after a minute.

Lynn let a few seconds pass before she said, very softly, "Then it's probably not a great time to buy a house, Cor. You just got out of a big commitment. And you just got your physical freedom. Why don't you live in that place for a while before you strap yourself down once again?"

I watched as a few people walked down the sidewalk in the sun. I couldn't argue with her. It made sense.

Gingerly, Lynn probed a little further.

"What is the one thing that's most important to you right now? What is the one thing you want to do above everything else?" she asked, and I knew right away.

"Move my body," I said in glorious defiance against the ghost of my illness.

"And where can you do that?" she asked.

"Green Lake," I said, popped it into my GPS, and oriented my car in that direction.

I BEGAN to move my body, slowly at first and not well measured, wake-shaking muscles that hadn't seen action in a while and discarding ideas of all that my body couldn't do, wouldn't do, shouldn't do.

At the same time, I was shedding the remains of what I had accumulated during a seven-year relationship and a four-floor house. It was all bound up in the same theme: purging.

There was a threshold to how much I could get rid of at once. The first layers of stuff came off relatively easily: the weight bench and treadmill I never used, the whiteboard, the copious table linens, fifty percent of an embarrassing number of vases. What I couldn't bring myself to get rid of went into storage.

When I went to Green Lake to find an apartment, there were only two buildings close to the lake and only one building that was outside the shadows of other buildings and bathed in sunshine. I only looked at units in that building and chose a two bedroom, two bath, corner unit facing North.

Not three blocks down the road after leaving, I called up the leasing agent and shifted my down payment to another unit: a 600 square foot studio facing South and drenched in light. When the Landlord and I had chosen the Palace, we specifically chose something sprawling, where space was abundant, in order to push out the walls of my enclosure. In this new life my weekly water infusions made possible I didn't want a space in which to luxuriate, I wanted to feel tightly swaddled and motivated to explore.

I also was crystal clear my home would be my sanctuary. After what happened in my home in Los Angeles, I drew firm boundaries before moving in as to who I would allow in. My dad, Jax, and Bart, when he visited, would be the only men given entry. Women would always be welcome.

I took my clothes, my books, and the guest bedroom bed to my new apartment, and surrounded myself with art. Both Kent's pieces hung by the front door.

This time is for you. Heal as you must.
Nothing will pass you by.
A whisper in the dark, Journal #5

∽

My cough would not go away.

"In Chinese medicine, the lungs are the seat of grief," Tuan said. "You are grieving."

Oh for the love of all things holy, I thought. Still?

Tuan was an acupuncturist. As he slid the needles into the fascia of my skin, I found myself hoping the small burr holes would act as pressure release valves, allowing the grief to escape soundlessly. My body was so expressive. It would be nice if, for once, my body could process something without needing to make an announcement. But grieving was a process, and I had made an agreement with myself to allow for it, learn from it, and not try to control how my body and soul processed grief or how long it would take to do so. I was a work in progress.

"It will be over when it's over," Theresa said. Healing would come when I released my grip on it.

My new apartment bedroom only had space for one bedside table, which was a perfect metaphor for this new existence: me, party of one. The rose quartz heart went back between the sheets. And to augment, I took a small piece of paper, wrote down a quote from the journals, and put it in a frame by my bedside. There is a moment in the morning when you first open your eyes, before the world takes shape, where you are suspended, floating, dancing in the fantastical, before what is real alights. I learned within this unique moment I had the ability to guide my thoughts and color my day. As new ground slowly began to build beneath me and a fresh layer of understanding would unfold, a new saying would be birthed and come to the fore. To guide it to its fullness within me, I would place it in the frame.

When you remove a breast from the mouth of a child it often cries, even though it's no longer hungry. That's what pacifiers are for that's what I needed: a soothing device until I could soothe myself. I was learning. This process was my healing framework. It was my way of finding my way back to my body and soul. The rose quartz heart, the journals, the framed journal sayings, I was putting together a small healing kit filled with touchstones to anchor me in the now, while pulling me forward toward hope.

I was also beginning to make friends, but I was awkward. In the eight years I had been off the earth, those my age sped past me. They had gotten married, had families, changed jobs, received promotions. They went to parties, saw movies, had dinners out, went dancing. They traveled, went on vacations, went to trade shows and sat on boards. While I, thankfully, did have a job and a relationship, we had done none of those things successfully. No standing dinners out or date nights at the movies. No international travel or beach vacations. No pool nights at dive bars or dress-up evenings at the symphony. No Sunday morning farmers markets or morning walks holding warm cups of coffee. The Landlord would go to work and I would stay at home. We had been together alone but mostly I had been alone alone. It was a strange vacuum. Life is a constant feedback loop and I had been out of it. In some ways I was old, having faced physical deterioration usually reserved for the aged, and in other ways, emotionally, I was very, very young.

In the process of my healing, I was following other people's footsteps out into the world in the same way I had Kim's. I was doing what other people liked to do, going where other people liked to go, engaging in what other people found fun. Theresa seemed to think that was ok for now. I was trying things on.

I sat on her couch with a picture on my phone. A Facebook

exploration led me to an old acquaintance of mine from LA. He studied Capoeira, a form of Brazilian martial arts, and was pictured with a huge Capoeira group. He was smack dab in the middle of a sea of humanity, leaning back and smiling, as the heap folded in on him. I held it out to Theresa.

"This is going to be me," I said with deep determination and equal skepticism. The phrase fake-it-till-you-make-it came to mind. I held it out again, even closer. "This is going to be me."

I didn't know if that meant I was going to take Capoeira, or what. I was still barely standing and would routinely get knocked down after small efforts of physical exertion, like walking around Green Lake two days in a row. Martial arts was probably a no. But something about the idea of belonging to a group that came together on common ground seemed appealing. Plus, he was laughing. And I wanted more of that for sure.

I also drafted off the business world. Steve Jobs, one of the world's most potent and effective businessmen, had been a man of intense focus. He'd famously held the leadership of Apple to three priorities, no more, no less. Anyone caught working on a priority outside of those three would be fired. It felt incredibly rigorous, but Apple's growth and market competitiveness were undeniable. If I was going to enter into a season of potent growth, I needed to set my own list of priorities so I wouldn't burn myself right back out again. I set the list at: community, impact, fun. I knew I needed community, as I had none. The illness had not killed me, but I knew if I didn't make friends and build community around me, the loneliness just might. Also, since I didn't die The Bag Lady, I wanted to begin trying on what it might feel like to make some type of social investment that would make an impact on the world in a positive way. It wasn't anything I had ever done before, but I was willing to allow for mistakes and learning as I tried things on. And I wanted to have fun. Lots and lots of fun.

Shortly after moving into my Green Lake apartment, I got

set up on a girl-date with Melody Biringer by a former Baby-Legs coworker. Per my coworker, Melody was the consummate connector, circle expander and force-multiplier. In my quest to build community, Melody was the jackpot.

I was working on a product launch for Agio and had been up since the very early morning and needed a break. When Melody's call came in, I was holding the phone in my hand, willing it to ring.

"Hi," Melody said. "I'm at Starbucks. Where are you?"

"Hi!" I said, glancing at my calendar, laughing. "We aren't supposed to meet until next week."

"Oh, shoot," she said. "Well, I'm here now. Any chance you can come down?"

"Already walking out the door," I said. And I was. I touched the "good in bed" phrase on Kent's painting, unlocked the door and walked down the hall.

Green Lake was a hive of activity, as always. Situated just North of downtown Seattle, it's a small man-made lake with a 5K circumference. Three miles. A perfect meeting place for outdoorsy Seattleites, rain or shine, and an easy forty-five minute walk. Melody and I lapped Green Lake easily, by foot and by mouth. We were quick friends, although I was fairly certain everyone who met Melody felt the same way. We weren't finished talking by the time the lap was done, so, free of demurring and without hesitation, Melody invited herself over. On our way up to my apartment we passed by the community room.

"What's this!" she asked excitedly. I clicked us in with my key fob.

The community room was wide and broad with a large deck at the far end, overlooking the courtyard, and a circular island in the kitchen that could seat at least twelve.

"We're going to throw a party here," Melody stated, as if it was already booked. And that's exactly what we did.

Melody threw a party and graciously called me the co-host. I provided the space, she brought the women, and over the course of an evening we all shared the real story of our lives. I shared the real story of my life. Out loud. Sharing my story allowed me to step back into the feedback loop I had long since stepped out of. I watched as my story took hold in the hearts of those who heard it. It surprised me and made me want to retreat and step back into the shadows I had become so familiar and comfortable with. But it also made me want to lean in. The ground floor forest of my soul had been so dry. Melody's party dropped a match to the dead undergrowth. The loneliness caught flame and was consumed. There was much more to burn, and more ground to cover, but Melody and her dinner party lit the first match.

And then she put me on stage in the middle of an urban campfire.

It turned out Melody didn't just host parties in my apartment community center, she hosted parties everywhere. A long-time propagator of living a life you craved, Melody hosted weekend workshops where hundreds of women would show up to open themselves up to what was burning inside. Melody asked me to keynote her August 2015 Urban Campfire event. It was an obvious yes, per my priorities, but at the same time, I couldn't have been more terrified. Melody wanted me to talk about living a life I craved, of which I had no clue. There is a vast difference between trying to survive and learning to thrive. I was still stuck somewhere in that expanse. So instead, I decided to just tell my story. Start from there. And talk about the fact that I didn't know how to live a life I craved when all my energy had been poured into the struggle of surviving. I wondered if other people felt that way, too.

The hour before the speech, I was lying down in Melody's hotel room at the Hotel Max in downtown Seattle, the conference venue.

"Normalize the adrenalin," CJ, a friend and former Agio coworker had said when he heard I was giving a speech.

I was trying.

The weekly IV's had begun stabilizing my energy over time but anything that overdrew on that bank account would knock me right back down to non-functional. If I was going to get on stage in front of hundreds of people, I needed to marshal all my resources to that end. Things like small talk with conference goers, or even standing upright, drained what precious little I had to give. I was holed up in Melody's hotel room, both conserving energy and collecting steam.

When it was time, I walked down the corridor, got off the elevator and stood at the back of the room until I was called to the stage. My heart was pounding as I took the stairs up to the platform. I was wearing a white dress, just like the white t-shirt of my dad's, the color of a fresh start. I leaned forward, my breath on the microphone as it had been on the guest bedroom mirror, and watched as the flicker became flame.

Wake up to who you truly are.
Theresa, Journal #8

❧

I WAS VORACIOUSLY DEVOURING all Seattle had to offer. I became a patron of the ballet and bought two season tickets, one for myself and a revolving ticket for a friend. Sometimes, if a ballet was very good, I would see it again, alone, because I wanted to and I could. I would sit alone in the theater, surrounded by humanity, and breathe in the collective air. Sitting in the dark with strangers, drinking in entertainment, was cathartic. Especially watching those who moved their bodies for a living. I reveled in their physicality.

I also began devouring music of all kinds. My life with the

Landlord had been void of music. I knew he was a big music lover, as was I, but if I ever walked into a room where he was listening to music, he would turn it off on my entrance. Music spoke to his heart and he had a practice of withholding his from mine.

Listening to music loudly was also a physical test of my healing. After Dr. Boatman had diagnosed me with dysautonomia, he cautioned me against listening to loud music or singing. Anything that would stimulate the vagus nerve was a potential trigger. I began listening to music and singing quietly and, low and slow, turning up the sound. If I had found peace in music once before, I thought, maybe I would find it there again. I had quickly fallen in love with Justin Bieber because, honestly, what forty-year-old woman hadn't.

As I left the ballet and walked out of McCaw Hall one evening, I noticed a huge line outside of the Key Arena. Justin Bieber was in town. Without a ticket, and in the pouring rain, I stood outside of Will Call, hoping against hope that I would get in. I was not the first in line, or the fiftieth, but I was the only one there alone, so when an agent appeared and said, "We have one ticket, is anyone here solo?", I found myself the only one walking through the arena door. And in the nosebleed section of the Key Arena, surrounded by screaming and adoring fans and being one of them, when Justin popped up from under the stage, I, along with thousands of twelve-year-olds, hit the floor and screamed the roof down.

FOR ALL OF THE NOISE, activity and sound that was coming into my life, I enjoyed finding the quiet, and hiking had become a favorite past time. On my way out the door to go hiking with my new friend Dizzy, I touched the phrase "good in bed" with the fingertips of my right hand.

"Not today," I said to no one and everyone. "Not today." And closed the door.

I'd like to say Dizzy was to blame for the decision to hike Rattlesnake Ledge in 80s get-up, although it just as easily could have come from her brain, as from mine. Regardless, I showed up to her house in black hot pants, a neon sweater shrugged off one shoulder and hiking boots. It was a good look. Sheena Easton would have been proud.

The Rattlesnake Ledge Trail is one of the most popular hiking trails in the Pacific Northwest region for three reasons: it's short, it's easy and it's easy to park. Hikers, spanning all ages and footwear decisions, file upwards on well-engineered switchbacks and around exposed cliffs and steep drops. After a 1.9 miles ascent, there is a junction and just to the left, Rattlesnake Ledge. The Ledge itself is a series of flat rocks upon which elated hikers could stop, rest, eat lunch and take in the view of Rattlesnake Lake below. It is a large pay-off for relatively little investment.

With each step I took forward up Rattlesnake Ledge Trail, I left where I'd been further and further behind. I thought about his mom, who said I needed a man who sat in an easy chair all day, and I took a step. I thought about my best college friend, who had abandoned me for having the audacity to be sick, and I took a step. I thought about the neurologist, who took my hands in hers and said I had a social anxiety disorder, and I took a step. I thought about the word selfish, and I took a step. Broken, and I took a step. Not good enough, and I took a step. Disabled, and I took a step. Labels kept falling off me, other people's notions of who I was, and who they said I would forever be, step by step by step. I was lifting them off my shoulders, but I was still dragging them somehow behind me. My body was light but my legs were still straining.

Dizzy took a series of photos of me at the top, arms wide, Stella the dog between my legs, both of us wagging happily. I had made it to the top but didn't want to hang out there just in case I didn't have the energy to make it all the way back down and an airlift off the mountain would be required. The fear of sudden physical implosion was still a constant.

We made it down the mountain fueled by stories of international travel (I had yet to), first kisses (a new door still in front of me) and whatever else two girls on a hike talk about. I had made it to the top and this new notion of frivolous but delicious banter delighted me all the way back down.

When the trail deposited us in the parking lot, I felt like I could finally relax and breathe out. My feet were light on the gravel, my elation turning to levitation. The view from the top had been clear as far as the eye could see. I carried it with me. But the view in the parking lot of Rattlesnake Ledge was almost as good. The sun was washing everything in a pink and orange glow. Dizzy was occupied cleaning up Stella's paws, I was occupied taking in the life all around and inside of me. My pulse had not yet settled, and I could feel the circulation warming my thighs. I ran my hands along them, rubbing down the prickling sensation, and closed my eyes.

"Thank you," I whispered quietly.

I opened my eyes again and shifted my gaze outward, looking up at the glistening rock face I had topped with my physical body. My breath caught and then unfurled slowly. It was so big. Majestic. Tears slotted into the outer sockets of my eyes. I blinked them back and turned my gaze to the expanse in front of me. The plane at the base of Rattlesnake Ledge had flooded years before, littering white birch tree stumps across the plane. The sun was setting, stacking layers of pink and orange and cream like a rocket popsicle.

The sun set, the rock face, the life-force coursing through me, the joy of a new friend - it all became an overwhelming cocktail of gratitude and the tears I had been holding back crested and ran down onto my cheeks. I couldn't believe I was here. I had spent so many years thinking I would never use my body again. I looked back on my life where I had made so many decisions based on the belief that I wasn't good enough, but I was surrounded by mounting evidence that belief was simply not true. I had broken in two and formed a belief I was unlovable yet here I was, so full with love.

Something was aligning. I felt liquid, fluid. I was swimming in gratitude and swallowed in love. A giant space began opening inside me, stretching me wide, a warm cascade filling my center, spilling over. My body rocked slowly and methodically, backwards and forwards, a pulsing answer to the setting sun. Inside, like a mantra, a phrase formed and repeated in rhythm: "This is beautiful. This is beautiful. This is beautiful."

And in the expanse of that moment I heard one thing back, *"So are you."*

There was, in my body, a great boom. The powerful chasm that tore apart after The Fall slipped, with tectonic force, back together. It was violent and it was instant and it was complete. Something cataclysmic had happened, from which I knew I would never recover. In an instant, I had been made whole.

The reality within me was at once silent and sonic, and I knew, beyond a doubt, I had been altered at the very core of my being. I didn't know what to think. I didn't know what to call it. I thought it might be God.

From that day forward, God took his place at the very core of my being and I began developing a personal, restorative relationship with him. Over the next few years, he would transform my beliefs, my behaviors and eventually all of my life.

$\sim$

I WENT BACK to New York again. With hydration flowing through my veins, I felt unstoppable. Lumen's illumination brought awareness to my need for IV hydration, and in an awesome act of provision, a company called The IV Doc opened at the very same time, girding my ability to travel again.

Regardless of living in states that are meant to be united, each state has its own healthcare parameters and plans. So although I had national healthcare, as well as what was called a "standing order" from my doctor allowing me to schedule and receive a saline infusion up to once a week at my discretion, it was only valid in the State of Washington. If I were to travel to New York, I would need to see a doctor in New York and secure the authorization all over again. This would include: finding a doctor in New York who specialized in my condition and took my out of state insurance; explaining my diagnosis and existing treatment plan; convincing that doctor to follow the same plan (and in my experience doctors have an inherent need to find their own reasoning, diagnosis and treatment plan); and then, with official New York prescription in hand, finding an infusion center that would take my insurance; and setting up an appointment. By the time I did all of that, my stay in New York would be over and I would need to head back to Washington again, if only to get hydration. The IV Doc removed all of those barriers and provided door-to-door IV hydration on demand.

The IV therapist I scheduled upon landing at JFK was already in the lobby waiting when I arrived at the Gansevoort Hotel. Within fifteen minutes, the fluid of life was running through my veins in the comfort of my hotel room and the IV nurse and I, yoked together for the next hour, fell into easy conversation.

Most of the nurses I encountered through The IV Doc were emergency room nurses and I took to them immediately. They held stories of tragedy and trauma with reverence and wit. They leveraged dark humor to compartmentalize urgent situations with empathy and distance. Most ER circumstances required both. It was a line they seemed to walk with grace and I marveled at their dexterity - emotional and physical.

The IV Doc nurse got the needle in on the first attempt. I felt very little. His hands were quick and sure. He worked in an ER in the Bronx and I imagined any person needing care would feel more comfortable with him around. I certainly did.

Trauma has a mildly addictive quality to it so it was funny to me, but not surprising, that an ER nurse, who had been shot and still had shrapnel in his body from gang violence that found its way into his hospital one night, would choose to put us in an imaginary emergency situation while we were sitting peacefully in the comfort of the Gansevoort Hotel.

"What would you take with you if your house was burning down?" he asked.

Sure, I thought bemused, the house is burning down. Let's go with that.

I reclined on the couch and looked up at the ceiling. The IV liquid had a sedentary effect on my body, as if the incoming fluid caused the dryness in me to open up, receive and exhale.

"I'm not really a sentimental person, so - " I started, but immediately cut myself off. "My journals," I said resolutely. "I'd save my journals."

Since the day I lay on the floor and watched Aunt Siggy read in her journal, I began compiling notes in mine. I had gathered sayings from all over; from friends, from family, things I had read or heard, nuggets of wisdom from therapy sessions with Theresa, song lyrics that stuck with me, I wrote them all down in a journal. What started out as one journal was now over thirty.

If my house were burning down, I would, without a doubt, want to save the journals. Those words in those books lifted me when I was face-down. Suddenly, I had this sinking feeling I was sitting on something that wasn't mine to sit on. What if those words weren't given to me just to inspire and lift me? What if they were meant to lift others as well?

And no sooner was it out of my mouth when I heard in my mind, *"They're not yours to keep, they're yours to give away."*

I had no idea what that meant.

Nothing will be wasted; everything will be used.
Theresa, Journal #14

TAKING AUTHORITY

Spring, Seattle, 2015

Facebook had become my new favorite thing. I was creating a version of myself as a woman who was out and about in the world and I couldn't wait to share it. Facebook provided a reverberation I would review in the evening hours, once the day was done and night had fallen, looking at the moments I had captured, thinking excitedly, "I did that! I'm that girl!"

When a co-worker from Agio flew in and drove me up to the base of Mt. Rainier and I got out and played in the snow. Captured.

When I went out to dinner with a few new friends and made it through the night without having an episode. Captured.

When I went to the Nutcracker ballet in a gorgeous plunging dress and posed by the giant Christmas Tree, my head thrown back in laughter. Captured.

So, when the Landlord got engaged less than a year after we split, Facebook captured that, too. And those who received the broadcast, who felt responsible for carrying my heart, their texts started flooding in.

Facebook had been a sore subject between us long before then. Four years after we had been living together, he refused to change his relationship status from single to anything that acknowledged we were attached in any manner. And since I barely left the house, he wasn't at risk of me posting pictures of us together.

"I use it for work," he said sheepishly, trying to deflect my inquiry, but we were already in a fight. He had received an invitation from his mentor to a festive gathering and on the envelope it was addressed to the Landlord and Guest. I was unacknowledged in his circle, by his family and even by him.

Unnamed.

Unclaimed

Unseen.

Uninvited.

There are things in relationships that mean nothing or something. Not claiming me on Facebook, I was aware enough to know that meant something. A few weeks after we broke up, he changed his Facebook status to, "in a relationship." And less than a year after we broke up, he was officially, per Facebook, engaged. My presence in his life had been almost invisible and whatever evidence there had been, minimized or evaporated now that we were in the rear view. He claimed her from the very beginning, as did his mom, who made her the cover of her own Facebook page.

I learned the news while on the road to IKEA. I pulled in, sat in the parking lot with my engine running and called Theresa. I wasn't sad as much as stunned.

"You would not be who you are without that relationship," Theresa said. "And who you are is going to touch so many more people. It prepared you for something else. It just continues to take time."

It was an irritating notion that whatever changes my life was going through would continue to take time, while he seemed to be moving with lightning speed forward, forward, forward. My life felt empty by comparison and I said something to that effect.

"You have not been emptied of your personality or of your gifts and talents," Theresa challenged, before redirecting my focus. "And ask yourself, are you being emptied of everything or is your slate being cleaned for something entirely new? Maybe you're being wiped clean so you can be used. There is real value in where you are."

I looked out the window and watched as a father of five pushed a flat cart stacked with boxes behind the back of my Jeep. The littlest one, maybe five or six, wanted to climb up the stack and ride on top. The mom was having none of it, pulling her off by one arm. The father, slightly sweaty by the exertion, ignored the commotion entirely and had a dead-lock focus on the back of his suburban parked next to my car. I heard what Theresa said but I was not picking up the where-you-are-has-so-much-value vibe she was trying to put down.

"This is where God does some of his most regenerative work and there's nothing for you to do. It's being done for you," Theresa continued. And was there ever truth to that.

Theresa was an unexpected bomb planting machine. Seasoned by adventure, with a full and exotic life behind her, Theresa was someone who had been through the valley of unbearable battles herself and had come out the other side an overcomer. She was short-statured and solid and looked like a friendly grandmother you couldn't wait to hug. Her unassuming exterior left a person comfortable and wide-open in such a way that she was able to insert small landmines of life-altering thought that would detonate without warning. If God had closed the schism between who I was and who I believed myself to be,

Theresa was in the business of blasting the foundation of what I had previously built on top of my mistaken identity to make way for all the new I could feel in my bones was coming. Presently, however, I was living in a whole lot of rubble.

Time, possessions, opportunities, relationships - it was all running through my fingers like water and yet I was supposed to sit still and be the mother-loving dot?

"In my heart of hearts I honestly believe this is so much bigger than a man, or a job, or family. You are being called back into relationship with God. That is where you'll find peace. And when that is restored, you will find all the other things thrown in as just abundance. God has a plan to work out in you, Cor, and believe me, it's going to be great."

Jax came over to my apartment later when he got off of work. He took off his coat and settled into my couch. I had found a certain level of peace after the days events, but was still pretty shell shocked.

"Whether he waited sixteen years or sixteen minutes, it doesn't matter," Jax said to the he's-getting-married-so-soon news. "It doesn't matter to you at all."

I wasn't sure I agreed. I found the velocity of the Landlord's race to the altar after seven years of sitting on me, like a chicken on an egg, a little hurtful.

"Of course it hurts," Jax said in validation. "The entire process hurts. You're not just bringing yourself back to life, you're bringing online your spiritual, emotional and physical sides, too, so you can live whole."

I went into the kitchen to make us tea and turned my back to him. I closed my eyes. The idea of wholeness smoothed the tension in my temples. I knew I had been made whole at the base of Rattlesnake Ledge but what Jax was saying was that there were more steps required, more things for me to learn, more beliefs for me to shed, in order for me to actually live whole. But truthfully, it was all I could do not to put my fist through a wall.

"You don't have to react to this news," Jax said. The thought of non-reaction seemed deliciously provocative. "You can respond and say, 'I am not going to be upset by this because I choose not to be upset.' You've changed from that part of your life so moving forward, it doesn't matter."

I brought two cups of tea over and put one cup inside his waiting hands. I sat down on the carpet and held onto the other. Jax took a sip, put his teacup back down and leaned forward.

"You overcome, every day, because *that's.what.you.do*," he said, staccato. "In this moment, you get to respond and if you truly believe how powerful you are, you get to choose. None of your human reactions are going to help you move forward. Sure, feel them. Acknowledge them. And chose to move forward."

I breathed in deeply and let the impact of the morning's news move through me. A small tear formed in the middle of my eye and slid down my face. I looked at Jax and, biting the inside of my lip, let out one short sob and shook my head.

"I know," Jax said, holding my eyes. "I know. Don't blame yourself for feeling the way you feel about this news. It's an outside physical force. But Cor, trying to be healthy trumps all of this. The only thing that's going to heal you, is you. There is no more Landlord. It's done."

Just give yourself 1,000 pieces of grace. For not being as far as you wanted to be. For not feeling good enough. For feeling stuck. Forgive yourself. Say, "I hear you, I love you, and you are forgiven."
Yaela, Journal #14

After Jax left, I sat back down with my tea and my thoughts and thought more about the idea of it being done. Really done. Over and done. What if his walking toward this new chapter in life meant I could walk, in freedom, toward mine? The problem was I didn't know how to sever the tie.

I slid down against the white leather chair until my neck cradled on the seat and looked up at the ceiling.

Something Jax had said came back to me, "The only thing that's going to heal you, is you."

When my brother was little, he had this saying he would yell at my mom to assert his independence.

"You're not the boss of me!" he would shout in defiance. It made us all laugh, except him. To him it was stone-cold truth. Which, of course, it was. What my brother knew when he was barely out of diapers, I was just now realizing in my mid-forties. I was the boss of me. Or, at least, I needed to learn to be.

Theresa introduced me to the concept of developmental delays - the arrested development of emotional maturity - and when she did, I knew exactly what she was talking about. I had experienced it firsthand. When I lived in Chicago, I dated a man briefly who was a recovering alcoholic. My dysautonomia symptoms were flaring and I had been diagnosed with mono to boot. I was wracked with exhaustion and he stepped valiantly in to save me, doing all things for me big and small. But as I began to recover and required (and desired) less and less of his doting, his symptoms also flared. The last time I saw him, he was on top of a cement pylon, wasted and directing traffic outside Wrigley Field after a Cubs game, while the police were trying to talk him down. I hadn't experienced alcoholism before and struggled to make sense of a guy who looked put together on the outside but struggled with demons on the inside. I wasn't at the point where I could see that we had been drawn to each other because *game recognize game* and our broken parts had simply magnetized.

In my research, I found that the moment an alcoholic takes their first drink, they stop maturing emotionally. Clearview Treatment Programs says, "When you live day-to-day in survival mode, emotional growth takes a back seat and gets no priority in life. Every single problem that has been brushed aside is still there, waiting to be dealt with once you become sober."

So, I wasn't dating Clark, the executive in his mid-30s. I was dating Clark, the 14-year-old kid who, when he took his first drink, stopped growing emotionally. Theresa gently let me know that I had some of those same markings, that trauma does the same thing. And I fell out of the window at seven.

The immediate result of trauma on a life is the interruption of growth and maturity. It is one of the easiest signs to spot in people who have experienced significant trauma. Not all trauma stunts maturity. Sometimes, things happen that overwhelm the system and a body shuts down critical thought and begins running a fight-or-flight protocol. Often, after the over-whelming event passes, a person can return to normal func-tioning as before. But trauma called "neglect," which can include things like malnutrition, abandonment, insecure attachment bonds or lack of joy in the home - that kind of trauma always inflicts damage and leaves a hole in maturity. I had such a hole.

If the only thing that could heal me was me, I needed to learn how to be the boss of me. I needed to learn how to be ridiculously in charge of myself. I needed to hold onto only those behaviors that would move me forward toward maturity, which meant I had to let him, and everything having to do with him, go. I had other things to do. I needed to learn how to Boss.

You are responsible for the stability and order of your environment.
Theresa, Boss Training, Journal #15

∽

IF THE LANDLORD had been my sun and my moon, Bart, and Agio, had been my North Star. Inexplicable to me even now,

Bart had found me by happy accident from 3,000 miles away. A breadcrumb from BabyLegs led him to me.

My first project for Bart consisted of creating the brand identity for an iPhone bike mount he was launching. He flew to Seattle from New York so we could do the initial brand strategy session in person. He arrived looking New-York-fabulous. I opened the door in yoga pants.

Three months after delivering the project, Bart called me again to help him to name, develop and launch a managed IT service provider positioned to serve the world's leading hedge funds. After the company was launched, neither one of us wanted to let go, and I, home and bed bound, physically devastated but cerebrally in tact, became a founding executive team member of what would grow to be a 150-person company with offices in Oklahoma and New York.

If Bart and I were separated by a great distance geographically, there was no distance at all between our hearts and minds. We had an uncommon bond. Bart often introduced me as family and the first person hired, which made the thought of leaving it all hurt like hell.

Bart had brought industry into my life when I was flailing. He gave structure to my days when time threatened to lump together. He made me feel seen when I was nearly invisible and spoke validation into my life in the exact places and spaces I was broken. My love for Bart and for Agio was inseparable but if I was to separate myself from everything I was, to step into everything I was becoming, I had to let go of the proverbial shore.

A new friend had flown up to Seattle to visit and we were walking Green Lake. A fresh invitation was at the door. If I wasn't going to move to New York, if I wanted to build a rich life of community, the two could not co-exist. New York, and all my coworkers, were 3,000 miles away and I could simply no longer stand to be alone. I struggled with a conclusion all the way around Green Lake until my friend asked me to answer this one simple question.

"Fill in the blank," she said. "This is it and this is perfect. Who I am is a possibility for…?"

Her voice trailed off.

My answer was the makings of pure desire. I didn't calculate. I didn't pontificate. I simply closed my eyes and whispered, "*More*."

The next morning I texted Bart and asked if we could talk. By the time he called back, I was in the bathtub and I stood to answer the phone. Dripping wet and symbolically naked, I gave him my notice and hung up the phone.

When a road comes to an end say, "we did the best we could do together," and move on.
Paloma, Journal #2

13

FAITH TOUR

October, Los Angeles, 2015

I was sitting at the gate when Amina called. When I had come back to life, I dug up old friends and Amina, a friend from college in Germany, was one of them. For a decade I had been absorbing all I could on health, nutrition and the nervous system. Hungry for more material and a broader pallet of interests, I began polling people on their inputs. Old friends were first up. What were they listening to? Reading? Or watching? What was capturing their attention that might also capture mine? I was wide open and absorbent so when Amina suggested I listen to the sermons from the church she and her husband Paul attended in Franklin, Tennessee, I did. I thought, if my life was to open like a book, why not start with the Bible? I also figured that one sermon was about forty-five minutes long, which was also approximately one lap around Green Lake. Two birds. One stone.

Somewhere between one and ten sermons, Amina and Paul moved from Tennessee to LA, swiftly and unexpectedly. For two people knit so tightly into a community they loved, the move was hard and the absence of their friends, jarring, and Amina had shared her desire for new community with me.

"Amina!" I cried. "You should try out Mosaic!"

While listening to the sermons from Paul and Amina's church, I happened across one by a visiting pastor from a church in LA. The pastor was fresh, and funny, and his name was Hank. And Hank was from Mosaic. And Mosaic was in LA.

I stood at the gate waiting to board my plane for LA when Amina called. She and Paul had been to Mosaic and she wanted to tell me all about it. At the very same time, a JetBlue gate agent lit up the waiting area with this announcement: "Will the group from Mosaic please board the plane." Amina and I laughed at the coincidence.

I was headed down to LA for an adventurous weekend with Yaela - a woman I had crossed paths with earlier but was just beginning to get to know - lured by the scent of community, sensuality, magic and potentially a little bit of dangerous fun. The video Yaela had forwarded was cryptic and alluring. Shafts of wheat released their pollen payload in the harvest sun. There were a few trees, some music, some dancing, fire (but also possibly a sparkler), and the single phrase: *Hallow's Eve*. Yaela's email to me was an equally cryptic one-liner: *Come to LA for an adventure with me!*

I booked my flight.

Immediately on touchdown in LA, the EDM and trance music slogan PLUR (Peace Love Unity and Respect) was back in full effect. It was the 90s all over again. Just like in Germany, in the days of underground dance parties and secret raves, Yaela and I had the car packed and were waiting for the email to come in, telling us where to go. It came and off we went. We had two hours to get there before the gates would close. Oh yeah, adventure had begun.

We arrived at the tree reserve, dust licking at the undercarriage of the vehicle, as we drove down the narrow road and onto the expansive dirt parking lot. One hundred and fifty people would drive down this same road and open onto this same parking lot, and then the gates to the reserve would close us in, and the rest of the world out. The exploratory experience, put on by a group called Habitas, was the testing ground for their still-forming concept; one where a global community could find a global home by fostering a space of connection and release, an intoxicating combination. It was a pseudo-Burning Man but exclusive, luxurious and elevated.

A woman in a top hat sat behind the check in desk. Through red, full lips she issued community rules and handed over a little satchel. In it was a long brass chain with a circle pendant, a compass of sorts, with three crossed arrows. I slipped it over my neck where it bounced lightly against my heart. Yaela and I crossed the threshold carrying our luggage and followed a dirt path onto a flat promenade that wove around a small lake. White canvas tents slipped three-quarters around the lake, the first of which was a grand communal tent. We peeked inside as we walked by, it's curtains flung open, it's mouth welcoming and wide.

The sun was setting by the time we unpacked and ventured into the big tent again. We would spend the evening there, reclined on Persian rugs, propped up against wine colored pillows, legs elevated on leather poufs, Moroccan lanterns throwing a yellow cast against the white stretched canvas walls. Somewhere in the evening, Yaela and I stepped out onto the sand and followed the path to the dance floor, where down-tempo beats were bending in the hands of a man with a pitch-black beard and impenetrably dark glasses. He hovered over the tables and wove the musical fabric for the rhythm of the night. Yaela and I moved to his beats, first together and then apart, and then I walked back to our tent as Yaela kept dancing. The first morning came.

The entire weekend was designed to be intimate and communal. I approached sleeping in a tent full of strangers with caution, pressing myself up against the very edge of the tent with Yaela protectively on the other side. The borders of my energy still felt porous and open, too much, too close to too many people, and everything would leak. I was learning how to self-contain. I did not wake drained.

Yaela and I were roused by the warming sun and walked back to the big tent together. We pulled food onto our plates from the buffet and sat down on leather Moroccan poufs across from each other at a round hammered brass table. There were two other people at the table already; one bearded and older, wrapped in layers of fabric, his face covered in a long white beard; the other fresh faced, clean shaven and acerbic, his calling card. The conversation wrapped around spirituality. The older gentleman was Jewish by birth, Kabbalist by evolution. The kid, atheist.

Two other men entered the tent. I didn't see them approach but I felt them as they sat down. Something had electrified. They sat beside me, one on each side, flanking me. They were both way too close. I was suspicious immediately. Both wore white from head to toe, but then, so did I. We didn't take pause when they sat down. The Kabbalist, who went by a chosen name, was talking about the recent movement within Judaism and Christianity to come together based on the shared history of both. The man to my left, his salty beard the only testament to his age, said, "Yeah, the head of Mossad came to my house and was trying to get me to be a part of it."

I would see a picture of our conversation later, my knees oriented toward him, my body leaning away. That may have been the very moment I leaned away.

"I'm sorry," I said, astonished and incredulous alike. "Who are you that the head of Mossad is showing up at your house?"

"I am the pastor of a church in LA," he said.

I closed my eyes slowly and opened them again, taking in his face more fully. I didn't want to ask but the moment was unfolding faster than I could contain it. I already knew the answer.

"Which church?" I asked quietly, knowingly, eyes closed again, breath exhaled, shoulders bent, leaning forward into the serendipity.

"Mosaic," he said.

My heart stopped with a thud. I shook my head slightly.

"And you are?" I asked, turning to the younger man on my other side.

"Also a pastor at Mosaic," he said. How many pastors did Mosaic actually have?

I looked at Yaela, eyebrows raised. She knew the story of the aligning coincidences concerning Mosaic. I could tell by her face she found it as strange as I did. I would confirm this later on the car ride home.

Another man joined our table. He would tell me so later, as in the rush of the moment, I hadn't even noticed. He and I would meet later that evening, officially, by the fire. He would be in a rabbit suit. I would look like a Christmas Tree.

I AWOKE in our tent when the music stopped. It was cold. And quiet. I had grown accustomed to the sound. Our tall tent mate returned with his girlfriend. They whispered to each other as they undressed, two bent reeds quivering by fairy light. I was awake and loosed. Something inside me felt wild. I felt for Yaela next to me. She was quiet and asleep. I sat up.

"Can I borrow your coat?" I whispered to the tall man, who was still layering his sleepwear. I surprised him.

"Sure, it's not mine," he said. "I think it's Bob's. He was wearing it last." He gave to me what had been given to him. It was a condonable exchange in communal living. What's mine is yours. What's yours is mine. Bob was tall. In his coat, I was swimming.

The fake fur was exceedingly warm and fell almost to the floor. When the reeds laid down and were put to bed, I took the string of fairy lights that illuminated our tent, wrapped them around me, and set out into the night. It was dark. In the distance I could see the fire pit still burning.

I moved through the night like a wandering Christmas Tree, bulky, furry, and lit up with fairy lights. I approached the fire silently from behind and slid into a canvas recliner. I was not alone. One person was sleeping. Another was smoking. Yet another was nodding to the beat of the music still playing in his head. I leaned back into the chair and let the cool air caress my cheeks. It felt so good to be up at night. I looked up at the sky and thought about my conversation with Emerson, the junior pastor from Mosaic. When he was young, he had been engaged. But before he and his fiancé were able to be married, she died, and through a cascade of sorrow and circumstance, Emerson ended up in prison. But now he had a wife and a son and a new life in Jesus, preaching to thousands about the healing in Christ. I thought about how sorrow sets you on a collision course with the absolutely unexpected. You think you know where you're going. You think you know where it all leads. You don't.

"I have been waiting to talk to you all weekend," he said, sliding into place beside me. He was handsome in a way that was familiar to me. Israeli. Curly dark hair. A personality that was broad and embracing, magnetic and enveloping. I had met a man like this when I had been out one night with Krish. I called him The Mayor. This man's name was Maor and he was dressed as a rabbit. Maor's rabbit suit covered his entire body except for his face, which he turned to me, open and probing. We talked all through the night and into the morning. We ebbed through moments of engagement and deep pockets of silence. The fire died. The sun rose. And by daylight we separated, attached warmly at the heart.

~

"I LIKED it but I'm not sure if it's my tribe," Yaela said, as we drove home from Habitas in shades of reflection.

I knew about Yaela's quest for tribe. It was foundational to us both. We joked about how we were on the hunt for a place to belong, approaching every situation like a Dr. Seuss book, asking inquisitively, "Are you my mother?"

"What did you think?" she asked.

I looked out the window, my eyes unfixed as the landscape blurred past. For most of my life I had felt like an outcast, an outsider looking in. Something in my physical brokenness and following fifty-cent story instilled a belief that I was inappropriate for consumption and unwanted in most company. I believed no one would want to sit at my table or invite me to theirs. It was untrue in fact, but alive in feeling.

"I can't explain it," I said. "I feel welcome at every table." No one was more surprised than me. I smiled at this new awakening of acceptance.

"That's great, babe," she said, easy and open, and for a minute or two we drove on.

A lone cloud appeared, littering the brilliant California sky and my spirits sank slightly, along with my smile.

"But I don't know where to go from here," I said.

"What do you mean?" she asked, both hands on the wheel, her gaze soft. We were still in the bubble of the weekend.

"I still feel invisible. Like no one knows me. Like I can't catch up. I lost so many years when everyone else was making friends, getting married, having kids, growing their networks. I did none of that. So few people even know I'm alive. I feel like everyone else knows, like, five thousand people," I said, leaning into the exaggeration. "And me? Maybe five people know my name."

Yaela and I were growing together, both caught in the wake of our past beliefs, both reaching forward, necks out, stretching for more. Growing confidence and lingering insecurity made strange bedfellows.

Offer up your insecurity with a prayer and it will be replaced
by spiritual strength.
Paloma, Journal #7

My phone pinged twice on Monday. Once from Maor and once from Emerson. Emerson invited me to Mosaic for mid-week service on Wednesday. Maor's text said, "Can you come for dinner? I want to welcome you to my table."

I went to Mosaic alone on Wednesday but arranged for Amina and Paul to meet me there. As I walked up the front steps to the entrance, I saw Emerson. He was waiting for me. We embraced and - quick like lightning - he began pulling people in and introducing me to them. With every introduction of, "Hey, this is Cordila," came a quick gasp for air or a shout of delight. At first, I fell fluidly against the acknowledgement, assuming Emerson had shared our connection with a few of his friends. But as the wave kept coming and the sphere kept growing, so did my discomfort. Emerson stepped into my closing door.

"Is this feeling a little weird?" he asked, a pitch-perfect reading.

"A little," I responded, trying out my new muscle of being honest in the moment.

"Erwin was really moved by your story and talked about it from stage during the services on Sunday," he said. And without missing a beat and speaking right to my heart he said, "I bet five thousand people know your name."

Time was collapsing all around me. What I knew I knew,

and what I thought I knew, and what I didn't yet know but had a deep sense of knowing was congealing into the same sanctified moment in time.

If churches are meant to feel sacred, this felt divine. If I was meant to feel special, I felt seen to the core of my being. If the experience of God was meant to feel personal, this felt specific to degrees unbelievable, yet I was falling, headlong, toward belief.

Emerson guided me through the dark sanctuary as the wake of greetings continued and showed me to my seat. The entire row had stickers on the back of each velvet-lined chair, which read: Reserved for Cordila. By the time Amina and Paul showed up my legs were weak and everything in me was crumbling. The music swelled and carried me away on a notion of worship I was only beginning to understand. And when it died down, Emerson chased up on the stage to do quick series of announcements and at the end said, "I know she's going to kill me, but I wanted to let you all know that Cordila is here," and he pointed in my direction. With that, the congregation, which was already standing, turned to me and cheered.

I looked, in utter disbelief, at the sea of smiling faces. I looked with the widest of eyes at Emerson who was looking back at me, smiling. The musicians started playing again and the large space filled with music. I didn't know what to do. I wasn't expecting any of this. I wasn't ready to feel this tsunami of overwhelming love, not from Emerson or Mosaic or Maor. Not from Yaela or Dizzy or Melody. Not because of new friends or a renewed body or a new chance at life, but from this growing and visceral understanding of God. Could it be possible he was real? Could it be possible this was love? Could it be possible that in all I had lost, I was found all along?

The music surrounded me, reverberating within me. In that moment, I did the only thing I could do, the only thing I wanted to do, the thing I felt magnetically pulled to do. I closed my eyes. I raised my hands. And filled my mouth with song.

YAELA and I had come together as both our relationships were ending and our friendship had become a safe place for us to explore new ways of being in life, in relationships, and in faith. We were learning to live life boldly, love tightly and loosely, and step toward faith with intention. Yaela would come with me the next time I went to Mosaic and was the loudest praise-giving, worship-singing, Jew in the Christian bunch. I would reciprocate by attending synagogue, Jewish High Holidays, and Shabbat dinners. We invested mutually in each other's exploration of what was, and what could be, and where we might fit in the world. It was beautiful and wonderful and supportive and freeing. We called these excursions Faith Tour. Something about it felt like home.

14

LEANING IN

My trip to LA had been lavish and indulgent. It had knocked everything loose, strewn my life on the floor. I was threads held together; my seams had all sprung. And I couldn't deny it, I was hungry for more.

I had jumped off the end of the dock with Agio but had no plans for what was next in my life. On Theresa's urging, I was practicing vision-casting, learning to identify my core needs and vision-cast a life for myself that I would like to lead. She said it would be fun. I thought it was excruciating. All I knew was *community, impact, fun,* and I held onto that like a dog with a bone.

After my successful hike of Rattlesnake Ledge, my daily walks around Green Lake, and my invigorating time on Faith Tour, I went looking for more opportunities to enjoy the outdoors. On MeetUp, I saw a walk in Discovery Park, the largest natural park in the city of Seattle, with the local Lean In Seattle Chapter and signed up to go.

Driven by my multi-faceted fascination with Facebook, I read the seminal work of Sheryl Sandberg, Facebook's COO, called *Lean In: Work, Women and the Will to Lead*. That book served as a battle cry and movement igniter for women globally who wanted more from their careers and their lives. I recognized the cry as my own.

Shortly after the Landlord and I had started dating, he had come home to the loft one night elated and told me he was going to be initiated. His mentor, an Ivy-League grad, successful entrepreneur and influential investor in the Seattle tech landscape and beyond, had built a tight men's group committed to investing in each other. What the Landlord was sure would be a night of drunken debauchery, instead was an induction into a sacred and powerful group of men who would meet monthly and go on large trips together, all for the purpose of moving their lives and careers forward, individually and collectively, through community. It influenced me greatly, if only by proxy. When I came back to life, I resolved to build a similar group for myself, though I had no idea how. This Lean In walk in Discovery Park, a mashup of both community and fun, seemed like a very good place to start.

I arrived to find eight women and one support dog and we quickly set off. I was fundamentally scared of small talk. I felt like I carried a conversation bomb from which, once deployed, it would be impossible to recover. I'd already seen the aftereffects of the sentence, "I was bedbound for eight years," now several times over and so far hadn't found a conversational path that let me avoid it. It was a verbal showstopper.

After filtering through the lightest conversation possible with several of the women, I stopped short and split off every time the dreaded moment threatened to come. I was forging a solo path when the co-founder of the Lean In Seattle Chapter, Pam, came up alongside me and picked up rhythm with my steps. We walked silently for a while and then found our way into easy conversation. This time, when the bomb surfaced, for some reason, I didn't shy away from it. I told Pam the bomb and it didn't explode. Instead, it expanded.

As a group, we emptied ourselves onto the beachfront and walked on damp, smooth rocks toward the lighthouse. We stopped and took a group picture. With the dog, too. I would look at that photo for weeks to come. It gave me a sense of a life to look forward to.

On the way back to the parking lot, Pam asked if I would be willing to keynote the Annual Lean In Seattle Chapter meeting in December and, with it, offered another beacon of hope.

Shortly after I left Agio, Pam officially asked me to co-host the Seattle Chapter as she was, after two-years of exceptional volunteer service dedicated to helping members accomplish their professional and personal goals, ready to move on.

When I went to the December planning meeting, Pam was unable to attend. The two other women slated to share the future leadership of the chapter with me were, and we all sat down. This would be my second keynote in Seattle but my first business-centered one and I was eager to learn what kind of content they thought would be most helpful for me to deliver.

"So," I inquired with an overexcited grin. "What's the plan?"

They looked at each other, a little surprised.

"Oh. We're not stepping in until January of next year. Until then, you're leading the chapter." In their minds, it was settled. It didn't take me two seconds to settle it in mine.

"Yes," I said, a stiffness raced up my spine and across my shoulders, changing my toothy smile into steely resolve. *Community. Impact. Fun.* "Yes. I am."

And just like that, I stepped into my new chapter.

The right choice for growth is expansion and evolution.
Activate what's in your hand.
Theresa, Journal #14

∿

I THREW everything I had learned drafting off Bart and co-building Agio into this new venture, setting up the foundational framework and business model to run the chapter like a business. Since it was a volunteer position, I sat down with Lynn and Theresa to discuss the pros and cons of taking a sabbatical and investing myself in building the Lean In Seattle Chapter for a year. We determined it not only met every pillar of my priorities, it also would provide an opportunity to build a powerful business network, lend visibility and be a resource for career opportunities moving forward.

The two women slated to co-host the chapter in January opted out of moving forward into leadership, and I quickly executed a merger with another local Lean In team and shifted the leadership structure from two leaders to many. With my health improving but still tenuous, I knew any structure built solely on my back could not, and would not, survive.

As a team, we developed mission, vision and values, and identified three core priorities to determine where we would focus our efforts. We established key performance indicators with metrics, and set up weekly calls to stay in alignment and execute against our stated mission. Our aim-for-the-fences metric was that we would do something so big, and so impactful in the Seattle community, that Sheryl Sandberg herself would have to come up to Seattle and check it out.

Twenty-eight women showed up to December's Lean In Seattle Chapter Annual Meeting and heard my keynote. I hired a videographer to capture the talk so we could share it on YouTube and begin spreading our new message: that we were in the business of moving women forward.

Within months, our membership exploded and attendance at our monthly meetings doubled and then tripled in size. We moved out of the community room in my apartment building where Melody and I co-hosted that first dinner and began looking for corporate spaces to accommodate our burgeoning group.

I was comfortable here in this space where I could build friendships and a network by proving what I could do. During my keynote, I had even said if you do great work you won't have to look for a job, opportunities will come to you. I believed it wholeheartedly and became a magnet for women looking to stretch their legs in leadership and prove what they could do, too. I had no idea I was perpetuating the very same cycle of do, do, do, prove, prove, prove.

Recovery is a journey.
Theresa, Journal #10

Our Chapter was comprised mostly of women in transition and our leadership team, itself, was home to an eager and assertive bunch. Many leaders saw their contribution the same way I did: a career opportunity wrapped in community, impact and fun. Every last leader poured out of the soul of herself and eagerly waited for opportunities to come, while employing every strategy available to make them happen. In the process, we were lifted and buffeted by the notion that we were involved in helping women learn, achieve and grow, and were galvanized to be part of the critical and global conversation of advancing the careers of women at a time when the whole world seemed to be watching and listening.

Two months after refashioning our chapter, a few of us were selected by LeanIn.Org to sit on the Regional Leaders Team with a group of top performing women from around the globe. One of them was Lieutenant Colonel Erika Cashin, United States Air Force, who led Lean In Military and was, in my mind, one of the coolest cats around. The feeling turned out to be mutual and mere seconds after the Regional Leader's group call was over, Erika and I jumped onto a call of our own and that's when we started to really get down.

Erika had a heart for women veterans and shared with me the horrifying suicide and homelessness rates that strike women veterans at a higher percentage than the men. She spoke with deep passion about the impact loss of community and mission had on those accustomed to the military brotherhood/sisterhood camaraderie and the high calling of serving God and Country. Leaving the military to serve in the private sector, where individuality reigned supreme and mission was sometimes indiscernible or uninspired, many struggled with the transition. Erika told me about the opportunity for the private sector to come alongside these transitioning veterans to help them bridge the gap from one world to the other, and also provide the private sector the opportunity to learn from the valuable traits those with a military background had to offer. She was going to start a chapter of Lean In designated specifically for women veterans and I was clear about one thing if nothing else: wherever she was going, whatever she was doing, I was doing it with her. If these women veterans needed a sense of community and a place to belong, I was going to do whatever I could to give them one.

Learn to stand back, relax, and let a larger purpose be revealed.
Theresa, Journal #8

Through Lean In, I was speaking more and more, not just at our monthly meetings but at a host of other forums. Cate Goethals, a University of Washington Professor, asked me to come speak to her Women In Business class and I happily complied.

In the years leading up to The Accident, whenever I was feeling particularly unwell, I would hole up and watch Jeff Bridges and Barbra Streisand in *The Mirror Has Two Faces* over and over again. Streisand played a professor at Columbia University and I always found the idea of professorship romantic. It had been a decade since I'd watched that movie but as I walked under the cherry blossom trees and into PACCAR Hall, it was like picking up a pin my soul had put down. I walked through the doors and into the lecture auditorium.

Cate and I had discussed my lecture in advance. I'd tell a bit of my career story in brand strategy and then walk them through a few brand strategy exercises. It had been a while since I left Agio and I was eager to stretch my strategic legs again. I so loved it. And missed it.

At the halfway mark, after I had rolled out some pretty juicy tools from the brand strategy toolkit and how, along my career path, I had discovered them, Cate said something unexpected.

"We want to hear your story," she said.

I looked at her perplexed but tried not to let my apprehension show.

"This *is* my story," I said with a smile, too big and too tight.

"No," Cate said gently. "The Story." She nod-prodded.

I looked out at the students. They were all so young, the oldest was maybe twenty-one. I couldn't be sure. They all looked incredibly innocent and new. Sharing a story of brokenness with this group felt like walking across a field of freshly fallen snow. Nobody liked that person. I certainly didn't.

I stood in front of the classroom with no place to run, and ran, instead, to the recesses of my mind.

"I fell out of a two-story window when I was seven years old and spent the rest of my life thinking I was broken and didn't deserve love."

I slipped into the story of how I developed a mistaken identity that had me thinking I was fifty cents on the dollar and how the decisions I made out of that damaged belief almost cost me my life. Although I had told the story several times by that point, I tried to ignore the gnawing embarrassment that I was telling such an emotional story from such a cerebral platform. The repetition brought a verbal cadence that allowed me to slip back a bit from the telling and disassociate myself to minimize my discomfort. I had long since perfected the out-of-body experience. With profound relief I reached the end and brought my mind back online to complete the wrap up. Only then did I see their faces, wet with tears.

A new feeling of confusion rained down. What had I done? Why were they crying? I wanted out of there as fast as possible. I wrapped up quickly and turned back to the lectern to gather my things when a lined formed. Woman after woman came up to me. Many to put their arms around me, not to hold on to me, but to have me hold on to them. Who were these women? Who were these young broken hearts?

A very thin Asian woman was next in line. I would like to say that I remember what she said but I don't. I was running an escape protocol in my brain so all I can relay is the feeling that remained. She was disheveled. She was desperate. She stayed with me too long. I felt anxious. At some point, looking at the continuing line of women I still had to move through, I, gently as possible, moved her along.

A few months later, the University of Washington Women in Business group asked me to be a part of a panel on women in leadership. After I was done speaking, another young Asian woman came up to me and very respectfully said, "You don't remember me, do you?"

Lean In had grown to several thousand members by this time, a statistic the team and I were extremely proud of, but it removed some of the intimacy we'd had at the earlier meetings. People stopped addressing me as Cor and started calling me Lean In. I was once in a bathroom at Starbucks when a woman came out of the stall next to me and in delight screamed, "Hi, Lean In!" It was pretty cool. But also pretty weird.

I had no idea where I had met this young woman, but I

suspected it was through Lean In. I tried to just smile graciously and prayed she'd continue talking to close up the space made by my lack of memory.

"I came up to you after Cate's class," she said. The minute she did, I saw her. And in a way, I saw double. I saw the drawn face of the girl who had come up to me after Cate's class in an over-sized sweater that hid her entire body, her sorrow-filled eyes brimming with desperation from which it was tough not to want to look away. It wasn't hard to believe this was not the same person, this actually was not the same person. She was fundamentally altered. Someone's belief about themselves seeps out from their skin. Self-sabotage, self-recrimination, self-doubt, desperation - it all had a smell. She now smelled like a new car. Her presence was exciting. The moment I realized who she was, I threw my arms around her and we hugged for a long, long time. When I met her, I was embarrassed I had shared my brokenness and she was embarrassed to be broken. Our hug was an acknowledgement that regardless of how we felt in our original meeting, hidden forces were at work. Her story of transformation told me my own story could be used in a way that could bring healing to others; that everything given to me could cause me to be a conduit for connection for someone just like her. Hugging her was such a heart opening that I couldn't understand why, in the middle of it, I felt the backdraft of a closing door.

15

THE SELL SIDE

Los Angeles, 2016

I'd escape to LA whenever I could. I was essentially free but still beholden to Seattle because of the monthly Lean In chapter meetings. Our chapter was growing like wildfire and I didn't ever want to let the team down. The magic of our team was we all felt that way. In our Operating Norms, we created a protocol for when a person needed to "lean out," to make doing so ok. Once it was, people did it with regularity. As did I. Yaela gave me a key to her house and I treated her bungalow like my second home.

Lean In had only added fuel to my cheerleader fire. Catapulting from obscurity to the stage in a nanosecond didn't allow for much space to adjust to life slowly or gracefully. It was still tremendously exhilarating to be in a world with other people in it and my excitement knew no bounds. I was overwhelmingly cheerful and awkwardly oblivious to personal space, other people's and my own. I had been streaming Pastor Erwin's sermons after our initial encounter at Habitas, so when I surfaced in LA, I bounded into Mosaic like we were best friends and I owned the place, which, of course, we weren't and I didn't.

Yaela was friends with a very well-known author and invited him to crash at the bungalow with us once when he was coming through town. I had seen his TED talk, and read his book, so I made the assumption I knew him and we were friends. Polite company knows to observe adequate personal space when sharing a single bathroom but not me; I went bounding in, in my negligée, like that was the most natural thing to do. The author, thankfully, was just brushing his teeth, but I bellied up right next to him at the sink and brushed right along with him, chatting, brushing and co-spitting like I had with my brother when we were kids.

I ran into Emerson one day while at Intelligentsia coffee shop in Venice. It was tense right away and I felt it. Though I was desensitized to normal interactions, to rejection I was hypersensitive.

I had felt such a special bond to him after my initial experience at Mosaic, but he had distanced himself quite a bit each time I returned and I felt hurt and confused. When we ran into each other unexpectedly at Intelligentsia, he asked me to sit down with him for coffee. I was braced and reluctant. Speaking right into the chasm our awkwardness had created he said, "Cor, you're super nice, and it's easy to take it the wrong way."

I didn't really know what to make of that but it felt terrifying to make new friends only to quickly lose them.

As my circle grew bigger it filled with the most interesting characters. One of them was Emily Mitchell, the Ritual Coach. Emily made bath salts and candles and guided people through rituals honoring different seasons in life. She offered to come to my hotel room after I had hosted a client off-site and conduct a special ritual for me. I wasn't sure what to expect but I was all-in.

I sat in the middle of the white, fluffy King bed in a hotel bathrobe as Emily built a circle of candles all around me. As she did, I told her what had happened in LA. When she finished, she sat down in a club chair outside the candle circle and talked me through it.

"Cor, you walk into a room like an energy explosion," Emily said. "You shift the room. But it's all energy out. You give away all of your energy without a second thought. But there's another option here. You can walk into the room and not give all your energy away. It's possible. It's possible to walk into any room, fit in, fit out, and remain intact. The wise woman comes in, scans the room, feels where she wants to give her energy and samples just a little. She then decides where she wants to invest her energy because she knows it's safe and she does so in exchange. You have to start putting boundaries around your vessel, so you are not giving your energy away indiscriminately. There is no doubt your presence is powerful. But the energy you have is hard energy. It's forceful. You needed to deploy it because it was your defense mechanism. But you're not there anymore."

Wait. Was my signature positive energy a defense mechanism? And to what degree?

Emily was right. I exploded into rooms and was incredibly excited just to be in them. On entrance, I was excitable and positive and overflowing. The positive energy I exuded also came with this notion of, *"This is amazing!"* And every person I met was received with, *"You are amazing!"* The final aspect in the Amazing-Trifecta was, *"I am amazing and you should like me, love me, accept me, and want to spend time with me!"*

And that might have been the real point of it all.

Because I was constantly battling internal and external messaging that I was not amazing and not worthy, I went into energetic overdrive to prove that I was. But that was all before Rattlesnake Ledge. Now I was secure in my value. And if I was secure in my value and didn't have to prove anything anymore, if I knew my value had nothing to do with any personal amazingness and everything to do with God's complete acceptance of me, how much of that positive personality was actually me?

Understanding will come as time unfolds.
Theresa, Journal #2

I shared what Emily had said with Theresa during our weekly session, as we sat in her back yard sipping tea.

"I would say that's accurate," Theresa said. "What is the belief that says you have to give all your energy away? Is keeping energy for yourself in direct conflict with being open in the world? Is deciding some people suck in direct conflict with the desire to be accepted for who you are, and accepting others for who they are? Is it important to be seen as nice? Ask yourself, Cor, what parts of your personality are a mask? What parts of your personality would you be willing to give away? And, more importantly, what do you miss while you are busy smiling?"

I furrowed my brow. It was a lot at once. I felt instantly defensive. As I put my tea down and crossed my arms, Theresa pivoted to the third person to take the pressure off, slightly. Her questions-deluge had successfully knocked me off balance, but she still wanted keep me open to absorbing the conversation.

"There is a difference between critical thinking and fantastical thinking," she said, eruditely. "When people become enamored with someone or something, they stop thinking critically about some of the obvious disconnects that arise. When you follow fantastical thinking you take in only the initial input and you don't leave any room for deviations from follow-on experiences. You ignore things that don't fit the paradigm. You just blow right past them."

It was interesting enough to unfurrow my brow, but my arms stayed crossed.

"Much of your life has been spent trying to convince people to want to be a part of you. You have been giving all your energy out in the hopes that doing so would make you safe and happy. But it's never made you safe and it's never made you happy. It's a false promise. It makes you blind to your surroundings and actually puts you at risk."

Although wound pretty tightly, I was definitely listening.

"Everything you do has to have some measure of self-protection considered. Walking into situations like you do, is like walking in stilettos and a vera wang dress onto the battle field. People don't want to see your style, they want to see your armor. Boundaries, values, beliefs, and standards - that's your armor. That's what's attractive to healthy people and what makes them feel safe."

In the face of this truth, my guard had dropped, but I remained embarrassed: embarrassed at this assessment of what I had called my personality, and embarrassed to be developing such fundamental skills and awareness as an adult. Theresa cautioned me from using this moment to pile blame on myself, as my fifty-cent behavior was wont to do. She put down her tea and doubled down.

"This response that you're always at fault, or to blame, removes the use of critical thinking and renders situations even more emotional. When problems arise, and are couched as your fault, by virtue of you being "selfish, dramatic, too sensitive, or crazy" - all words that heighten emotions and add additional emotions like shame, guilt, and condemnation - it shifts the focus to you and off of the actual problem. It leaves you holding a bag of blame, instead of challenging both parties to work through conflict with critical thinking, perspective, detachment and problem resolution. It's a cop-out. But because you were tied to other people for validation, critical analysis of a person or situation became less important than managing their feelings about you. If your critical thinking is being overridden by taking on other people's emotions to try to get them to like you, how effective is your critical thinking? What would it take for you not to absorb all the blame?"

I felt like I wanted to lie down.

Sometimes and hour with Theresa felt like a lifetime. This was one of those times.

She leaned forward and kept going.

"This concept you have that you're responsible for other people's feelings by virtue of them blaming you is what's derailing. Because if something happened and you got blamed and you were to get "emotional" - because now you feel unjustly accused and you dared say so - you've now played right into the loop that gets you labeled as crazy, sensitive and dramatic. So instead of setting yourself up to have to manage this firehose of blame, you opted to wear rose-colored glasses instead. You choose to automatically believe everyone is amazing and has the best intentions at heart, but that's not always the case. The truth is, you have all the tools you need to see situations critically. You have empathy, intuition, sensitivity and even - contrary to your belief - the capacity for critical thought. You've just been so busy selling yourself you haven't yet deployed this incredibly powerful asset."

Tears rose up to my eyes. My porous mind was bloated to capacity. I wanted to learn, I wanted to change, but didn't know if I could take it all in. Theresa stayed with me, holding me with her eyes, but allowed for space to let what she'd said wash over me until I could breathe again.

"You did what you did for a reason. You created these parts of your persona so you could feel loved and accepted. You are not there anymore. That season is over. You are loved. You are accepted. You don't have to sell yourself, Cor. Cut the ties."

I sat in my Jeep in front Theresa's, gathering myself. My mind was equally heavy and light with these new learnings: people are a sovereign state; energy should have borders; rose-colored glasses are no match for critical thought; and my very favorite, I didn't need to sell myself. I was not for sale. I was just beginning to learn what it meant to have been bought by the blood of Christ.

It had been a saturated month. Recovery, I learned, came and went like the tide. A wave would come in and rinse over the beach of my mind, until I was submerged, steeped and swollen. Then the water would be pulled back out to sea, leaving treasures behind for me to pluck from the ground and dust off the sand. In front of Theresa's, I went beach-combing once again. And in the quiet of my Jeep, I looked down at the treasures in my hand.

16

BODY AND SOUL

MEMORIAL DAY WAS sunny and bright, but I wasn't. The end of May had been Lumen's due date. I continued to clock time around her: conception, heartbeat, miscarriage, due date. When she had formed, I had bonded. I walked into my living room and looked at the small urn bearing the remains and the engraved stone I had made as a headstone. Instantly, I had a thought: what if I let go?

I thought about her every day. I never got to see her fully formed face, kiss her tiny feet, play with the head of curls she undoubtedly would have had, or blow bubbles on her tummy. I held her in my hand but never held her sweet little hand and still, she brought me life.

In the months that followed the miscarriage, I had begun weekly saline infusions. Within a month my life had been restored. Apparently, the trauma to my brain and resulting nervous system had caused a malfunction in maintaining blood volume. The symptoms of blood volume loss included everything I had become so familiar with, the relentless nausea and profound fatigue the most life-draining ones. Lumen's departure pointed a big arrow to a treatment plan that got me up out of bed, and back into life, in a way I had long stopped hoping for.

I had heard her name a year later from one of my nurses, in passing. Inserting an IV in me was not an easy task and the nurses frequently had to make three or more attempts. They would successfully insert the catheter in the vein but, for some reason, my veins would clamp down around the tube, blocking the flow of water. It was frustrating and confusing for the nurses and painful for me. We weathered it together with humor and grace and I would do slow and deep breathing and encourage them along. The nurses had a protocol that, if they tried twice and were unsuccessful, they would bring in another nurse to try again. Sometimes they stayed and kept trying. But most of the time they brought in another nurse. A fresh start for us both.

I knew all the nurses by name and, over time, also came to know the stories of their lives. Karen had made two attempts at my veins when Susan came in to offer relief.

"What's going on?" Susan asked. "You trouble again, lady?" she asked, with a laugh.

I shrugged and smiled an apologetic smile.

"Same as always," Karen said, getting up off the stool and letting Susan sit down. "I successfully get it in the lumen but then her veins clamp down."

I waited until I got home to look up the definition.

Lumen: an opening; the cavity of an organism, vessel or cell; the hollow of a needle or catheter; the space through which water flows.

I marveled at the coincidence that the very name we chose in thirty seconds or less, having no idea of its secondary definition or reason to believe at the time it was anything special or significant, was precisely the name that held both my hope and my healing. Lumen was my beacon for healing and her name carried the healing methodology. When we first chose the name, I looked at it one way but in this new light, her name became something else entirely. I had come to know this as the beauty of healing; it is both pleasure and pain, darkness and light, a prism refracting light differently at the advent of each new day.

I walked to the edge of Green Lake and sat down in the sun. I watched the water dance for a long, long time. I thought about Lumen as the sun lay on my face. I felt the weight of the rock and turned it over and over in my hands. It read: You were here. We saw your heart.

As I sat quietly by the water, I dug a small hole with a broken off branch. When it was deep enough, I slipped the small, square urn inside and moved the earth over top of it. This would be her place of rest.

I stood up and dusted off the rear of my shorts. In order for me to move forward, in order for me to live into the life her life made possible, I had to return it all to dust. I held the stone to my mouth and whispered these simple thoughts:

You were born November 18, 2013. I held you in my hand. Your name is Lumen. I am your mom. From this day forward, the life I live is your legacy as much as it is mine.

I arched my arm back and let the rock fly.

There is no greater power than the acceptance of loss.
Theresa, Journal #17

∾

I WASN'T JUST TAKING authority of my healing; I was grabbing it by the horns. I engaged Josie Rice, a local Seattle artist, and a graphic designer to help me design elements for the healing kit and spent $10,000 bringing it to life. I had no plans for what to do with it but when I heard, "They're not yours to keep, they're yours to give away," I felt internal pressure to action it. I made one hundred boxes and began giving them away. I became rigorous in looking for signs where I had clamped down around my pain and did everything I could to reopen the flow.

I wasn't sure how long I had been doing it, or when it started, but the moment it came into my awareness I was clear it needed to stop: I had been showering with the lights off. For years I had been at war with my body so deep I had developed a disregard for my flesh. It wasn't so much that I hated my body; I stopped acknowledging it existed. It was a systemic problem. I had become numb.

Physically, my dysautonomia had impacted my nerve endings and robbed me of a lot of physical sensations. I didn't feel hunger, I didn't experience thirst and when I worked out, I had no indication of waning energy until the floor dropped out. Emotionally, I had also become numb to the signals my soul was sending, perfecting the out-of-body experience or cheerleading my way through emotional pain. If you protect what you value, I didn't value a body that couldn't be relied upon, a body that had tortured me from the inside. Consequently, I hadn't protected it from the outside, which meant I let danger in and ignored it when it came. My body and I had separated long ago. Shutting off the lights was tantamount to divorce.

When people are acutely uncomfortable or desperate for a new life, they often talk of shedding their skin. If shedding was rejecting, I had done that. But if I was going to step into a wholeness of being, if I was going to be responsible for healing myself, I needed to find a way to put that skin back on, accept it, and somehow learn to embody it once again.

A woman I met at Melody's Urban Campfire event had posted a picture on Facebook of a boudoir photoshoot she had done for her husband for their anniversary. It was discrete and her body looked beautiful. I thought that maybe, through another's lens, I might be able to see my body anew.

The boudoir photographer, Dana, and I met at a coffee shop in Ballard and quickly bonded when I shared with her how I had detached from my body. She had struggled with her body, too.

"Well, you look great," was always the response I received when someone was shocked to learn the state of my health. It was meant as a compliment but only served to make me feel even more invisible. I was hoping, with a click of a camera lens, I might show up.

"Where do you want to do it?" Dana asked. "Do you have a great bedroom or hotel in mind?"

The idea of shooting my skin-reclaiming moment in bed, the seat of my physical torture and years of isolation, caused a stricture in my throat.

"No Dana," I said, a warm rush of panic spreading up my neck. "It can't be inside."

She knew just the place. She showed me a shoot she had done outside in the mudflats of Moses Lake and very close to Vantage, the halfway point between the home of my parents and the new life I was building in Seattle. I liked the symbolism of the half-way point. Half-way between death and life. Half-way between healing and embodying wholeness. In the middle of transition, covered in mud, a molten hot mass of forming new life. It was the perfect spot. We would go there. And as planned, we would shoot by the light of the full moon at midnight.

We drove out to Moses Lake and shot a few images in the mudflats and sand dunes at high noon. It was sweltering hot and if I started out clean and shiny, I ended up dirty and wet. As Dana wrapped up her gear to move to our next location, I leaned against the hood of the Jeep, mud streaked my arms and thighs and caked in my hair. I breathed out against the heat. My

Jeep had always felt like freedom and shooting my body outside felt like freedom indeed.

I showered and we spent the evening in separate yurts. Around midnight, Dana came calling and we slipped out into the night. We took no lights with us and walked quietly to a field we had scouted on arrival. It was a wide-open plane, surrounded by vineyards on three sides and a road on the other. We were hoping no cars would pass by. The ground was dry and hard, the topsoil thin, dusty and unforgiving. I thought briefly about snakes.

We found a spot that caught the moonlight and Dana set her camera down. I opened up my gold scarf, draped it over the harsh ground, stretched myself out across it and lay naked in the dark. The thinness of my scarf was little protection and brittle grass poked up out of the compressed earth, through the scarf, and dug into me. I pressed my body into it, wanting to feel the earth even if it delivered pain. I lay, looking up at the sky, aware of Dana's gaze but ever-distancing. The night air was careful and warm. It whispered over my body like the down-stroke of a song. The moon hung swollen and low. I could see her craters. And in the dark of night, I showed her mine.

Here, I would lay down my pain. Here, I would press my body into the earth. Here, I would lift my throat to the heavens and open my voice against the roar of the sky. Here, I would embrace that I was made of shattered stars and let their light litter over my physical offering. Here, I would accept that my body was a vessel, made of earth and filled with the heavens. There was no distance, no space between. We were, every last one of us, one. One with heaven. One with earth. Made of dust. Filled with song.

You are loved by the creator of the universe beyond
comprehension.
Theresa, Journal #19

DANA and I sat in front of her computer screen in her apartment a few days later. She gave me a moment to prepare myself for what was about to come.

"Are you ready?" she whispered quietly, in tones of excitement and anticipation. I nodded and braced myself.

I allowed the images to lift off the screen and make their way into me, coaching myself to enlarge the opening. I forced my way past any critique of my body and found my way to it's beauty: the twist in my wrist, the curve of my thigh, the lift of my neck, the length of my arm. In the end, I found myself most fully in two images: one predictable, one surprising. The first was of me standing in the moonlight before I laid myself out on the ground. The moonlight rinsed over the contours of my face, it's harsh light cut contrast to the peace within, self-evident in the tilt of my head and the ease behind my closed eyes. The scarf, gold and flowing, stretch out on both sides, arms open wide. Behind me, way off in the distance, six miles away, were the red lights of a few cars, night owls on the road. Lights on my runway and I, a winged eagle, prepared to take flight.

The second image I turned away from the moment it popped up.

"No, Dana, no!" I yelled, horrified. She coaxed my hands down that had flown up and covered my face.

I had been so emboldened when we captured the shot. Brazen. Trailblazing. Fierce and free. It was high noon in the desert. The sun was overhead, it's white-hot heat, unmerciful and unrelenting. And rushing forward, like a semi on the highway - my thighs clapping thunderously, my forehead tilted forward, my eyes squinted against the sun - right down the centerline, naked and unashamed, I came barreling down.

I left Dana's house and embraced these truths:

I was an energetic body and a spiritual being.

I was made of dust and infused with divinity.

In response to healing and heartache and loss and life, I would take it head-on, naked and unashamed.

I would embody the vessel given to me and in it, come what may, I would come barreling down.

17

PLAYTIME IS OVER

MAY, SEATTLE / LOS ANGELES / SAN FRANCISCO, 2017

LEAN IN WAS STARTING to feel claustrophobic and right at the very weirdest of times. In May of 2016, we achieved our big vision when our chapter hosted, and I interviewed, Sheryl Sandberg in a beautiful evening event where she spoke intimately about her life after the loss of her husband, Dave. Four days later, the entire Lean In Seattle Chapter hosted a Lean In Women Veterans event, our largest event ever, and nearly four hundred people filed into the Fisher Pavilion at the base of the Seattle Space Needle to talk about going through transitions in life purposely, thoughtfully and powerfully. At the close of the event and after I shared my own story of attempting a powerful transition in my own life, I asked the photographer to capture me in the middle of the group, replicating the image I had seen on Facebook, a living reflection of my soul's cry of, "This will be me!"

The moment the photo was being taken, I asked each individual in the group to create an image in their own mind of something their heart desired. I asked them to hold in their mind's eye a visual of something they wished for deeply, and asked them to dare to take a stand and say, "This will be me!" For one woman, it was a visual of herself holding a baby, a bold stand after she had suffered a miscarriage. This will be me. For another, it was the founding of a global women's empowerment movement of her own. This will be me. For another, she held a vision of herself holding a new business card with her name and the title of a desired promotion. This will be me. We put forward dreams audaciously and as the shutter closed we shouted, "This will be me!" It was the culmination of the work Erika and I and our Lean In Seattle team had been working toward for over a year. For me, personally, it was incredibly special. I looked at the image later and smiled and thought, *this is me.*

Lean In had delivered *community, impact, fun* all rolled into one package. It took me from the edge of death to a vibrant life. It forced me to increase my physical, mental and emotional capacity by learning to move around in a world with other people in it. It gave me the opportunity to build and exercise gifts I never knew were always in me. And whether I learned and failed, even publicly, I still found a place of acceptance and growth. And yet with every group phone call and every meeting, my attachment to my organizing priorities of community, impact, fun began to fade. The season was changing but to what I didn't know. It made me sad and confused and a little scared.

"This past year you have been rich in community and you really, really needed that," Amina said, when I called her and shared my surfacing feelings. "God gave you what you needed. You built something amazing and it has been a success, but you need to put that same time and that same energy into the next thing. There is something else waiting for you. Start thinking and praying about what that might be."

I began to lean out to make space for other leaders to lean forward.

I drove down to LA to visit Yaela. Again.

"You were learning to play," Yaela said, as I sat in the kitchen of her bungalow, my feet tucked underneath me and my hands wrapped around a warm cup of coffee. I hadn't thought of Lean In as play. I thought of it as work, very serious and important work.

"We need to respect that play looks different for different people," Theresa said, when I shared Yaela's comment with her. "Let's look at what play does."

We made a running list:

Play stops time.

Play brings rest.

Play rejuvenates the soul.

Play brings us into a place of joy, freedom, restoration, and vulnerability.

Play allows us to be known, build community and experience love, even if we're playing alone.

When we play, we experience some of the very best parts of creation, which often ignites delight within and actually causes us to worship.

For me, Lean In had done all of those things.

I left LA and drove through San Francisco on my way up the coast, stopping off at Creativity Explored, the little sweet gallery in Noe Valley, where I encountered Chocolate, Strawberry and Vanilla people and the artist who created Dinosaur. I sat in my Jeep - after being told the mark on my life was that I was from Middle-earth - floored. It was incredibly scary to feel the ground shifting underneath me again. I was tumbling through space and time, being pulled from solid ground and back toward the core of the earth once more.

"God, hold on to me," I prayed, and then started my engine and drove up the coast.

Allow it to unfold. You can't push. The flower has to be allowed
to open.
Lynn, Journal #14

Speeding up the coast with a mix of Justin Bieber, Tiesto, ODESZA and Hillsong UNITED worship music blasting, I thought about my next season. I had seen Lean In as a means to an end. I had expected Lean In achievement to lead to industry and when it didn't, when I had to recategorize Lean In as play, I also had to acknowledge I was still in transition. Jax had asked me a challenging question: was women's leadership my career path forward? When I listened to what was rising up inside me, I had to acknowledge it wasn't. And that meant it was time to lean out permanently. The backdraft I had experienced a few months back after the University of Washington speech had been the chill that comes with the change of season and the shift of air from a closing door. Playtime was over.

IF THERE WAS NO MORE Lean In, then job was an obvious priority. In fact, it was Priority One. Up-leveling my body had been a long-held desire, so I put that as a close second. I was doing so much better physically and I was eager to test my body's capacities and boundaries and possibly hire a trainer again. This was not the New York misguided attempt at reclaiming fitness, this was a carefully weighed assessment of my present physical state and a desire to continue to improve my healing. That's what I told those concerned about my goal and the potential for crashing. The fact that I held an image of six pack abs in my mind was something I need share with no one. And if Lean In wasn't filling up my evenings and weekends, it was time for love. So those were my three new action priorities: *Job. Body. Love.* I didn't waste a single moment before diving into all three at the same time.

In a season-shifting explosion, things started happening all around: I booked a consulting job for a local behemoth tech company with potential for long-term employment, tackling my top priority of job; I downloaded all the dating apps and after over a dozen dates had narrowed it down to one, locking in on the priority of love; and the focus on body took a turn I hadn't seen coming.

My apartment situation had come to a bitter end and I moved into my parents condo, selling even more belongings and putting the rest in storage once again. In the process, and in a stunning display of lack of spatial awareness, I returned from my storage unit one night and, while talking to Aunt Nancy, closed the hatch back of my Jeep on my face, splitting it wide open at the bridge of my nose.

At Urgent Care, the doctor suggested a prescription for strong pain medicine. Eschewing medicine, or the concept of pain altogether, I walked confidently out the door. Not eight hours later, with stitches in my face and heady with pain, I stumbled into the bathroom and broke my toe on the door frame. Only a few hours after my first visit, I was back at Urgent Care, setting more bones in place. The same doctor was still on call.

I was dating and working and working out with a boot on my foot and stitches holding together the skin on my face, all while newly ensconced in my parent's condo. Stress is defined as anything which challenges our survival, joy, prosperity, security, or stability. It is anything that forces our system to adapt. The season hadn't just changed, it had been triggered and I was lost, once again, without sound.

"You're probably going to have to kill off your dramatic princess," Yaela said, in one of our frequent phone calls. "Drama is movement but it's not the kind of movement you're looking for."

I did not feel like I went looking for drama. I distinctly felt like drama came looking for me. And as I was coming to the close of the year, I had a feeling of screaming through chaos.

Moving out of my apartment had not been a desired outcome. A new tenant upstairs had brought with her a nocturnal working schedule and while I was sleeping below, she was doing laundry, opening and closing drawers, playing music loudly and making hay while her sun was shining smack in the middle of the night. After trying to handle it personally, I began following my building's protocol for noise complaints with no discernible result, until the tenant came down in the middle of the night herself. Seeing this as an opportunity to rectify the situation, I let her in. It was after 2 AM. We talked for a while about her schedule, her life and her live-in girlfriend. She apologized about the noise and promised to be more circumspect that someone, namely me, was sleeping below her. I opened up a bottle of wine to smooth over any hard feelings and to toast to a new world order. After we clinked our glasses and I took my first sip of the wine, she leaned forward to kiss me and, in doing so, sealed my awareness that the place I had so carefully created as a sanctuary, had become a torture-trap. The kiss gone wrong did not change things, if anything, it made the situation more incendiary. I tried to get out of my lease by renting another apartment in the building but my status of unemployed left no opening. By the time I got the contract job, I had already moved out.

It had been almost twenty years since I had worked in an office and three years since I left my relationship, and while it wasn't actually a job, and it wasn't actually a relationship, the cadence of the project and the dailiness of male text communication made them both feel like one.

I would arrive to work most days around 6 AM. The project

was patched together with external contractors, of which I was one, and from the very beginning it was clear that the road to permanent employment was incredibly uncertain. Behind the scenes I was managing yet another relationship that showed no signs of real engagement, so naturally that was precisely the relationship I chose.

I had been through a season of date-roulette but the moment I saw Jake, a bullet dropped into the chamber, and I knew it instantly. We stood beside each other in the elevator, not talking. It felt good standing next to him. Foreign and familiar. The door opened and he slipped a hand on my lower back to guide me out of the elevator. All it took was the touch of one hand and I was caught in jet wash. I quickly gave myself over to a situation that sent my value plummeting, starting with that night.

Jake took to texting me day after day after day after day but made no plans to take me out. Any mention of the disconnect, or a request to stop the maddening and meaningless texts, sent him down a tangent of how I should be confident in what we had and not need anything more. When I said a daily text exchange did not constitute even a whiff of a relationship, a blame-game would ensue. It was stupid and exhausting. I was exhausted. We weren't headed anywhere but his bed, from which I was struggling to pull out.

At my second to last Lean In meeting in October of 2017, one of our newer Lean In leaders, Nidhi, found me in the corner and asked me to write a book of my journey of recovery and coming through to the other side. I was struggling to see evidence that I had been brought through anything. This didn't feel like the other side. This felt like a very long journey through hell right back to the exact same shore.

～

Trust yourself to know what to shut down.
Lynn, Journal #40

"HOW MANY TIMES can a man fall and be forgiven?" Shellie asked rhetorically. "Seventy times seven."

I was caught in my same, age-old cycle with Jake. A vortex of skin and a pattern of rejection. It was magnetic. Intoxicating. And crushing in equal measure. I wanted to know Jake and be known by Jake, not just the pattern of his freckles, but that wasn't our present trajectory and I knew it. For that, and other reasons, I had pulled the ripcord. When I called Shellie, I had been up all night crying. I felt hopeless. I felt helpless. And I felt really, really angry.

My heart ached layers and layers deep. I had been in a desert for so long. Not only had it been three years since I left my relationship, but all seven years we were together had been starved of oxygen sexually as well. Jake had reignited something I thought was dead. And he hadn't just reignited it, he obliterated the entire previous decade. I ached from the separation from a body that promised intimacy, but the only intimacy that remained was my anger at myself. And that I knew inside and out.

"Nothing has changed, Shell," I cried into the phone. "How can I look at my life and say anything has changed? How can I say God changed my life when I'm still this person? I'm still fifty cents on the dollar. I'm still accepting a lame substitute for a relationship, still giving myself away and calling it love." I caught the thrill of the vice in my voice, devastating me all over again. "I'm not new at all."

Shellie caught my descent with both hands and her heart.

"Stop right there, Cor. Do not beat yourself up if you find yourself repeating behavior. It's how you get out of it that matters. You identified it quickly and got out of it. Grace keeps us from falling. You may stumble. But just because you stumble, doesn't make you un-new. You're new. You stumbled but God kept you from falling. He caught you. You had a revelation moment and you disconnected from the pattern. It took both you and Jake a minute, but you cut it off. We over complicate what God does. I don't think it's for us to understand. He is able to keep you from falling. That's what we need to know. When you're new, you're new."

Her voice sharpened slightly.

"But now that you've caught yourself, you have to be diligent, Cor. You always have to ask the Holy Spirit to help. You can ask for understanding and assistance and support, but that's really where you are."

It was one thing to talk about God and understand the concept of Jesus as his son, but the Holy Spirit was next level. I didn't always know what to make of it.

"It makes me sad that my stumble was so...public. That I told so many people," I said, thinking of all the friends I had whispered secretly to in the back of restaurants, laughing about midnight exploits and escapades, covering up my breaking heart.

"Get down off that cross, girl. Jesus already did that. Look at you gettin' on that cross like you're saving souls. You're not!" She laughed, that rich, full laugh I loved.

"This is a test. You see it. But because you know better, you gotta' do better. You're no longer in your wilderness moment, you hear me? You are no longer where you were. Don't be so hard on yourself. Just reset, Cor. It's ok to need to take a minute to regroup. Get really clear on what you gravitate towards. That "you-can't-have-this" man? You don't need to have that. You know the signs. You don't change what you gravitate towards, so you have to change your pattern. Jesus did not ask you to join him on that cross. We own too much. I'm real good at trying to own what this journey is for everybody, instead of what this journey is for me. And on top of that Cor, you have to be transparent. Authenticity is real. People only want to see the real you. The problem with people creating their own version of your story for themselves that includes perfection is it erases all the beauty of this journey. This journey includes flaws and falls. That's the whole point. Give people everything and how they digest it is up to them."

I lay quietly for a moment, looking up at the ceiling.

"I miss him," I whispered against the dark of the room, to God and Shellie.

"I know, love. I know. Now you need to allow yourself space and grace to reset. You let him into your heart. That's going to take a minute to heal. And what you said about a half-dollar, I sure hope you put the other fifty cents in savings because somebody's going to need to know you stumbled. This is not just for you. None of this is. The Holy Spirit will tell you what to share, with whom and when. Just so you know, somebody's going to need to know you had this moment. It's not about you anymore. You're the daughter of a King. You belong to eternity."

In the space of the next two months, I let myself unfold through the lessons from Jake. There were many, most important of which was that God holds everyone in his hands.

I thought back to one of the few conversations I'd had with Jake. We knew each other so little, yet spoke frequently of God.

"Who is God to you?" he asked me once, as I lay on his barrel chest.

"He's slowly becoming everything," I said, not knowing exactly what that meant and ignoring the obvious. He slid a finger up and down my spine as we lay in the peace of quiet.

"I don't know Jake, that moment on Rattlesnake Ledge changed how I feel about people and about love. I see God's beauty in everyone now and I have a deep reverence for that and a sense of love. I love people now, on the spot and without conditions. It's awkward sometimes. But I also believe people are sovereign beings as a child of God, as am I, and that comes with boundaries and mutual respect."

Jake flattened his palm on the middle of my back and I breathed out against the warmth of his hand.

"I'm trying to learn how to love well and I'm just beginning to understand what that means."

We settled into quiet again and I popped up on my elbows and looked directly at him.

"I love you, Jake." I said directly, surprised at the ease with which I said it. It didn't feel awkward at all. "This may go somewhere, or this may go nowhere, but I love you and that won't ever change."

Jake asked me for coffee after I had ended it and I agreed to meet him in a public place. He arrived wearing a suit and tie. We spoke of nothing of consequence, but it was nice to see him again and we held space together easily.

"I love you, Cor," was the last thing he said to me. I knew exactly what he meant.

The greatest gift God offers is the healing of a soul.
Theresa, Journal #10

I SAT in Aunt Nancy's kitchen, drinking tea. There were two things I knew I wanted: to do the will of God in my life and to learn to love well. I was questioning how to love well in release.

It was officially over with Jake. To his proposition of an ongoing text relationship that was going nowhere I had said what my friend Amanda called, "Thank you, no thank you. Hashtag Full Dollar," and we had moved forward with love. So why was I still thinking of him? A sermon would come up that I loved and I would want to send it to him. Or he would cross my mind and I would close my eyes and wish him well. But truthfully, I wanted it to stop. We'd had such a fleeting connection. I was embarrassed to still be thinking of him, and I was beating myself up about it pretty badly.

Aunt Nancy sat next to me at her kitchen bar and took it all in. She gave a lot of space for me to come to the end of my musings and then more space before she chimed in.

"I was listening to a podcast the other day," she said. "It was of a mother and her son, who had autism. Pretty severe, from the sounds of it." I quieted into her story. I felt relieved that I could set my mind to listen and not have to worry about needing to respond.

"When her son was born, her husband left. And as the boy grew, she stopped going to church, self-conscious of how her son would respond in public and worried he would be too disruptive. She stayed away for years. One day, when her son was in his teens, she decided to go back to church but only at the end of the service when the people emptied out into the lobby and there was other noise. As she did, a few men on the tear-down team noticed her and one of them spoke to her son. 'We could use your help stacking chairs. Would that be something you'd be interested in doing?' he asked, and the boy nodded, and also agreed to come back and help again the following Sunday.

Sunday after Sunday this went on and the boy was not only helping with tear-down but setup as well, which meant he and his mom would stay for the whole service. They even made the boy a special place at the back, standing with the production team. One Sunday, the pastor asked those who wanted to participate in communion to come forward. The boy raced to get in line. Instantly, his mom got nervous. As the line inched toward the front, the boy's excitement grew and so did his utterings. He would shout and moan and clap his hands wildly. With each excited outburst, the mom's tension grew. Would he be shunned by those in the church, she wondered? Would they be asked to leave? She wanted to do everything she could to save them both from the painful rejection she had been experiencing for so long. By the time the boy reached the front to receive communion, instead of taking the small piece of bread offered to him by the pastor, he reached up and took the entire loaf! The mom was mortified! The pastor just smiled. 'Looks like he needed a little extra Jesus today,' the pastor said, and laughed."

I could totally see it.

"The mom felt so bad," Aunt Nancy continued. "As she looked up to apologize to the entire congregation, she noticed everyone was smiling! She hadn't expected that. With tears in her eyes, she turned to the pastor with a quizzical look. He smiled gently and said, 'They're loving him forward. We all are.'

That's what you're doing for Jake," Aunt Nancy said simply. "You're loving him forward. We all need that."

I wondered if, in all of this, God was loving me forward, too.

18

LOCK AND LOAD

December, Seattle, 2017

"You're unfocused," Theresa said. I thought she could have been a little more generous. I was focused on finding a job. That wasn't nothing.

"You're not looking for a job," she said. "You're still looking for validation. The enemy of destiny is distraction. That is what steals your efficacy."

Looking back over the cacophony of my life, the truth of that was self-evident. I was marked by distractibility. I had been distracted my whole life. Distractions like illness, unavailable men, spending time proving myself, following other people's paths to happiness - all had me spinning my wheels or going in circles and all of it dragged me down.

"'Get off me' is a very legitimate prayer," Theresa said. It was clear I needed to double-down.

By contrast, Erwin, whom I was still watching, listening to and following, had been diagnosed with, and treated for, cancer. He had come back after his surgery and one-month recuperation and looked dramatically changed. The experience seemed to burn things away to make him even more effective and compelling. He was the antithesis of distracted.

"He looks like a rocket," Yaela whispered, during service at Mosaic amid another Faith Tour in LA. It was true. He did. He looked like freedom. Lean. Unencumbered. Directioned. Potent. During the short period of time he had been unseen to us all, he had rocketed through the night.

"I want you to know there is a tremendous amount of crap that God has to strip away from you in order for you to become a rocket," Theresa said, when I shared with her that I'd like to become a rocket. "There is a shedding of stuff. God will remove anyone that distracts you, anyone you want to absorb into yourself, anyone who diverts you from your purpose. God will strip you naked so that the only thing you are left with is what's been poured into you by him."

I thought back to what Yaela said about how drama was not the kind of movement I was looking for. Drama was uniquely delicious but it wasn't destiny. I was so completely over drama and was ready to put it behind me.

I got into the business of identifying the hallmarks of drama, so I could I identify when I was in a drama vortex and strip it off me. I noticed drama was present when:

My voice or the cadence of my voice would change (higher, faster).

The conversation turned into a monologue or a blame-game (theirs or mine).

The retelling of what happened would get me wound-up and overly excited.

And drama was definitely present when I'd shared the story of what happened with three people, and yet was looking for opportunities to tell it more.

In ending drama, I had to let go of what were two very powerful drivers in my life: I had to let go of needing people and I had to let go of needing to be needed. Loving people and wanting to be connected to them was a legitimate and healthy desire, but injecting need into relationships whipped up drama like nobody's business. In fact, I was noticing that in needing people less, I had space to love them more.

To that end, I also had to let go of the idea that I could, or needed to, "fix" anyone. Firstly, I couldn't. Second, nobody liked being "fixed," not to mention, I was still shoring up wholeness myself. And lastly, it wasn't my job. Even if I wasn't actively trying to fix someone, sometimes my version of help and support was cumbersome. Jake had even noticed it.

He'd said, "I want you to learn to champion yourself like you champion everyone else."

When a guy you barely know can spot that coming like a freight-train, it's a problem. I had hung up my pom-poms in high school but never let them go. I was still on the sidelines cheering everyone else on, while my own scoreboard blinked zero. I didn't need to need people. I didn't need to save people. And I certainly didn't need or want any rescuers myself. I needed to do whatever it was that God wanted me to do in life and be about the business of figuring that out and let God handle the rest.

But would God actually handle the rest? I still had needs. I still needed a job. I was trying to trust God as my provider but, honestly, it was pretty hard. I was pursuing all job leads but nothing was materializing. I had seen God manifest jobs when I was home and bed bound, not even able to leave the house. I had to trust he would do it again.

If I was going to trust him as my provider, I had to look at my provision very differently, starting with how I felt about living at my parents' condo.

I had been persistently and consistently angry about my situation. I piled blame on myself for what I called "a stupid decision" to leave a secure job, while trying to rebuild my life.

Whether it was or whether it wasn't, was yet to be proven out. The only things that remained were my circumstances and my bad attitude, and while I wasn't wholly in control of the former, I was fully in control of the latter. My parents would come over from Liberty Lake once a month for a few days or so and during that time, naturally, they'd stay in their condo. My bad attitude met them at the door every time. Whether my parents said something to Aunt Nancy, or she saw it for herself, she pulled me gently aside and spoke to me about it.

"Your parents are letting you use their place, that's a gift," she said. "I know you don't want to be there, and we all know you're really trying to change it, but your parents have never, ever said to me they want you out or feel like you're not trying. This is their gift to you. I think there's room for you to observe how you're receiving that gift and consider if you'd be willing to receive it more gracefully."

She was right. My parents had never made me feel badly. In fact, quite the contrary. I had watched my dad's heart crumble along with mine when I had to move in.

"Cur," he said calling me by my childhood nickname, "everyone has something. Some people have a wonderful marriage. Some people have great health. Some people have a trust fund or a great job or siblings that love and support them. Right now, you don't have those things. But you have this home and we'd like you to use it."

We sat across from each other, both of us crying.

"Everyone gets provision," he continued. "This is yours."

On a call with Theresa, she stepped in to block any feelings of inadequacy and redirect my thoughts toward purpose.

"When you allow other people to help you, that is when you see how much you are truly loved. To reject it is to reject God's hand giving you what you need. Begin to look at your resources differently. You have to be a rocket with a little give. You have to be a rocket with one percent spandex and focus less on where you are and more on what you do. You direct people toward having a deep knowing that they are loved by God. The inspiration you bring comes out of this purposeful, lightning-rod personality. Think about it, how would you see yourself as a rocket? What would being a rocket look like to you?"

I made a list of Cor-As-Rocket characteristics:

Directioned

Sleek

Aerodynamic

Elegant

Propelled

Powerful

Not looking to the left or the right

Delivering a payload

The only thing I could think of that might be a payload, or the work aligned to the will of God for my life, might be the telling of my story. The notion of "it's not yours to keep, it's yours to give away" had never left me. I designed the healing kits and they were beautiful, but somehow that wasn't it. Nidhi from Lean In, who had prompted me to write a book, had approached me three more times about doing so, and it started to take root in my mind. If God's power was released in my focus, if my payload was released by doing what Shellie called Divine Assignments, as best as I understood them, then I had to make my Assignment my focus.

I immediately went back to the drawing board on my priorities: *job, body, love.* Job was a necessity. I needed income. Body would crush me if I didn't tend to it. The contract job and affair with Jake had exasperated all of my energy stores and my cough had returned. Body was no longer about shredded abs as much as it was about staying out of bed. And if the book was my Assignment, love had to go, at least for now. I deleted all the dating apps from my phone.

I made a checklist for myself and stuck it by my bedside on a sticky note:

Wake up.
Pray.
Ask for guidance.
Follow your intuition of what God is saying to you.
Everything else must go.

I now had a vision of what a life of fierce and focused faith would look like. In Erwin, I had a model of how it was done. If I wanted to take on this battle, this life of faith - and I really, really did - then I had to become a warrior. I told my friend Yuliya about my revelation over dinner.

"Once you decide to become a warrior," Yuliya said, "battle begins."

III

TRANSFORMATION

GOING TO GROUND

JANUARY, SEATTLE, 2018

I COULDN'T BREATHE.

I went into the living room to get a Sharpie and got back in bed to lie down. The room was darkening around the edges and closing in. I felt urgency to prioritize communication, so I put down the Sharpie, picked up the phone and contacted my doctor first.

"I'm going down," I texted. "But don't worry. I have a Sharpie and will write what's wrong with me on my arm so when I am found unresponsive, they'll know what to do."

Before I got a chance to write anything on my arm, the lights went out.

I woke up to texts from my doctor. She was not pleased.

You will not be writing anything on your arm. Get to the ER. Now.

New Year's Eve had come and gone and I had spent it in bed again. The previous New Years, a little over two years after my first infusion, I threw myself a ReBirth Party as a celebration for coming back to life. I did my best to remake the environment of the Habitas Hallow's Eve event, transforming a subterranean apartment into a cave from Morocco, with floor seating, layered carpets and finger foods featuring saffron, figs and pomegranates. I collided people from my past with those from my present and stood at the base of the staircase and gave a speech about how grateful I was to be still standing, still alive, still blessed to see another day. Then the DJ started spinning and everyone started dancing. It was all very poetic and beautiful and moving, but from my present vantage point, such a sham. I was right back where I started: sick, in bed and living at my parents again. The irony wasn't funny, it was bitter. My heart sucked on it like a lemon.

I lay in bed all of January 1st and 2nd. By the early hours of January 3rd, I was struggling to breathe.

Trips to the ER had never been fruitful and I avoided them at all costs. But even for me, who had lowered the bar on required physical functionality, not being able to breathe was, admittedly, pretty subpar. I waited until a reasonable hour and called Aunt Nancy to see if she could take me to the ER.

"You have very little iron in your body," the ER doc said, as he leaned back casually and crossed his legs. "We'll have to admit you to the hospital so you can get it immediately via IV."

"Can it wait until tomorrow?" I asked.

He looked at me quizzically, his eyebrows furrowed and then shot up towards his hairline. He had just told me he was concerned I'd have a "cardiac event," which is doctor speak for a heart attack. Who asks to postpone treatment that might stave off a heart attack?

"I have a meeting with my hematologist tomorrow. I promise. It's already scheduled," I said.

My low iron had been a point of discussion for the better portion of a decade but after being prescribed an antibiotic in

December for a suspected bladder infection, it tanked. But iron infusions were toxic and sometimes fatal, so I had been avoiding them for years. With everything my body battled, I hadn't wanted to add iron infusions to the load. And so far I had been successful at staving it off, but that ship had clearly sailed. However, if the ER doctor was willing, I was going to buy myself a tiny bit more time.

"Why do you think you have low iron?" he asked.

"I don't know. Nobody does. I have low blood volume, too. I have dysautonomia. So, whatever," I said, trying to dismiss and make light and avoid a crazy assignation.

"Why do you have dysautonomia?" he asked. It was a reasonable question. Dysautonomia was never a primary condition, expect for rare occurrences only in the Ashkenazi Jewish population.

"I don't know that either," I said.

"When did it start?" he probed further.

"The dysautonomia symptoms? Like the very beginning?" I asked.

He nodded.

"After I fell out of a window with my brother. That's when it started. And then it got really bad after my car accident," I said.

"Did you hit your head both times?" he asked.

"Yes," I said.

"Did you pass out, both times, or even once?" he continued.

"Yes," I said. "Both times."

"So you've had traumatic brain injury. Twice," he said simply. "Who's on your care team?"

"A primary, an endocrinologist and a hematologist," I said.

"No neurologist?" he inquired.

"No," I said flatly.

Neurologists had been a hard nut for me to crack. They were famous for dismissing me, even with my diagnosis of dysautonomia. I had fired so many I'd lost count.

The ER doc leaned forward and placed his forearms on the metal rails of the hospital bed. Deep compassion washed over his face.

"You've got to get a neurologist and not a regular one," he said. "You need to find someone who specializes in traumatic brain injury. That's a necessity. Any other neuro is going to look at your brain like it's a normal brain. And it's not a normal brain. You do not have a normal brain," he said, driving it home. "The traumas you sustained fundamentally altered your brain, so you need to find someone who assumes anomaly, not someone who assumes normality and looks for anomalies. You won't be served well."

"Also," he said to my already blown mind, "I'd like to see you get some support. TBI's are no joke. They can be life altering. It sounds like yours have been. Get people around you who know what that's like. That will help."

He walked out and returned with a number for a TBI center. I was swimming in the relief only medical validation can provide, especially to land as parched as mine.

Rest. Find your YES tomorrow.
Kent, Journal #24

I RECEIVED my first iron infusion, as promised. I also found a neurologist and went in with my mom. My dad sat in the waiting room, not wanting to inconvenience the doctor. They had come over to Seattle specifically for the appointment, such was the heft of hope. My mom sat beside me, quietly nodding, as I recounted the whole story again for what felt like the hundredth time. On the drive home my mom and I shared excitedly with my dad how much the neurologist had listened. He had even known about dysautonomia and POTS (Postural

Orthostatic Tachycardia Syndrome), my specific variety. On the heels of my ER visit, I was eager to see if there was any evidence of the TBIs. The neurologist said he was going to run tests to find out more.

In the end, he ran tests for his personal specialty, epilepsy, and when they came back normal, he referred me to mental health suggesting I had a panic disorder. When I fired back that I had medically documented evidence of dysautonomia that he reviewed and confirmed, he added, "This in no way detracts from your existing medical diagnosis."

Instead of treating me for my condition, he passed me off. I took a slow breath in against the rising anger. It felt hot and tight in my chest and I tasted incredulity in the back of my throat. I couldn't believe that, after all this time, after all these positive test results, I was still fighting to find the help I so desperately needed. I felt cement pour into my chest and pull me under.

During the meeting, the neurologist had taken so much time to speak with me. I'd felt heard, seen and understood. He knew about dysautonomia and validated my diagnosis by looking at my chart. That was so rare. Usually I had to educate the doctor in front of me on my diagnosis. But I had let the balloon of hope obscure a warning sign. At the end of our initial meeting, in an aside, he'd said, "Do you think this is PTSD?"

"PTSD?" I said in my mind before it came out of my mouth. I was confused by the question but lulled into the sense of safety his listening had afforded, so I remained open and curious.

"Um. I'm not sure," I said carefully. "Isn't PTSD where you have flashbacks and nightmares and stuff?"

He nodded.

"And doesn't it come after, like, a single traumatic event and you relive that event over and over again?"

"It can," he said simply.

"Well, I don't really have those things and that's not what

happened to me so I'm going to say no. I don't think so. I don't think this is PTSD."

He shrugged almost imperceptibly. I tried to let it go but I couldn't. I felt the growing need to prove myself again and disprove the crazy that had found its way into yet another conversation with a doctor.

After the visit with the neurologist, I had engaged a PTSD therapist to disprove the validity of me and PTSD. In my mind, PTSD was for soldiers. I was not one. I also wanted to arm myself for the proving exercise that would surely follow.

"I'm here to gather data for my neurologist, so when I see him next we're able to have an actionable meeting," I said, to my very own Dr. Phil.

I liked how I sounded. Smart. Self-aware. Put together. Not crazy. I told him how I fell out of a window with my brother and the resulting physical trauma. Mine. Not his.

"I'd say your brother really owes you, wouldn't you say?" Dr. Phil offered.

I stopped.

"I'm not sure what you mean by that," I said.

"Well, you both fell. He fell on you. You caught him with your body and you have never been the same. It changed you, it changed your family and it changed everything in your life from that day forward. If you ask me, it sounds like you bore the brunt of the fall. He might owe you a bit of gratitude for that."

I walked out of Dr. Phil's office with that comment in my mind. In the months to come I would wonder where else, in my past, I had been a shock absorber.

When I got home, the neurologist's findings were waiting for me: I did not have epilepsy - no kidding - and he was happy to refer me to mental health. Scathing mad and feeling abandoned by the medical industry once again, I composed a response to the neurologist and, for the first time in my medical career, filed a complaint with the medical board. My parents sat in silence as I shared the results over the phone. The journey stretched endlessly in front of us. Hope, once again, gone.

I don't remember if we said our "I love yous." We didn't need to. We were tethered together, swallowed whole. I put myself on the walking path in front of my parent's condo and stepped slowly through the first mile, a tender expression of life. The setting sun met me in pink, our soft underbellies, reflected.

"God, are you here?" I asked silently, but I knew the answer by now. I felt him in the air around me. Hanging. Hovering. Gentle. My words were gone but his presence moved out before me as I moved forward through the night. He was there. He was always with me. And in that moment, that was all I needed. I was heartbroken, but whole. Still, but moving.

Aunt Nancy called to hear the results. All who loved me had been hovering, waiting.

"Oh man! I so wanted a pill or surgery to fix things," Aunt Nancy said, exasperated. "It's so American."

"Yeah," I smirked. "It kinda is but I get it."

I walked on in silence. I no longer felt responsible for how other people processed the news.

"What's next? Where do you go from here?" she asked.

"I take the step before me," I said. It was simple and wrapped my spirit in rest.

I hung up with Aunt Nancy and let *Surrounded (Fight My Battles)* sung by UPPERROOM fill my headphones. I was stronger the second mile. And by the third mile, silent tears slipped down my cheeks and entered my mouth through the corners of my smile. The neurologist had disappeared from view and I knew, once again, I would rise. I came down the hill and opened the gate. Only three miles and a song and I had found my way home.

～

WHEN I SAW Dr. Phil again, I shared with him my response to the neurologist.

"I wasn't super gracious," I said, with a hint of pride for standing up for myself but it immediately disappears. "His email took me several days to recover from. I wish it wouldn't impact me like it does. But it does. It makes me so unbelievably mad."

"Why is that, do you think?" Dr. Phil asked carefully.

"I don't know," but immediately I do and I tear up and my emotions explode. "It's like he sat right in front of me and didn't see or hear me at all. I mean, how could he acknowledge I have a neurological condition that he's licensed to treat and refuse to treat it?" I was crying at full-bore.

Dr. Phil let me cry it out. It wasn't long before I got myself quiet again.

"By the way," I said, once my spirit settled. "What did you mean before when you said I bore the brunt of The Fall?" I asked. "What does that mean?"

"Well," he said. "When you fell, you got hurt and, because the doctors couldn't see it at that time, you were told you were a hypochondriac and selfish and jealous of your brother. Consequently, you didn't get the help you needed and you felt scared and alone and angry. In short: you were not seen; you were not believed; and you were unjustly accused. That's the pattern that's been set up and has repeated itself multiple times over the course of your life. And anytime it comes up, it curls you up in fetal position for a while. It's a trigger, and your system is rigged to respond."

I nodded.

"And that is PTSD."

And at that moment, I stopped fighting.

WAKING UP TO SEED

With the PTSD diagnosis, the part of my heart that held The Fall closed like a book and made a sound. There had been trauma. And it had been traumatic.

In the quest for more information on what living with PTSD was like, I reached out to Kayla Williams, the former Director of the VA Center for Women Veterans, whose husband had also been diagnosed with PTSD. In her book, *Plenty of Time When We Get Home*, she walks the reader through love and recovery in the aftermath of war. When we hosted our big Lean In Women Veterans event, Kayla had been there as one of our extraordinary speakers. After she heard my talk she came up to me and said, "I wrote a book. I'm sending you a copy." And she did, which I read in a compassionate but detached manner. Her husband had PTSD, clearly. At that time, the thought I might, hadn't even crossed my mind.

When I reached out to her again and told her I had been diagnosed with PTSD, she said, simply, "That makes sense."

My work with Erika and women veterans had put me in rooms in front of soldiers - men and women - on a not infrequent basis. During my last year with Lean In, I'd had the opportunity to speak to Team Red, White and Blue, whose mission is to enrich the lives of veterans by connecting them to community through physical and social activities. I was asked to speak to their West Coast Leadership Team. It both humbled and embarrassed me as I struggled to understand what I could possibly say that would be applicable to their situation at all.

The tables were set up in a U shape and I walked up and down through the middle. To my left sat a soldier whose face was covered by the bill of a baseball cap but his energy was palpable. He sat slumped very low in his chair with his chin to his chest, looking up at me through the narrowest of eyes. His presence was thick and deep and magnetic. I knew, if I wasn't careful, his energy could derail me entirely. Because I wanted to be fully present with the team, I shut him down by not looking in his direction.

The speech went off fine. I spoke of leadership and culture, motivation and inspiration, galvanizing action and managing teams. I spoke very little of having been home and bed bound, but I did make mention of it. After I was done speaking, I opened up the floor and took questions. The soldier waited until the very end of the Q&A and then raised his hand. My spine stiffened when his hand went up.

"Yes?" I motioned confidently in his direction, opening up the floor to his question. But inside I was deeply nervous.

"I see veterans all the time who are wounded but they're kind of...stuck...you know?" he said, tapping one finger on the side of his head. "They can't get past it."

I looked at him straight on. I couldn't imagine what he had seen. I couldn't imagine what these veterans had been through, or struggled with, on a day-to-day basis. He had my full attention.

"I recognize you as someone who has suffered. But you got past it. You got to the other side," the soldier said. "I need you to share how you did it, so I can help them get to the other side, too."

I hadn't known what to make of the soldier's comment or his call to action. At the time, his statement only made me feel even more unqualified.

Seeking clarification, I brought it to Theresa.

"God created you to make a unique contribution, whatever that is," Theresa had said, in our session that week. "Even if it's stacking chairs in the church."

Still unclear, I approached Shellie, a veteran who had served twenty-five years in the US Army, and, as a soldier, asked her for insight, too.

"There is so much more God wants to do through you," Shellie said. "You are not your condition. Your name is Cordila, and everyone calls you Cor. You need to get right with that. It means something. You need to figure out what it means."

I THOUGHT about the soldier again in the aftermath of my PTSD diagnosis and Kayla's response. Though I had spent a lifetime unseen by doctors, I was now *seen* by those who mattered most. Those who knew exactly what they were looking at, and what they were looking for. Those who, like me, had experienced trauma and who, like me, wanted healing from the core.

There is a mark on those who had been in the pit - challenged by life and dirty from the battle - *but had made it to the other side.* I was awakening to the understanding that I bore that mark. And for those looking for healing and recovery, that mark was a sign of hope.

Play the role that destiny has for you.
Theresa, Journal #11

AT THE TURN of the year, I was still no clearer about my future. The brand strategy contract job had come to nothing. Jake and I were dead and gone. My body was back in the pit. The only place showing any signs of life in my career was through speaking requests, which was rough because the iron infusions had me pretty much bed bound again. And after three years of no consistent work, my bank account was empty. But the speaking requests kept rolling in.

By January 16th, 2018, I had received sixteen speaking requests. One per day. Only two of those were paid. Since I had been running around Seattle speaking on behalf of Lean In as an unpaid volunteer, that was the expectation: that I'd show up for free and wouldn't ask for a thing. But that season was over. It had to be. My priorities were now *job, body, book* and job was first on the list. I accepted the two paid speaking requests and said no to the rest.

When Nidhi encouraged me to write my book for the third time, I'd given it thirty days and had spent the whole month of December 2017 writing. The idea of writing terrified me because the practice was something one could only do alone, and I had lived so much of life alone. To combat isolation, I found the loudest, most chaotic, most social environment in which to write - the Starbucks Roastery - and sat myself and my computer down.

The Roastery was filled with the cream-of-the-crop baristas. Not only were they deft at making an extraordinary cup of coffee - full of theater, zest and charm - they were also extremely fascinating individuals in their own right. Each person embodied a dynamism, in background and personal interests, that made them fascinating to talk to. If Starbucks was Cheers, I was Norm. I started the book three times and burned it right back down. At the turn of the year, I shifted from writing the book to looking for work and put the book, and thought of the book, behind me. The Roastery, I didn't.

By Spring of 2018, my daily presence had earned me the unofficial title of Mayor of the Roastery. I would go in every day at opening, or as employees and self-proclaimed insiders like me liked to call, "The Howard Hour," because then Starbucks CEO Howard Schultz would often be there. Eyeing Howard Schultz at the Roastery was like spotting a celebrity in New York or LA. If you were a tourist, a celebrity sighting would be an event. Having lived in LA and New York, I would watch over and over as tourists or non-locals would run up to a celebrity and ask for an autograph. Natives and residents didn't do such things. It was seen as gauche. The same could be said about seeing Howard at the Roastery. Approaching him was a no. I'd watched tourists do it over and over again and would cringe a little each time. Although Howard is an incredibly charming and magnetic man, I always gave him his space. Until he stood right in front of me. Then I caved.

"Howard," I leaned forward and whispered.

Howard Schultz was making a coffee for himself behind the smooth teak bar directly in front of me, a whisper away. For sensualists like me, the Roastery tripped all the senses. Where Seattle was a palette of overlapping cool blues and oppressive grays, the Roastery was a warmth explosion. Copper piping ran overhead carrying coffee beans from the roaster to the baristas below, where they would grind the beans and brew them fresh for your cup. The beans running through the pipes sounded like rainsticks from the Amazon. The space was layered with warm woods, from the beams overhead to the enormous teak bars, to the stools and chairs nested beneath them. The giant, hammered copper roaster pulsed at the very center, like a beating heart. And chocolate brown coffee filled every cup, the undeniable elixir of life. I loved it there, which is what I leaned forward and whispered to Howard.

"Howard..."

"Yes?" he said, his inquiry laced with the brace of self-protection. This was a man who was used to intrusions from strangers, which I was.

"I love it here," I said conspiratorially. His head snapped up, so I said it again. "I just love it here."

He came around the bar with haste and sat next to me, his smile open an engaging.

"This place," I ventured. "It's a heaven for the senses."

"You think so?" he asked, his excitement spreading across his entire face.

"I do," I said, and smiled equally large and possibly a little extra. All coolness gone.

"What are you working on?" he asked, looking down at my book and notepad. I suspected this banal question, asked by this extraordinary man in Starbucks worldwide, would net some of the most delightful responses. A book. A screenplay. A new business idea. Or maybe even the hallmarks of everyday life like a nanny schedule. A fitness plan. A personal budget breakdown. I wondered what it felt like to hold the heartbeat of so many people's lives and dreams in the spaces you created. It was evident he was still ignited by the answers as he waited for mine.

"I'm working on a speech, for Starbucks actually," I said, a little embarrassed.

"You are?" he asked, surprised. "What is it on? What do you do?"

His volley was a two-fer but because I was a little embarrassed to tell this formidable CEO I was speaking at his company headquarters on living from the core, I opted to answer the latter.

"I'm a brand strategist," I said, thinking that for him, of all people, the master of brands, my answer would be self-explanatory. Apparently, it wasn't.

"What does that mean?" he asked, genuinely confused but also perhaps a little provocatively.

"It means I connect people emotionally to brands," I said, feeling a little small.

"For yourself," he said. It was a statement, not a question. What did he mean? Like for myself, as a person? No. I did not do brand strategy for myself.

"For companies," I said, starting to feel weird in addition to feeling small.

"Yeah, but for yourself," he stated again.

"Well, no," I said, not knowing where to go from here and also wanting to get out of this death spiral stat. "I'd like to do it for you," I said, driving the nose into the ground.

Whatever happened after that was a blur. It included taking a selfie at my prompting, just when I thought I couldn't go any lower. He exited quickly after that.

I raced to Theresa's.

"What on earth did he mean by that?" I wailed. "And why does everyone think I only work for myself? I'm so sick of being alone. I would like to work on a team, thank you very much! What about that is so hard to believe?"

"There is a calling on you, Cor," Theresa said. "An invitation to step up. An invitation to inspire. There is an aura of power that you project. That aura is a gift from God. That's what God has given you as a resource to attract the kinds of people who make changes. Howard is a change-maker. He was expecting that you were someone who drives change, too."

I was still not remotely over my epic swan dive in front of Howard Schultz or hitting him up for a job, because getting hit up for a job by a Starbucks customer surely never happens to him, I thought, swimming in my own sarcasm.

"You have to get comfortable with where you make a unique contribution. When you make your unique contribution, that's when you connect," Theresa said, waiting for me to get it.

"People can only really connect with you when you are contributing your highest and best. Otherwise, you're subterranean. They can't even get at you. The challenge for every human being on the planet is to be at peace with who they were created to be."

It stopped me cold.

"God gave you your identity, Cor. He made you who you are. You are exactly who you were created to be."

Something about what she said reminded me of this thing we'd say in junior high. "Who do you think you are, God's gift to humanity?"

I laughed to myself. But then thought, what if we *are* God's gift to humanity? What if that was the plan all along?

〜

Little by little. Step by step. Just keep moving.
Yuliya, Journal #34

"WE HAVE A PROBLEM, but we'll figure out how to solve it," Teri said. It was speech day at Starbucks.

It was only noon but for whatever reason I had been prompted to put on my game-face makeup early. I thought it was dumb but did it anyway. Teri's call came in shortly thereafter.

"What's the problem?" I asked.

"Well, the projectors are out. We can't show any slides."

Most of my speeches were more of a story and easy to tell with no slides. This one was content rich. If we had no projector, it was going to be tough. It was possible I'd have to deliver something completely different than I had planned.

"I hear that you're stressed. I'll come help. I'm leaving now," I said, and grabbed my already packed garment bag and headed out the door.

Teri met me in the lobby of Starbucks headquarters. We walked up to the room where the speech was to take place. A young man was there to receive us.

"Have you gotten it to work?" Teri asked him.

"No," he said, his face drawn. "But we're bringing a tech guy in."

Teri nodded, looking exhausted and exasperated.

"Go," I said to her. "I've got this."

"You sure?" she asked, relieved.

"Yes. Absolutely. Go."

Both of them left and shortly thereafter, another man entered with a toolkit in tow and the swagger of a problem solver.

"I hear we have a problem," Darryl said, good-naturedly.

"That's what they say," I said, eating the sandwich I had packed for lunch. I had left the house at noon and would go on stage at seven. I was ready to be parked in this seat for the duration.

I sat on the stage as Darryl climbed on the ladder. In the beginning we said very little. I balanced my laptop on my lap and followed his orders. Try clicking on your PowerPoint. Try it again. And again. That was the essence of our conversation. We were a few hours in, when he asked me what my speech was about.

"I'm giving a talk on knowing who you are at the core and living from it," I said, a little embarrassed. I still couldn't believe I was doing this. For a decade I had been a brand strategist and my work had been about strategy and alignment. Knowing your identity and living from the core seemed too personal to speak about from a corporate stage and I felt self-conscious. On my way into Starbucks I had been wrestling with the idea of changing the content last minute. If we couldn't get the projector fixed, this could be my way out. What a godsend.

"That's cool," Darryl said. He tried to sound intrigued by the topic, but I could tell he wasn't.

"What do you do?" he asked, looking for another, more cerebral and less emotional touchpoint.

"I'm a brand strategist," I said matter-of-factly, trying to recoup some of the credibility capital I was clearly losing.

"Oh yeah?" he exclaimed. "Would you look at my business card and tell me what you think?"

"Of course," I said laughing. Here we go again, I thought.

Opining on business cards was my standard party trick. Many professions have one. When a doctor surfaces at a party, they are presented with a list of symptoms. My back hurts. My mom can't wiggle her thumb. My baby does this weird thing when he sneezes. Every manner of latent, non-urgent concern comes forward for the doctor, who is at a party, to diagnose on the fly. If a pilot goes to a party, they are asked about turbulence or the likelihood of planes crashing or to describe the scariest thing that's ever happened mid-air. If a brand strategist goes to a party, we're asked to look at business cards, logos, or websites. Every time.

I suspected the card and logo were self-imagined, so I wanted to tread carefully. I'd been honest many times in the past and it turned out that being painfully honest was neither appreciated nor desired. What people were looking for was truth wrapped in validation. I looked for what was true and what I could validate about the card. It was black and white with an icon of a bowtie, an on-the-nose interpretation for a company called Black Tie Communications.

"Well, you're clearly a gentleman," I said, kicking off strong. "Your mannerisms and demeanor are sophisticated and elegant. I can also tell being considerate and professional is important to you."

Darryl was on top of the ladder in front of me, screwing in a new light bulb. At this, he dropped his arms.

"That's true," he said, looking down on me.

"So, your choice of graphic - the bowtie - tells me what I can expect from you: class, respectfulness, elegance, and first-class service. To that end, I would expect you to be a man who knows his stuff," I said.

He lifted his arms back up and started working on the light again.

"Hm," he said, lost in thought. "That's really very interesting. Thank you."

I smiled and we fell back into silence. He continued to work on the projector as the hour was getting later. I had resolved to speak on different content because it really didn't seem like this was working out. There was some talk between Darryl and the young man who came back to check in on his progress about a part needing to come from China. Even if sent via FedEx, it obviously wouldn't get there in time. I felt a sense of relief.

But suddenly something worked that previously hadn't, a projector light went on, and in very short order we were back in the game. Darryl climbed down off of his ladder and went over to the room light switches so we could test it. On his way to the light switches, he walked along the front of the stage.

"You ready?" Darryl asked, rendering the room dark.

"Yep," I said, and pressed a few buttons to pull up my Power-Point. It worked.

"There you go," he said to himself more than me. He was pleased with his work. As he should be. I wasn't sure, however, if I was.

Darryl turned the lights back on and came up onto the stage to walk back over to his ladder, crossing directly in front of me. He strode confidently across the stage until he reached me and then he halted, as if forcibly stopped.

He lifted a hand up over his mouth and looked at me, eyes wide, and slightly bewildered.

"What is it?" I asked, concerned.

His eyes narrowed as he looked at me potently. Searchingly.

"What?" I asked. I was starting to get uneasy.

"It's just," his speech was slow in coming. I could tell he was struggling with something. "I shouldn't say this. I shouldn't. But I've not felt it like this before."

Oh man, I thought. What's this about? Yikes.

"Is it ok if I say something to you?" he asked. I could tell he was conflicted about it, which of course made me ultra-hesitant.

"*Okay,*" I drew out. We both braced for impact.

"I feel God around you," Darryl said. "The feeling is so strong."

I looked at him, stunned.

"If you're having any reservations about what you're doing, don't. God's hand is on you. This is your purpose. I believe it's his design for you to take this message all around the world."

Darryl packed up his things and left the room shortly thereafter. Thirty minutes later, I was on stage at Starbucks talking about knowing your identity and living from the core. Three hours later, I was driving back home to my parents' condo.

BEARING THE MARK

MAY, SEATTLE, 2018

AT THE VERY beginning of my leadership tenure of Lean In Seattle, I met a woman named Jana who had also started a chapter in Seattle along with her friend Alicia. The original co-founder of the Lean In Seattle Chapter, Pam, had co-founded our chapter with a two-leader model. But by the time I encountered the chapter, Pam was the primary leader. When Pam and I met to discuss her experience, she confessed it was incredibly gratifying work but it was a lot. I knew I'd have to reimagine the existing model to create a more stable base. Anything built on my back was dicey on its face. Stability would only come if I amortized the risk by enrolling other leaders to co-lead with me. Since the slated leaders Pam had previously enlisted had opted out, I went looking for more leaders, fast. Jana, Alicia and I met, hit it off instantly and decided to merge our efforts. We jokingly called it an M&A deal and agreed, still many years later, it was the best decisions we made.

Jana and Alicia were extraordinary women and added

incredible fuel to the Lean In Seattle chapter fire. Unfortunately, as soon as Jana leaned in, she had to lean out. She had a health battle of her own to contend with. She had a bad heart and it was failing.

When Jana was newly married, she had contracted a virus that settled in her heart. Within short order, she was in need of a heart transplant and pretty quickly after we met, she received one. Our whole, newly combined chapter had a front row seat to the unfolding.

Throughout her battle, Jana remained a force of nature. After she received her heart, she proudly and unabashedly wore plunging shirts to highlight the vertical incision that was evidence her core had been cracked and opened. The scar was beautiful. Brutal. Savage. And I wanted one.

I didn't want a scar like Jana's. I certainly didn't envy her seven-year quest for a donor heart, nor the weight of what it must feel like to carry one. But I wanted evidence, physical evidence, of the war I had been fighting within. My body sustained all of its battles without a single mark. Even the loss of Lumen produced no visible child. Moreover, Jana's scar wasn't just physical evidence of a vicious battle, it was proof of the gift of life. The scar gave Jana an opening to talk about the generous, astonishing, and game-changing gift she received through sacrifice. One person and family made a decision to leave a legacy in order to infuse Jana with the life she eventually would have lost. The battle was both a mark of death as well as an opening to tell a story of life. That is what I wanted. I wanted a visible manifestation of my invisible reality. I wanted a mark to provide evidential proof that I too had been through a battle and received the gift of life. Since I had no mark, I would have to make my own.

I LAY BACK as Mike Barker, owner of Jackson Street Tattoo

Company, came at me with his vibrating needle. We were entering into a very sacred relationship. He was going to leave a mark on my body that would never go away. Yuliya, my Russian friend who flinched at nothing, came with me to commemorate the day Mike would tattoo my body with Lumen's name. Lumen had been here. I was still here. Together we were proof of life.

"You're right. Your life is her legacy as much as it is yours," Aunt Nancy said potently over post-tattoo tea when I shared with her the thoughts that had formed when I laid Lumen to rest. She would talk to me about Lumen, one of the few who did. "What would you want her to see if she looked at your life?"

"I wouldn't want her to see me contract," I told Aunt Nancy. "I would want her to see me expand."

In ancient Israel, a woman who never had a child carried an enormous load of shame and disgrace. The word for such a woman was "barren," which by definition means bleak, lifeless, and too poor to produce much or any vegetation. In a world that prized procreation and tied a woman's worth directly to her fertility, a barren woman was seen as useless, dried out, and her life, bleak.

When Israel found itself in Babylonian exile and captivity, they felt the same shame, disgrace, and humiliation. God spoke to Israel, likening Israel to a barren woman, and promised release from not only the exile and captivity, but also from the burden of shame, disgrace, and humiliation. He promised the shame of barrenness would be so completely healed, that they would be so completely made whole, that they would be fruitful to overflow such that they would have to expand their living space.

The opening verses of Isaiah 54 visually reminded me of the big, communal, Moroccan-style tent from Habitas. When the Lord spoke to the people of Israel, he encouraged them by saying:

"Expand the place of your tent, stretch your tent curtains wide, do not hold back; lengthen your cords, strengthen your stakes. For you will spread out to the right and to the left; your descendants will dispossess nations and settle in their desolate cities."

It was a message of audacious expansion after a season of restriction and desolation. Easy to say. Hard to do. It was a calling to hold onto a promise of fruitfulness, when there was no visible or physical evidence to warrant it. The Lord was asking them, while they were still in a desert of barrenness, to hold onto the hope of abundance. And to not just hope for it, but to walk in it. To boldly expand the place of their tent in expectancy of a promise fulfilled. It was an incredibly ballsy stance and one I was determined to find within me.

If I was going to move forward and be used by God, I couldn't waste my miracle on my pain. God brought me through what he brought me through for a reason. How I chose to look at what happened in my life would determine everything. I was determined not to waste his grace.

If I was determined to be used by God, I knew I would be. I was still a useful and valuable person in the world. That was inherent in my identity as a child of God. But it was on me to decide if I would contract or expand. And I resolved that no matter how big the square patch of earth would be on which I would stand, I would expand the place of my tent. I would speak fertility over the notion of barrenness on my life. I would refuse to let anyone or anything determine how I would set or orient my heart every day. I was bound so tightly but refused to be kept down.

I surrounded myself with people who refused to be held down. With Helen Keller, who was blind and deaf, but that did not keep her down. With Frida Kahlo, who was maimed by accident and disease, but that did not keep her down. With Steven Hawking, who was crippled by illness, but it did not keep him down. With Mother Teresa, who was burdened by a deep sadness in her heart, but it did not stop her from lifting the hearts of those around her whose pain and suffering was unspeakably great. They were all individuals who, like me, were physically bound and still dared to expand and in doing so, touched the world. I didn't know what God had in store for me, who I would touch, or how. That was out of my hands. But I did know that no matter what happened, or what didn't, I would expand.

I was a woman with no husband, and still, I would expand.

I was a woman with no children, and still, I would expand.

I was a human whose body was broken, and still, I would expand.

I had no job.

I had no home.

I had very little to call my own, and still...

I would expand.

I would expand.

I would expand.

I LAY in the bathtub a few days later and looked down at my tattoo. It was a mark that would never see the light of day, but it would be my daily reminder, a monument to the work God had already done in my life and a promise of what was to come.

Then it dawned on me that I was one. I was the mark. I was the living monument. I was the embodiment of the promise. The game-changing gift I had received was not so much in my physical recovery but in understanding who I really was. That was the gift. God instilled in me identity intelligence and that was the truth that changed everything. It did not require physical burden of proof to make my story more believable. I was the evidence. I was the proof of life. All that changed in and around me was all the proof I needed.

Unleash a unique, original, extraordinary, wonderfully untamed faith.
Theresa, Journal #30

I sat in Dr. Phil's office a few days later and shared how I was still struggling with the infinite delay in the face of such a strong desire for expansion. I laid out all the activities and actions I had done to try and proactively move my life forward.

"I don't know what else to do," I said. "It feels like it's in God's hand."

"Then it probably is," he said. "This whole time you've been feeling like you're alone, but you're not."

The barrenness I had been experiencing had not just been in my womb, but in the whole of my life. I so deeply desired industry and to be working as part of a team again.

"You and God are partners," he said. "You're already on a team."

Tears instantly sprang out of my eyes and down my face. There was no holding them back. I smiled and breathed that new truth deep into my bones.

"I'm already on a team," I repeated, inhaling and closing my eyes.

"You are, Cor. And you always have been."

If God and I were one a team, I wondered, what would be my code with God?

When a company sets its brand strategy, it does so by establishing two powerful tools: the Coressence, which I had learned about powerfully in Hollywood during the Wilbur Weiner audition; and the Code, or the operating agreements by which the brand is run. The Coressence answers the question of who a brand is at its core and drives the emotional experience customers have with the brand. The Code answers the question what can this brand be counted on to provide? How will the brand interact with me? How shall I anchor my expectations?

With brands, the Coressence is crafted very thoughtfully and carefully. At the Starbucks Roastery, the warm woods, the smell of coffee, the choice of the music, all of it - all of it - had been carefully selected to give an emotional feel to the brand. Mythologically speaking, Starbucks was the Siren, the wooing sea maiden who pulled men to her by the lure of her song. She is an intoxicating, captivating, and magnetic myth and these enigmatic characteristics were woven right into the Starbucks brand. These characteristics sit at the core of the brand as its Coressence. I went to Starbucks specifically for the heady intoxication this Coressence provided.

There is something that walks into the room when I do. I have little control over it. If I was to accept that my identity was formed by my Creator, then I must also acknowledge that the characteristics that made me, me, were part of His hand-crafted experience. They were purposeful and by design. All of it was beautiful. All of it was purposeful. Any thoughts otherwise would be mistaken identity once again.

We cannot control how we are received by others. Some will walk into the Starbucks Roastery and feel, as I do, that they are transported somewhere heavenly. Others will walk into the Roastery and walk directly back out. They may find it too loud, the coffee too acidic, the crowd too oppressive, the brand too touristy. Starbucks, and all those who manage the brand, can do nothing about that. Nor should they. They are not in the business of pleasing everyone. They are in the business of pursuing their mission, which is to inspire and nurture the human spirit - one person, one cup and one neighborhood at a time. And let those who are drawn to the brand, be drawn to it. Full stop.

The characteristics on me were equally self-evident. I was a ball-buster, for one. I also knew that the majority of people considered me provocative, deeply layered, sensual, and fun. Provocative, in particular, was something I had been extremely sensitive about. It had brought forward some interesting and often unpleasant circumstances in my life and was the seat of a great deal of shame because of it. Before I realized my full value, I considered this attribute a character flaw, when it wasn't. It was something God had placed in me. I could walk into a room and not even open my mouth to speak and people would find me provocative. I could not control how people would receive and experience me, no more than Starbucks could. Nor should I. My traits, my Coressence, was intentional and by design.

And yet my provocative nature was there for a reason. When placed in the toolkit to be used by God, it could be an incredibly powerful weapon for good. It could, and had, challenge people to examine their own underlying sense of self-worth, causing dynamic change for the better. It could, and had, conjure up very strong and magnetic reactions in people, pulling those to me who were interested in making changes on a large, corporate, or global scale. I have been at the apex of change, and often an instigator of change, because of this characteristic that God put inside me. It is an extremely potent tool and when I allow myself to embrace it instead of reject it, and in doing so reject myself, I set free the tool for God to use it in ways that would honor him and bring about change beyond what I could ever even imagine. This is the purpose of our unique personalities, so that each and every one of us can be uniquely used by God.

And yet if these tools of my personality and Coressence were given to me, they were also entrusted to me, and it was one hundred percent on me to determine how I would use them. God created me to be who I was, but it was on me to decide who I would become.

Calling all lightning.
Theresa, Journal #24

~

"How do you handle disagreements and personality conflicts among the leadership team?", a student had asked when I was at the University of Washington, guest-lecturing about how we ran the Lean In leadership team.

We were a team of over forty leaders, all working for free. Functioning by a Code was paramount in order for us to work together seamlessly. Very early on, we had established a list of five operational agreements. It was our Code. It was not only how we ran our team but how we ran the whole chapter. The Code tenants were easy and repeatable and designed to live on the tip of every leader's and member's tongue:

Show Up
Energize
Add Value
Build Community
Leave a Legacy

During the course of the second year we added a sixth value: *Spread the Word.* This Code was one of the most powerful in that it gave ownership of the future growth of our chapter to each and every member.

"The Code functions like an agreement," I answered, "which we agree to mutually and collectively in advance. In the event a disagreement comes up, we use our Code to guide the conversation and in doing so, remove emotionality from the equation entirely. There should never be something as insignificant as personality conflicts. Every voice at the table is unique and valuable. Our Code drives alignment. It reminds us of what we agreed to and keeps us on purpose, which allows every team member to contribute powerfully."

I walked to the middle of the classroom to get closer to the students. I believed so wholeheartedly in this concept and leadership tool that the only way to press it into them was to get close.

"We have a call every week," I said. "And if someone doesn't show up to that call, routinely, I don't have to make it personal. Instead, I just pull that person aside and say, 'Listen, as a group we ascribe to the Code *Show Up*. You haven't shown up to the last five calls so we need to talk about that.' So now it's removed this idea that, 'Hey, this is about you,' and it makes it more about what we agreed to as a group. The Code is a mechanism by which we establish trust. It's a trust builder. If I, as a leader, let it go, then everything falls apart. When one person does it and gets away with it, then what's stopping another person from doing it, and another person? And then, before you know it, we're not who we say we are at all. And when one Code breaks by becoming invalid, how much will the group put stock in the rest of them? And then what happens, do you think?"

"Anarchy!" someone shouted from the back.

I laughed, my whole head tilted back. I loved doing this. I loved being with these kids.

"Yeah," I said. "Pretty much."

HOW MUCH OF my life was subject to anarchy, I wondered, as I left Dr. Phil's office and headed to the Roastery; the class had returned from the annals of my mind.

After making the rounds and greeting everyone, I settled into a chair in the corner and pulled my feet underneath me and slid a napkin underneath my glass to catch the moisture. The print on the napkin said Starbucks Reserve. The word jumped out at me and I looked it up.

Reserve: to be kept specially for a particular person or purpose; to be set aside for future use.

The word reserve is similar in meaning to the word marked, which, among other things, meant to be anointed by God. Both the words contained both inaction and action. To hold oneself in reserve felt inactive but to be kept for a future use contained action. What if that was the Code God was asking me to agree to: to be held in reserve and used by him for the time, and purpose, of his choosing?

I slid the napkin up the side of the glass to catch a little bit of sugary sweetness that had cascaded up and over the rim. I held the napkin to my nose and inhaled its scent.

"What fragrance is being diffused by your life in the Kingdom?" Theresa had asked me once. "If you were to pass by, what would remain?"

I thought back to the Rebirth Party. In a desire to recreate the sensual and enveloping experience of Habitas, a woman I knew by way of another friend offered to create a signature scent for me. The process had been luxurious and intoxicating.

Kate's lab was below her shop in Pioneer Square. This older part of downtown Seattle was characterized by large warehouses and small brick buildings, home to many mom-and-pop storefronts. Hers was one. The basement lab of Essential Apothecary below E. Smith Merchantile was lined with shelves of bottles of essential oils. I wiggled stoppers out of the amber glass bottles Kate selected and one by one inhaled their scents. The heady and sweet scents of ylang ylang, rose, and lily. The spicy scents of cumin, coriander, and anise. The incredibly sensual and alluring scents of cedar, leather, vanilla, and tobacco. Each scent took me on an olfactory journey. How would I ever choose? I loved them all. Kate, an alchemist, set aside every bottle I inhaled with intensity. The ones I smelled and quickly set back down, she put back. She began to make a list with the bottles she had in front of her and with a small dropper, filled them in three separate containers. In one she added a bit more cumin. In another, more vanilla. In still another, she dosed a healthy base of leather. My time with Thickskin had turned me on to something I treasured by scent, and though that bag line was long gone from my life, it lived on - by scent - in my body.

Leaving Kate's shop with a perfume named "Cordila," I realized that I was the alchemist of this life. God had given me so much to choose from. Each scent made available to me was heady and intoxicating, but the concoction was mine to combine.

I sat in Roastery and thought about the scents I would combine for a life in the Kingdom. I would put in a drop of **Reserved** to remind me that I was held apart by God for a use and a purpose. I knew I was a person with limited energy and because of this I would do less to be able to give God more. I added drops of **Wholehearted**. "You need to be experienced," Dinah once said to me. My life would be a full-bodied experience. Anyone who would come into contact with me would be enveloped. They would feel me on all levels. I included drops of **Humble**. I had embraced the idea that every individual was a child of God. Every person was a sovereign being in their own right and on a journey with God and of God's design. I had learned that loving well was founded on a healthy dose of humility which looked like respect: respect for myself, respect for others, and above all, respect for God. And lastly, I poured in fun. Life was meant to be lived, and no matter the circumstance, no matter the situation; anything short of living fully alive, was death. I called it fun; the Bible called it **Filled with Joy**. This would be my operating agreement with God. Any moves I would make with God by my side would carry the unmistakable scent of God's hand in mine.

EMBRACING TRAINING

May, Seattle, 2018

By May, I was two rounds of iron infusions in and my first paid speech was coming up. My body was wrecked. I surfaced at my endocrinologist - a man so signed up for me but still part of the same old system - and complained of feeling full. I had been doing so for three months.

"I have so much pressure in my stomach and it won't let up," I complained.

"You keep saying that but you're very thin," he said. "I can see your waist. I think you need to be careful of the messages you're telling yourself. I think this is body dysmorphia."

Yet another flavor of mental illness. It was a losing battle and not one I wanted to fight. I ignored his comment and the sensation in my stomach and kept moving right along.

The speech for the Washington State Department of Licensing was to take place in Lacey, Washington, close to Washington's Capitol. It was the DOL's Annual Convention, pulling in four hundred people from around the state. I was their opening keynote. I was excited and overly prepared and eager to receive my first and only paycheck of the year.

Five days before the speech, the stomach pressure I had been experiencing for months had turned into a stomach pain. I was doing my best to ignore it. By soundcheck, sweat from the pain was rolling down my back. As I stood on stage while the tech team tested the mic, I tried to stabilize the pain. I can handle this, I thought. If this pain level stays the same, I can handle it. My speech was meant to be ninety minutes long. If the pain level stayed the same, I rationalized, I could manage this level of pain for ninety minutes. I was incredibly relieved when sound-check was over and I was released back to the hotel.

Shellie had planned to come over after work to go on a walk with me. It wasn't often I was in her neighborhood, so we jumped at the chance of getting to see each other. She called me on her way over to the hotel, but when I picked up the phone, she knew right away something was wrong.

"Uh oh," she said. "I don't like the sound of your voice."

"Yeah, Shell. I'm not feeling great," I said.

"I'm still coming over," she stated and hung up the phone.

By the time Shellie arrived, I was in pajamas and white as a sheet.

"I brought you some ginger tea, chicken broth, and crackers," Shellie said, setting everything down on the console by the TV.

"You're going nowhere," she said, after taking one look at me. I agreed.

By 4 AM I was in searing pain. I was standing up but bent in half. I grabbed the chair by the desk with both hands and rocked myself back and forth, willing my back to open and release. It had tightened around the pain and clamped down.

I spoke to myself in increments of time. "Cor, let's see how you feel in 5 minutes. Then you can call Samantha," the woman who had booked me for the event.

When five minutes passed and I was still in white-hot pain, I pushed out my deadline a little more. I desperately wanted to speak. If I didn't go on, I wouldn't get paid. More importantly, I couldn't stand the thought of letting anyone down. This was their annual convention. Four hundred people were coming. There were only a few hours left to go and news like this would send the whole team scrambling. I couldn't stand the thought of it. The minutes kept counting down until I couldn't put it off any longer. I texted Samantha, tried to do what I could to help manage the situation, and then, contrary to all logical thought, got in my Jeep and drove myself home.

I couldn't escape the pressure. It was in me and all around me. I knew my parents, who were in town, would be waiting for me at the condo. I dreaded seeing them. I knew my pressure was their pressure and they would be sad right alongside me. The pressure in my financial situation was strangling me. I had applied for job after job after job and wasn't even getting interviews. It didn't matter that I had internal employee references. It didn't matter that I had a network. For whatever reason, the doors were all closed going on three solid years. The pressure in my stomach made me angry. Angry that I couldn't ignore it away. Angry that, even though I felt like I did my time in physical purgatory, I was still being sidelined. Angry that whatever was happening now would *probably* have to be dealt with and would *probably* lead me down another road of dismissals from doctors.

By the time I tore into the condo driveway and rolled my luggage through the front door, I'd had it. I threw my sunglasses across my room and they broke. I dealt with the screaming pain for two more days before going back to the ER, Take Two for the year, waiting until my parents had left town.

The basement of your soul is far deeper than you know.
Unknown, Journal #32

"Lord what are you doing?" I cried at the top of my lungs in my mind.

When Jake asked me who God was to me and I said he's slowly becoming everything, I meant he was slowly becoming everything. I didn't know how to orient myself anymore if not rooted in my small but growing understanding of him. I couldn't totally explain it but the conversation of God had taken over all my thought-tracks and wasn't letting me go. Anything that came up for inspection - resentments, desires, motivations, distractions - all came up for review under this new light. It was exhausting and exhilarating and engulfing. I released expectations on relationships, old resentments on friendships, and a desire to control how things were going to go. As my finances dwindled even more, I eliminated my storage unit and got rid of even more of my possessions and tried to find humility in the fact that my healthy six-figure income was no more and may never come again. I torched all of who I had been and watched as fire burned everything to the ground.

But where was God in all of this? Didn't this life of faith come with some type of assuredness of holy protection? Surely the God who stepped in and told me I was beautiful and rearranged everything I thought about myself and life could step in and fix this, too. Whatever was going on in my life, whatever this full-scale undoing, it totally sucked.

I had driven myself to the ER and was in the white paper hospital gown with the back open, rocking my back out again, when the ER doctor walked in. His attractiveness was off the charts.

"Ok, the results are back. It turns out you have about fifteen pounds of fecal matter impacted in your colon. That's what is causing the pain."

I needed a moment.

"Are you seriously telling me that backed up…"

"Fecal matter," he filled in.

"Yes. Is causing this level of pain? How incredibly embarrassing," I said, rolling my eyes. Having to talk about this at all was unpleasant but having to discuss it with a stunningly hot man was unnecessary, God, if you ask me.

"No. No. You shouldn't be embarrassed at all," he reasoned. "One night on rounds I dropped to my knees in massive pain. It was unbearable. I thought I was having a heart attack! And I'm an ER doc in the ER so we ran all the tests and everything but I was fine. It turned out it was gas."

He laughed. I smiled tightly. My embarrassment was complete.

"I never underestimate the level of pain this type of situation can cause."

He prescribed a course of action and I walked back out the door.

Two days after I ended up in the ER with compacted fecal matter, I flew back down to LA.

God is always advancing his purpose in your life, even if it looks like you are losing ground.
Theresa, Journal #55

"CALL 911," I ordered. It was the second time I'd issued that directive in four years, and the third time I'd be visiting an ER in six months. Yaela called them immediately.

I had been in LA for a few weeks trying all manner of natural remedies to release the blockage in my body. The day before I was scheduled to leave LA and return to Seattle, all hell broke loose. It was in the dead of night, but something was wrong and it woke me up. The second I opened my eyes, there was no ground. The room pitched uncontrollably. Violently. I flung myself on my back and grabbed both sides of the bed, my arms and legs splayed for balance. None came. Nausea rushed forward. As if crawling up the side of a plane in flight, I flipped over and clawed my way up the bed, grabbing for the anti-vomiting pills in my bag. With shaking hands and bouncing eyes, I peeled back the corner and tossed a pill in my mouth. Nothing. I needed to get to the bathroom, fast. Something was horribly wrong.

I rose from bed, gripping anything steady, and pulled myself forward to the bathroom, calling quietly but firmly for Yaela along the way. She arrived instantly.

"What's wrong?" she asked with the heat of deep concern.

"I don't know," I got out. "I can't....find....ground."

I slid to the floor in the bathroom. Everything was hard. The porcelain bathtub, the cold marble floor, the rim of the toilet. The room was pitching, the edges were turning black, and I was terrified I was going to vomit and pass out and hit my head on something hard.

"Do you want me to call the paramedics?" Yaela asked.

Not waiting a mother-loving second, I said yes.

I had come to LA to escape the pressure of my circumstances and also treat some of the side effects from the iron infusions that had holed themselves up in my abdomen, in a more natural way than prescribed. If not LA, then where? I tried juicing, colonics and abdominal massage that were all, in their own way, effective, but the process had caused deleterious dehydration - the kiss of death for my condition - which landed me in the ER with no ground. Somewhere in the middle of the night I sent Yaela, who sat vigilantly by my bedside, home from the ER. She was pregnant and needed rest, as did I. On my discharge, Yaela's fiancé, Charlie, was waiting for me in the parking lot. After holding myself together, and after weathering what would go down as one of the most physically terrifying nights of my life, I closed the door to the car, and as Charlie sat still with the engine running, I put my face in my hands and cried.

I lay in bed several more weeks at Yaela's, weathering the aftermath of the episode and trying to get steady enough to fly home. My body was on a bender that was sending me back underground and although I didn't know how yet, I was determined to course-correct the spiral, whatever it took.

I called Kent.

On top of being an artist, Kent was in mortifyingly good shape. The kind that stopped traffic and tilted all conversation in the direction of fitness the moment he entered the room. I knew attempting to acquire the kind of shape Kent worked hard for, and enjoyed, would be a death-sentence for me, at this juncture at least. But I knew he knew the fundamentals. And like Michael Jordan said, if you master the fundamentals, everything else will rise. I enrolled Kent in my quest for a healthy body.

"Find a rhythm of fueling your body and resting your body," Kent said. "Try to do that for two to three weeks. Find the same thing to eat every day. Figure out what fuels you. You. What I do won't necessarily work for you. It took me a year and a half to get it down. You need to find your own fuel source."

There was something comforting in that idea; the idea that he didn't just know from one moment to the next how to master his body. The idea of experimentation gave me space to try things on and work things out.

"Start playing with your diet to see what you need," he continued. "Figure out a plan that keeps your body sustained so you can build from there. Just figure out how to fuel your body, Cor. Don't worry about anything else," he said, sensing remnant impatience and eagerness for health. "Your goal is simple: stay consistently on your feet."

Finding my own fuel source made me feel like a car and I laughed at the memory it conjured up.

Two summers prior, with wine in our hands and the sun on our faces, Mark, Alastair, Charlotte, Dinah and I played the game of what-car-would-you-be-if-you-were-one. We were sitting around the fire pit at Westward & Little Gull with a view of Lake Union. It was summer, Seattle was glistening and I was in heaven.

Dinah, it was decided, was a vintage 260 Mercedes. Cherry red. It was perfect for her as she had the feel of a woman brought forward from another time. She was sensitive and thoughtful and also capable and true. It was a car-match if ever there was one.

"I'm a Jeep," said Charlotte, not wanting or needing other input. She already knew. Charlotte was infinitely likable and easy-going and had an inherent, self-sufficient confidence that made her delightful. "Everyone loves driving a Jeep," she said cheerily with a shrug. And she was right.

Alastair, her husband, was a BMW. We all agreed. An engineer and a born thinker, he was the ultimate driving machine of precision and grace.

And Mark was Mark. He was a pickup. We all laughed when he said it because it was just so spot-on. He was easy, up for adventure, reliable, useful, and shared by community. Mark wasn't just Mark. He was "our Mark." Unanimously loved by all.

"Cor, you're a Lotus," Alastair said, and everyone was immediately on the bandwagon. I didn't even know what a Lotus was. Alastair slid forward his phone to show me.

"Oh," I said a little tightly. "It's a high-maintenance car."

"Yeah, but Cor," Alastair said. "It's a Lotus."

I was surrounded by friends who loved me and yet all, unequivocally, considered me high maintenance.

Dinah added I was also a Lotus because "men love them but don't necessarily know what to do with them."

"Or handle them!" Charlotte shouted. "Not everyone can drive a Lotus."

"Certainly not how it's meant to be driven," Alastair said, with characteristic softness and under bellied wit.

Some things are meant as compliments but strangely leave one crestfallen. This was one. I wanted to be easy going and reliable, like a Honda. I wanted to be able to roll up to any situation and be appropriate. I wanted to be a car with a steady engine and all-wheel drive with four doors and a low stairwell, so everyone was comfortable. I wanted to be the car that was acceptable for any and all circumstances, but I was apparently a Lotus. Hot on a track and a bit of a spectacle, but otherwise a high-maintenance machine requiring a pit crew. That was me.

I called Theresa, my pit crew lead, and told her about the Lotus analogy.

"They're right," she said. "When you come in you exude a ton of energy and power, it just pours out of you. It's magnetic. But then there's nothing left. In order for you to perform, you have to be really firm around your boundaries. These boundaries will allow you to get up and go the next day."

Theresa and I drilled way down. We talked about how many hours a day I could work. How many hours I would need for rest. What types of socializing I would do, how often, and how long. The guardrails were closing in hot and fast.

"Your environment needs to be clean, white, minimal, and relaxing. Soothing sounds or silence. You have to minimize the noise. Be careful how much noise you allow into your head. When the noise hits a decibel that vibrates your whole body, that's really bad for you," Theresa said, talking about noise in the literal and figurative sense. "You can still hear sound without needing to have your whole-body rattle."

After I finally made it back from LA, I lay in bed, still recuperating, and listened to the sounds of the Seahawks next door. Living right next door to the training facility of the sometimes Super Bowl champions had its pluses and minuses. It meant weathering loud music during summer outdoor Training Camp, and dealing with pulsing bass reverberation from extra-large cars with black tinted windows at four, five and six AM when players rolled into the parking lot to begin their day. But it also meant having a birds-eye view into what high-maintenance peak performance really meant. The players didn't apologize for it. At all. In fact, they were celebrated for the careful attention they paid to their bodies, schedules, and intense training. Any restrictions or parameters they placed on their lives or bodies were met with a level of awe and reverence. Of course they would need to be tended to differently. Of course they had special needs and requests. They were peak performers.

The acknowledgement of being a peak performer, however, didn't start when they stepped out onto the field in cleats and a uniform. The acknowledgement, and their commitment to peak performance training, whatever it would take, began much earlier on. It began in the dark. It began at the crack of dawn. It began when there was nobody looking. No assuredness of success. No bright lights or big stadium. No reverence for restrictions or screaming fans. Somewhere along the way, each player decided that they were a peak performer and they never looked back. I decided I wouldn't either.

Give yourself permission to be you. Finally.
Yuliya, Journal #48

My struggle in recognizing my identity as a Full Dollar had always been around this belief that who I was, how I was, was an illegitimate expression of humanity. Nobody needed someone high maintenance. That type of person was not useful to humanity but rather a burden requiring extra attention and care. As I lay in bed listening to the Seahawks it further solidified my new-found understanding that my original belief was not true at all. The Seahawks, and peak performers just like them, had a legitimate role to play in the world. As did I.

In Christianity, it is understood that every believer is part of the body of Christ. Every person, and whatever they bring to the table, is a valid and legitimate member of the body. Not only legitimate, but useful. Necessary. Without every single person's gifting, the body would not function. To the world, I might be high-maintenance but to God I was vital. The distinction made me want to lean toward him even more. I was determined to give all that I was over to be used by God. Whether I was able to consistently stay on my feet, or not.

IN ACCORDANCE with my health protocol, I was set to get another round of iron infusions. It would be my third series in a year. My body took a beating every time, but per the Mayo Clinic and my hematologist, iron infusions were supposed to help. I went to schedule another appointment to receive my infusion, but my endocrinologist emailed me and was concerned about some of my blood test results. By the looks of it, I was in acute Stage 3 kidney failure. Before he would sign off on another infusion, I had to wait and do additional blood tests to see if the kidney failure would resolve or require critical medical intervention. Thankfully, it resolved, and I went into the hospital for another iron infusion. I spent the next ten days suppressing vomiting.

I prayed silently as I lay staring at the ceiling.

My body was wreckage. My physicality pressed down. Breathing came hard and heavy. The helplessness within me, a sinking stone. I rolled over, curled into myself, and reached for my phone. I opened the music video of *No Longer Slaves* by Jonathan and Melissa Hesler and played the video again and again. Watching Jonathan sing, I felt the cold of the midnight air in the mist that surrounded him. He was tall. So tall. I wondered what it was like to tower over and rise above.

He opened his arms wide and sang, *"I'm no longer a slave to fear. I am a child of God."*

His voice broke and I anchored in it, in all of it, my face wet with tears. If I laid here too long, I knew I wouldn't get up. "The song is meant to lift you, Cor," I said to myself out loud. "Let it do its work."

I took a slow breath in. Slow magic, like Emily said. Slow down. *Slow.Way.Down.* I heard Kent's voice in my head say, "You are enough. You are enough and you are loved."

The breath left my lungs and I was left still.

"I'm no longer a slave to fear," Jonathan sang, and I pulled the words into me, ingesting them with my body, allowing each word to permeate my cells. I paused the video and, taking a long breath in, pushed myself up on my arms, swinging my legs off the side of the bed and bending forward. Only then do I unpause the video. My heart is ready for more.

"I am a child of God," he sings, and the last words of the song spread out into the night. I see his breath. I see the air rest on him, swirl around him.

I cross my arms over my stomach, grabbing each arm above the elbow. "I have breath in these lungs," I exhale into the room, staking claim through the very presence of my breath on this planet. I didn't have much, but I still had breath in my lungs. Laced with weariness. Full of grace. "With these legs I stand up." Once I say it, I do it, and walk gently over to the mirror.

"Talk about how the Funk is always there," Ottavia had said. "Talk about how you always have to manage it. Everyone can relate to The Funk. The Funk is heartache."

I feel my heart ache, but something new is in my core. I look at myself in the mirror, my eyes pour clear liquid. This is the same mirror in which I first saw the spark. Now I see fire.

My phone rings. It's Mom. "I'm worried about you. I think you're a little depressed, sweet girl," she says gingerly, but very matter-of-fact.

"I'm not," I counter but don't defend. Whether she believed me or not, didn't matter. I knew what was true.

Life lay heavy on me, no doubt. I felt burdened and exhausted by the pressure and strain of living in a body, and in circumstances, that did not let up. And while my muscles ached, something inside me had started to like it. Something inside me relished the burn. I was in training and I knew it. The war for my value had been won. That battle was over. This was something different. This was training. And as surely as the Seahawks leaned into their training, whatever needed to happen, wherever this would take me, I would unequivocally lean into mine.

Stay meditative. Breathe. Just being able to breath is a
relationship of exchange. You're part of the fabric of life.
Josh, Starbucks Roastery Barista, Journal #23

23

LEARNING TO FIGHT

July, Seattle, 2018

"You have got to be kidding me," I said to myself but aimed at God.

With every passing year without a job, I had made less and less ancillary money through clients. It also didn't help that I had been in the ER three times in 2018 alone. The only money I pulled in was from a few speaking gigs, and since they were all for the government I had given a substantial discount off my rate. I was sticky with worry when I received another speaking request from the Washington State Fire Chiefs Assistants. I sent my proposal and price over email and was on a nice long walk when I heard an internal prompt to do one for free. I banished the thought as soon as it came up. As I continued to walk along, the thought only got louder. Do one for free.

By the time I reached the second mile, I couldn't keep the struggle inside anymore. It started to come out of my mouth. I rationalized that I looked less crazy because I had my AirPods in but whether that was true or not, I couldn't stem the tide.

"You have got to be kidding me!" I said, forcefully and out loud. "No. Do you hear me? No. Absolutely not."

The prompting got louder. Do one for free.

"Why would you ask me to do this for free?" I asked the air around me. "It makes no sense. I am making zero cash here, God, as you know, so you're going to have to throw down some coin if you want me to start doing speeches for free. Not to mention, you know the toll they take on me physically. So, seriously, what's your plan?"

I'd like to say an answer came all neatly packaged and crystal clear. It didn't. But pressure was building, and I couldn't push back any longer. Do one for free, I heard again.

"Fine!" I shouted, thankful no one was on the path with me. "Fine. When the Fire Chiefs come back to me, I'll tell them I'll do this one for free."

I walked inside, threw down my headphones, ripped off my jacket, tore off my shoes, and after stomping around shoeless for a while, sat down at my computer to answer emails. A woman with no job doesn't have a lot of emails, so the solo new email in my inbox stood out: Subject: Governor's Conference. I opened it up.

On behalf of the Governor of the State of Washington, we'd like for you to keynote the Annual Governor's Conference. The purpose of this conference is to pour into the government employees who work for our state in a way that elevates and inspires them. Since personal and career development is not something the taxpayer likes to pay for, we ask that everyone who participates do so...for free.

So, not fifty-five people for the Fire Chief Assistants, but 3,000 people for the Governor of the State of Washington. My response had been predetermined. My heart had been primed. By the time I wrote yes over email, I had already said it out loud.

The Governor's Conference was to take place in November. It would be the third keynote speech in the speech trifecta. It would also be the largest audience I'd ever addressed.

You gotta' be stone enough to carry what God's going to put
in you.
Bishop T.D. Jakes, Journal #58

The speech for the Annual Governor's Conference was in Tacoma, Washington, only an hour away by car from my parents condo. But given traffic, and the state of my body, I didn't want to take any chances. I booked a hotel room in Tacoma for two nights.

The conference had two keynote speakers who would kick off each day and speak from the main stage. I was the keynote speaker for Day 2. The Hotel Murano was situated directly across from the Tacoma Convention Center and after depositing my luggage, I walked across the street to see if I could peek in and get the lay of the land.

Hollie Jensen, the Director of Continuous Improvement for Results Washington and the Office of the Governor, who booked me to speak, looked up surprised when I walked in.

"Hey!" she said, cheerfully.

"Hi, Hollie," I said. She was clustered in a group of other employees.

Putting on a conference of this size was no joke. "I don't want to interrupt," I said, feeling a bit badly. "I just wanted to peek into the space really quickly, if that's ok."

"Of course it's ok," she said warmly. "I'll take you up."

Tacoma had long been known as Seattle's lesser sister-city, often called the armpit of the state. It is theorized that the paper mills gave Tacoma its putrid, noxious smell of rotten eggs. Rumor has it the Tacoma Aroma, as it is so deliciously called, caused Bruce Springsteen to abandon a concert tour in the 80s at the Tacoma Dome. The smell was so intolerable to him, he left the state early.

But with top tech companies flooding into Seattle and the need for housing growing at an unprecedented rate, many were forced down to Tacoma and it was experiencing a bit of a renaissance. The Greater Tacoma Convention Center was built in 2004 and was the second largest meeting and event facility in Western Washington boasting over 118,000 square feet of space. Hollie and I took the escalators up to the top floor and walked through the doors of the grand ballroom. I felt suspended in space.

The cavernous room was a cooling grey and black. Large lights, equidistant apart, littered the ceiling like planets and chairs stood at attention like soldiers below them. Their precision and order calmed me. The room was incredibly quiet given its size. It could have easily held two 747 aircraft with room to spare. It sincerely felt like outer space. In the still, cool and quiet, I felt at home. I felt markedly different the next morning.

I awoke on Day 1 and ventured over to catch the morning's keynote. He did a great job, but I hardly would have known as I was pushing down the urge to vomit the entire time. I sped quickly back to the hotel thereafter, got on my pajamas, and crawled in bed. It wasn't even noon.

The night between Day 1 and Day 2 I didn't sleep at all. I had been up most of the night with anxiety. Why on earth would God choose to put me on stage with my illness and its unpredictability? How was I going to pay for this hotel bill with no money coming in? What could I possibly say to government employees that would resonate or elevate them to the level of inspired? It was an incredibly tall order and one I felt I had no way of fulfilling.

Around 3AM I broke down in prayer, "God, I believe I am here on Assignment. I don't know why. And I don't know how I'm going to do this. But I promise you that I'll stand on that stage and give everything I have. But I need you to do one thing for me. I need you to take this anxiety from me."

And before I had finished praying, my anxiety was gone and I was asleep.

The next morning 3,000 people entered into the space to hear me speak. I had only been speaking for three years, and never to more than four hundred people, and I was about to tell these people that they were a Full Dollar and encourage them to live from the core.

Upon arrival, I went to the tech team to grab the mic. I didn't want the small lapel mic. Something was stirring inside me and I wanted to grab the mic with both hands. I waited in the dark to the side of the stage while the MC walked through her prepared introduction of me. I looked out at the people and felt a sense of overwhelming peace.

"I don't know what you're doing God," I whispered. "But I know that you're with me. And that's enough for me."

The room began to clap, the MC came down and I walked up the stairs and onto the stage.

Make the most of every opportunity and expect God to move.
Theresa, Journal #42

IN THE WAKE of the Governor's Conference, I remembered back to a test I had taken to assess the health of my nerve endings. With dysautonomia, my nerve endings had been shot. The lack of sensitivity of these nerve endings got me into trouble on multiple occasions. We need sensations. They are vital for life. After a few years of receiving my IV saline treatments, the results of my peripheral neuropathy test were as follows: they could see evidence of trauma, but my nerves were rejuvenating. They were once again able to receive input and transmit stimuli.

The Governor's Conference had felt so good. It felt like flow. When so much of my life had been characterized by my over-reaching, leaning in, stretching forward, trying to make things happen, proving, proving, proving - the dance between me and God and people at the Governor's Conference had felt easy in comparison. In a strange way, it felt more like an opening. The wider I opened to God, the more there was of him and the less there was of me, the less I had to lean forward. In a very strange way, the opening was the opposite of giving. It was receiving.

Emily, the Ritual Coach, had talked to me about receptive energy long before I was in a place where I could absorb what I was hearing.

"Cor, you gotta shift from go-get 'em energy to the energy of receptivity. Instead of trying to go after everything, magnetize it. Receptivity is ethereal, subjective, and often unknown. Your surrender, your receptivity, is your power."

She was coming at it from a different perspective, but I heard a similar notion in a sermon from Pastor Steven Furtick of Elevation Church. In it, he talked about when Jesus approached his as-yet uncalled disciples. By trade, Jesus was a carpenter. These men were trained fishermen. Jesus walked up to them after they had fished all night and caught nothing and told them to get back in their boats, go back out into the deep and let down their nets again. I suspect, had it been me, I would have had a few choice words for a carpenter telling me what to do in a trade he knew nothing about.

But they did it. They listened and obeyed.

Closing the sermon, Pastor Furtick modeled a prayer in agreement with Jesus' invitation to receptivity. He said:

"We pray now the prayer of surrender. Not my will, but yours, be done. Because you say so, I'll let down the nets. No negotiation. No justification. We don't need an explanation. We just need a word. Speak, Holy Spirit."

A receptive stance is able to receive input and transmit stimuli. Stimuli is that which rouses activity or energy in someone or something; a spur or incentive. Quite literally, my willingness to surrender to God and be receptive to his leadings was the very thing that allowed me to receive input from him and transmit his life-changing energy that brings people to life. I was a conduit for connection. When I open my mouth and let God through, he speaks life. By triangulating with God, he does the healing. We do the serving.

After the Governor's Conference, after surrendering to God the best I knew how and opening myself up to have him speak through me, three people came up to me fed up with life. One person said he had planned for that day to be his last day on earth. He had resolved to take his own life. Instead, because of something God said to him while he was listening to me, he decided to keep going.

Not my will, but yours, be done.

Pray that God keeps you and protects your pure and authentic presence, and that it continues to light up the world. You are a life-force.
Theresa, Journal #22

JANUARY 2019 KICKED off with a series of job interviews. Finally. It was the first set of interviews I'd had in three years. The salary for the position was half of what I used to make and, positionally, was at the very bottom of the totem pole. My last job with Agio had been at the top. I went in with gratitude and hopefulness but didn't get the job. My parents had come to visit and were sleeping in the bedroom next door when I learned the news.

I watched myself from above as my body twisted in pain. The pain, for once, was not physical, it was spiritual. The battle was inside of me and my body contorted to try and get it out. Would I trust God with my life or would I succumb to the pain of my present situation? The pressure was inescapable. The sadness I felt from the lack of work was indescribable. The isolation my return to the arms of illness had produced was unbearable. I opened my mouth to scream but my throat didn't make a sound. My body found a steady motion and rocked backwards and forwards again and again. Smooth. Rhythmic. Pulsing. My body was liquid, an ocean in a storm. I looked down at myself and saw the tempest. A liquid reverberation. I was formed but formless, my anguish unutterable, yet I was sound.

I wanted work so badly the lack of it ripped at my soul. The speaking engagements were nice, but they were fits and spurts, not sustainable, daily work. After coming back from the edge of death and crawling out from under the earth's crust, all I wanted was to be useful. All I wanted was to be on a team.

"This is not only a spiritual battle, this is an emotional deconstruction of your beliefs," Theresa had said. "You need to practice how to deal with this."

She offered me a sample prayer:

God, you made me to make a contribution. I give myself wholly to your will. I want nothing more than to live for you and be who you intended me to be. The enemy is using my past pain and this present annoyance as a distraction. It saps my energy and taxes my ability to produce. I need your Holy Spirit to tell me the truth, and ask that you come around me and claim me as your own. I want to fulfill my destiny. Satan be gone from me. I am my Father's child.

God had begun taking up more space in my heart and filled my mouth, but how could I trust God when I went, year after year, with no job? How could I reconcile the God of my heart with the God of my mind?

I heard my dad get up to go to the bathroom. I needed to scream; I needed to lift my heart in prayer; I needed to fill my mouth with song; I needed to talk to God out loud. It was 11 PM when I got up, got dressed, headed out to the car, fired up the engine and drove into the night. Over the next five hours, as I drove from one end of Washington State to the other, my Jeep became my battle ground.

You are the only one in your inner sanctum. You and God. It needs to be untouchable.
Theresa, Journal #41

No more feeling weak. Time to fight.
Yuliya, Journal #41

24

ACCEPTING THE ASSIGNMENT

FEBRUARY, SEATTLE, 2019

SOMETHING CHANGED in me after that drive. The words of faith that had taken up residence in my mouth, had now hidden themselves in my heart. I had accepted the Assignment of the Governor's Conference and seen it through to the end, but now it was a new year and the interviews were netting nothing and the speaking requests had completely dried up. I didn't know what to do next.

I was mainlining online sermons just to make it through the day when I came across one from Michael Todd called *Marked*. He said, if you're at a point in your life where you don't know what to do, do the last thing God told you to do and spend time in his presence. If binge-watching sermons was part of the latter, executing the former was trickier. Oh, I already knew what God told me to do but I didn't like it and negotiated with God that since I had no job, this clearly wasn't the right time. But the Assignment kept coming.

From the IV nurse in New York to the tech contractor at Starbucks to Jake to Nidhi at Lean In, I had received so many repetitive signals pointing me toward my Assignment, it was just a question if I was going to give in. The more I said no, the more the conversation would spring up like whack-a-mole. While I was running around to all my contacts, trying to get picked for a team, any team, messengers were streaming in with a single refrain: *write the book.*

You need to get into a trance. No questions. No nothing. You've been scared of this for a long time. You either go left or you go right. You have two roads. Choose.
Yuliya, Journal #41

On our first date, when Jake and I, foreheads pressed together, shared where we'd been, he'd said, "I feel honored to be hearing this story first hand, but I don't feel like I should be the only one to hear it."

I threw him down in the car a few hours later, if only to shut him up. When the contract job dried up and I texted him about it he said, "Time to write your book, Cor. Quit dancing around it. Ask it to tango."

I cut it off with him, ended up in the ER, got an iron infusion and landed back on the couch. (You can be lying on the couch and still be running.)

At the end of 2017 I gave in, set up shop at the Starbucks Roastery, wrote to 30,000 words, three times over, and burned the book down each time. By mid-2018, I had lost all momentum and didn't think it was ever going to come back. I wasn't sure I even cared. I needed work. The book could wait. Or whatever.

Then Shellie's call came in.

Shellie had traveled to Dallas to attend a conference and I was eager to hear how it was going.

"Hi Shell!" I said, greeting her with upbeat and cheerful energy. I wanted her to know I was down but not out.

The noise in the background was deafening, and I immediately pulled the phone away from my ear a bit before carefully leaning back in.

"Hey Shell? You there?" I asked, thinking maybe she had pocket dialed me.

"Write your book. Write your book. Write your book," she said rhythmically.

"Ha!" I said. "How are you? How's the conference?"

"Write your book. Write your book. Write your book," she said, still in rhythm, but louder.

I rolled my eyes.

"I know. I will. I just-"

"Write your book. Write your book. Write your book. Write your book," there was something in her voice I didn't recognize. Shellie was crying.

"Shell, are you-"

"Write your book. Write your book. Write your book. Write your book, Cor. Write your book," she was fervent and almost frantic.

The force of her message pushed me against the wall. I slid down it, in tears.

"Ok, Shell. Ok," I said quietly.

"Write your book, Cor. Write your book," the connection was horrible, but I could hear she was sobbing.

"I will Shell, I will," I said, with growing conviction and then the line went dead.

I sat on the floor in the hallway outside the bathroom for some time, crying. Hard.

Multiply all that is given to you.
Theresa, Journal #34

In not wanting to surrender my desire to be part of a conventional team, I completely missed that there was already a team around me. If I did not think God had heard me, knew me, or was speaking to me, then I was not even remotely listening. In all my moaning about feeling so alone, God sent a pit crew and put them on the track. In all my sermon-pounding looking for an answer, I had been filled with the directive that everyone who encountered God is to tell that story. And in all of my insomniac hours of tossing and turning, sweating with fear at my dwindling prospects of a successful and fruitful life, the one thing I heard over and over and over again was, "I gave you a story. Now tell it," and I continually ignored it. I was so determined to put myself on the path in service for God, while ignoring that God was providing one.

God had been running core alignment strategy all along. When I surrendered my life to Christ, he took hold. In all the no's and closed doors, he kept me standing still to train up my faith and make me strong. All that was left for me to do was to say yes. Would I say yes to my Assignment? What if the purpose of an Assignment wasn't to know the outcome or be assured of success once done? What if the purpose of the Assignment, in fact some Assignment's only purpose, was to just do it. Do it and do not delay.

I looked straight at myself in the mirror. My hair was wild. What if in my weakness, I was strong? I had heard it in a sermon and knew it was in the Bible, but what if I accepted that truth and actually lived it out?

The last few years had been a season of such great delay. I felt continually delayed. Weighted down. Isolated. Held back. Benched. It wore me out. It wore everyone out. I was looking to myself to be the source of strength, but God was offering to *be* my strength. I scrambled out of bed and threw myself to my knees.

"I want to align my heart with yours every day," I prayed, frantically. Fervently. "Please show me how to do that more and more. Holy Spirit, I invite you deeper and deeper into my heart."

The words were leaving my mouth before they even crossed my mind.

"Leave nothing untouched. Clear everything out. Take it all away if you need to. Make me a vessel to hold whatever you want to pour into me. Make me sensitive to your leading, your voice, your urging. Make me a spirit in this world."

I thought back to that voice I had heard in the middle of the night after I left my relationship, "You will be in this world, not of it."

It collided with me fresh again.

In Psalms 37:4 it says, "Delight yourself in the Lord and he will give you the desires of your heart."

I felt my desires changing, like water filling cracks in dry ground. It was liquid. Fluid. Visceral.

The Assignment wasn't about me at all. It wasn't given to me, it was opened in me. It exploded like a flame in the center of my being, from the core. When it says God gives us the desires of our heart, it wasn't about my desires or my preferences. It wasn't about finally attaining health or accomplishing achievements. It was about letting the fire now inside me consume me completely with an importance and urgency beyond myself. My Assignment wasn't a calling to serve people. The feedback loop I was being invited into was one where I would serve God, and in serving God by completing the Assignments he put before me, I was serving the people he wanted to reach. **My Assignment was my connection point to others.** This was the feedback loop of desire. My role was to do what he said to do and have that profound intention inform every area of my life. To give everything I have to the Assignments I'd been entrusted with, no matter the condition of my body or the circumstances of my life. To tell my story so that somebody else could encounter the love of God.

And if this was true, I had to pick up the Assignment and not put it down until it was done.

IV

HOPE

25

DIVINE ALIGNMENT

MARCH, SEATTLE, 2019

IN ACCEPTING THE ASSIGNMENT, everything shifted. The heat of transformation still burned within me, but I began to feel the cooling of the ground. I was, undoubtedly, on a more solid foundation. My eyes were adjusting to the light, my soul to the expanse of the plain. For the first time, I could feel the edges of ease. I had the radical thought that this might be hope.

During my season of transformation, I had slowly made faith my own. I pulled back from the need to seek advice from others. I pulled back from Facebook, no longer needing that type of feedback validation. I met with Theresa less and less. My need to verbally process my situation with my friends decreased as well, and consequently, so did the some of the relationships. God was now the source of my processing and there was great peace in that.

The notes in my journals also changed. The entries were no longer notes about me and my own value and worth in the world, they were notes about fighting battles with praise, learning discernment, and getting in tune with God's voice. They were about living on mission and doing so by letting myself be guided moment-to-moment by the Holy Spirit and, in a very real way, letting Jesus take the wheel. The result was an overwhelming sense of safety and trust.

In the past, I had outsourced my safety to other people and left myself with great vulnerability. In the entire animal kingdom, weakness always draws a strike. On the outside, I appeared confident, but the external belied the small, trembling rabbit on the inside who needed to be liked, treasured, protected, and valued to remain alive. I trusted people immediately and tried to manipulate circumstances so that I could get what I thought I needed: love, acceptance, and belonging. That included: being overly kind and generous to my own detriment, which is neither kind nor generous; trying to be liked by all people, all the time, and experiencing profound confusion and discouragement when my best efforts were not enough; and indiscriminately inviting people into my personal and private struggles until struggle became the defining mark of our relationship, which then depended on my continued struggling to stay alive. Even as an overcomer, a fighter, a warrior, a survivor, my personal pain was still at the epicenter.

Letting God sit at the core of my life absolved me of the luxury of falling victim. It caused me to hold the right expectations of humanity and myself. Being discerning about the friends, environments and situations I brought into my life would help, but it would never be enough. People were untrustworthy. Jesus was betrayed by two of his disciples, Judas and Peter, and three days after his death, when Jesus said he would rise, not a single one of his twelve disciple was at his grave. Intentions can be good. People can mean well. I can mean well. But we will all fail. God is the ultimate and only trustworthy repository for our safety, and it would only be living in him that would make me, as a person, safe. I would be safe with myself, and safe around others, not because I could always rely on myself in my own willpower to do the right thing, pick the right people, behave the right way, or not be overcome with my own needs; I would be safe within myself only when I continually reassigned my safety over to God and trusted him with my life.

I let people go.

I let my situation go.

I gave it all over to God.

I placed everything I had, and everything I was, in God's hands and developed a mantra of peace and release by saying to myself, "Cor, you can't know what God is doing with this person, this season, this circumstance. Let's let it all play out."

No maybe. There is no more maybe.
Yuliya, Journal #40

While I was moving forward on the book, it wasn't going smoothly. I was frustrated and stuck and a little bit confused. Why would God give me an Assignment, only to make it so difficult to execute? I had written and rewritten the book several times over and still wasn't settled on what, exactly, it was supposed to be about. God had given me a personal story of physical brokenness and I was telling it, but in my mind the blow-by-blow of my life wasn't incredibly compelling, and I was certain that was coming out in the writing. A few friends had asked to read it and the feedback was the same: write more of the sick. But I didn't want to write more of the sick. I just wanted to write about - and be - well.

I was also concerned about not having industry for so long and discontented with my circumstances. I wanted to be a good steward of the time I had been given and the generosity of my parent's provision, so while I was still writing the book, I hadn't stopped sending out resumes and attending interviews and continually looked for ways to build industry of my own.

Way back in 2010, I had been watching a Zappos all-hands meeting when Tony Hsieh, the CEO of Zappos, the online shoe company, made a big announcement that Zappos was going to get into selling clothes, too. Fashion was a billion-dollar industry and made business sense, but to me, something about the idea of Zappos selling clothing was jarring. I didn't know why. I loved the culture. I loved the Zappos experience. I loved online shopping. But never, in a million years, would I consider buying clothing from Zappos and I wanted to understand why.

As someone who, at that time, had been responsible for crafting brand and culture at Agio, the Zappos culture fascinated me, as it did thousands, and I became a student of Zappos culture. Because brand and culture drive the achievement of business goals, I also liked to watch corporate all-hands meetings or shareholders meetings, when they were open to a larger audience, to get a better understanding of the business goals companies cared about. Getting to watch the Zappos all-hands meeting was a mental boon for someone who loved business strategy but wasn't able to leave the front door.

At the end of the presentation, Tony put up his email address on the screen and an open invitation for anyone to reach out to him. So I did. In a short but thoughtful email, I shared how much I loved Zappos, followed their culture, was an online shopper, and had experienced the legendary Zappos customer service for myself. In my anecdotal experience, shopping for shoes was different than shopping for clothing. Shoes were augmentative, I suggested, clothing was an experience. In that way, shoes could often be searched for like auto parts: black pumps, running shoes, sandals, loafers; but clothing, that required something more: identity exploration.

In bullet points, I outlined the idea of shopping by archetype. As a brand strategist, I had studied archetypes for building brands. I knew those who employed archetypes in their branding outperformed market competitors by leaps and bounds. Brands like Nike, Starbucks, and Amazon all had mythology and archetypes at their brand's core.

We, as consumers, were more likely to be compelled by story and storytelling than by simple and direct product presentation. Why, I reasoned, should it be different with humans? Couldn't we, too, present ourselves as stories, and consequently shop by them?

I sent the email over, not expecting anything in return. Mere minutes later, Zappos head of fashion merchandising contacted me at Tony's request. I shared my idea of Archetypes of Style with his clothing department. They loved it, both Zappos and Amazon, Zappos parent company did, and implemented it.

But what I shared with Zappos was only the tip of the iceberg. Over time, I began to wonder if Archetypes of Style was an idea I could or should build out. Amazon and Zappos use of archetype categories established its validity and market usefulness, and I had seen personally how galvanizing a deeper understanding of one's Coressence and identity expression could be.

In the ongoing absence of industry, I kept working on the book, but tentatively began to work on Archetypes of Style as well. I gathered a few friends who were a strong expression of a particular archetype and shot a few videos. Next, built a small team of people who caught fire around the idea and wanted in. With each step, I held with an incredibly open hand. My prayer consistently was, "God, if this isn't for me, if this isn't my path forward, shut it all down."

I had long been a door opener. When illness came knocking, I tried every remedy available, and in doing so, became masterful at opening every door. I followed every lead. Twisted every handle. Tried every new protocol. Functioned only in desperation and hunger and hoped behind door number two, or three, or four, or forty, there might be an answer. It was the same in relationships. A twisted knob was yet another opportunity at validation.

Such was the door-opening mark on my life that for Christmas one year, the Landlord gifted me a necklace containing my favorite Emily Dickinson poem (another shut in): *Not knowing when the dawn will come, I open every door.*

But it's fifty-cent thinking to say, "I need. I'm hungry." It predetermines lack and reaches forward toward satiety. But I now knew hope was not hunger, but humility; a forward motion with an open hand that said, it's yours to give and yours to take away. If you remove it, I will let it go. I moved forward and made plans, but stayed open to God's leading through the closing of doors.

WANTING to keep some treasured connections from Lean In, I reached out to a few women from the team who'd had new babies and were mutually experiencing the stress of first-time motherhood. I offered to host a small party and while the mom's chatted, I could help watch the babies. They were all in.

We were all sitting on the floor watching the babies crawl around when Alicia and Brittany started talking about Brene Brown's book *Dare to Lead*. In it, they said, she talked about this notion that everyone in life had only two core values. Just two. Hers, Brene's, were Faith and Courage. My strategist mind piqued. Zappos famously had 10 core values, created by the Zappos employees. At Lean In, we had five and added a sixth. At Agio, we had seven and refreshed them from time to time. I found it radical, the idea a life could be guided by only two core values. Not believing it to be true but willing to try it on, I asked myself, what would be my two?

God had become the core of my life, so when I heard one of Brene's values was Faith, I recognized Faith was one of mine, too. The most important one. Courage also resonated with me but not in that same visceral way Faith had. Maybe not Courage but possibly Wholeheartedness, I thought loosely, and instantly it clicked. Everything I did, I threw myself at wholeheartedly. That was it! Faith was at my core, wrapped in Wholeheartedness, held loosely in my hand of hope. These would be my core values. They gained velocity within me and moved me forward.

Being able to receive The Divine is the opposite of effort. The only thing you are responsible for is openness and submission.
Theresa, Journal #31

For Shellie's fiftieth birthday I took her to see Elevation Worship in concert and treated us to the VIP Q&A session. As I sat in our seats, while she stood in line to purchase t-shirts, I thought back to Dr. Boatman.

"Dysautonomia is going to be hard," he'd said. "It will affect everything connected to the vagus nerve. You shouldn't sing, you shouldn't listen to loud music, and you shouldn't stand on your feet too long."

I laughed to myself thinking I was about to do all three simultaneously.

Shellie came back just as the band came out. I listened as, one by one, people asked their questions. Suddenly, I had one of my own and shot my hand up. The facilitator motioned in my general direction. Did he mean me?

"Yeah, you. With the hair."

The audience laughed. That's me, I thought, a Strawberry Person with big hair.

"How do you keep in alignment?" I asked the band in general. "You're a big church and spread the message of God all over the world. How do you stay connected to your core and stay on the same page?"

My thoughts on core values were coloring the whole of my thinking, even here at a concert.

Various band members answered. One spoke about always remembering their Why: to connect people to the heart of God. Another mentioned working hard and continually planting seeds, even while harvesting.

"You have to remember," Chris Brown, Elevation's long-time worship leader, said, "To you it's Elevation, but to us it's the local church. We just get sent out from the local church. We're on commission."

I wasn't exactly sure what commission was, but I knew I wanted to be sent out on commission. I came home after the concert and booked a trip to North Carolina, home to Elevation Church.

> *What you need to do is reach over into another dimension and*
> *stand flat-footed, and reel it in!*
> Bishop T.D. Jakes, Journal #45

I saw Dr. Phil cock his head to the side and right away I knew I had said something off. I told him about my upcoming trip to North Carolina and said I was hopeful to be finished with the book by then so I could bring it along. That's when he cocked his head and I knew I had once again uttered some fifty-cent thinking.

"You don't need to bring an offering to have something to offer," he said poetically. "You don't need a book in hand to incredibly add to the conversation. Who you are is enough. You are a living testimony. That's more than enough."

Fifty-cent thinking was just lurking in my cells ready to pop out at any time.

When our session ended, we agreed I didn't need to return. Occasional fifty-cent thinking wasn't something that needed to be worked through anymore, only to be recognized and quickly adjusted. There would always be remnant Funk requiring management, but no longer therapeutic intervention. The PTSD diagnosis hadn't entangled me, it had set me free.

I left Dr. Phil's office and met Ottavia for drinks. My friend Ottavia had walked through a transformative year of her own. She had married the love of her life, bought a house, and sold her company - all in rapid succession. We were out celebrating with drinks. It was still pleasure enough for me to be able to enjoy drinks out with a friend after so many years in bed, and I loved celebrating the wins and accomplishments of those I loved, but I couldn't help but sit in comparison. I was watching her launch successfully into the stratosphere. Although I had made it through a season of burning internal transformation, my rocket was still very much on the launch pad. She caught my wavelength though I said nothing.

"Cor, you're built to serve and service is opportunistic," she said, and my ears perked up. By this point I had trained myself to listen for the mind-blowing. I could tell insight was coming.

"Service is showing up when something happens and someone has a need. You surrendering to the process is critical to the mission. That is where you have the most value."

I began thinking of where I might have value. The job hunt wasn't providing many clues. I was getting interviews but not getting hired. I would consistently hear one of two things. The first was a version of you're too much. It would be presented in many forms. When interviewing with a megachurch for a staff position I was told, "People like you don't want to be on staff. People like you volunteer." In my second interview at that same church one woman said, "You're kind of a big deal, and we have our big deal," in reference to their globally-renowned pastor.

Never mind that I was living at my parents' house.

Never mind that I hadn't worked in three and a half years.

Never mind that I was interviewing for a low-visibility staff position and not requesting a pulpit of any kind, yet there was still this perception that I was a Lotus and nothing I said changed any minds. Every company needed only one Lotus, if they needed one at all.

The other comment I would hear, from the tech world in particular, was you don't have the pedigree. No matter what I had achieved or how many employee referrals paved the way, because I didn't come from a widely recognized and esteemed company or school, I didn't carry the appropriate pedigree, and therefore was not a compelling person to even consider.

I began to feel at once too much and not enough. It was a strange mixture and one that was a trigger hazard for my desire to prove that I was both inconspicuous enough or good enough, whatever the situation required.

But with God there was no burden of proof. God was no respecter of persons, which meant neither position nor pedigree would matter for what he wanted to do through my life. I could surrender my need to constantly prove I was worthy of selection or twist every handle desperately looking for any open door. He was the door opener now. Not me. He was the way maker. As a servant of the living God, my job was to follow what I believed to be God's voice, align myself to his Word, and get in the room. The need would meet me there.

You just go and bring Christ.
Pastor Erwin McManus, Journal #57

A BETTER WORD

MAY, NORTH CAROLINA, 2019

WHEN I BOOKED my trip to North Carolina, I also contacted Kent, who happened to live there. Although we had done several collaborations together since our first encounter over the broken canvas, it would be the first time we would meet in person. I thought about what the PTSD therapist said about being a living testimony. Kent was, in a way, a big part of mine. God had begun to speak to me about my worth and my value through the broken canvas I had purchased from Kent for Lumen. It had become an analogy for the work God was doing in my life, although I didn't know it at the time. When I told Kent I was coming, I floated the idea of doing an event together. We could call it the Broken Canvas event; it would be a living testimony. We would tell the story about how we met and I would share a little of my own journey of brokenness in the hopes that doing so would open the door for participants to share a little bit of their stories, too. Then we would all paint together, and I would get to paint side-by-side with Kent in person. Something was coming full circle.

Regardless of how bolstered I felt about my trip, I was also incredibly nervous. I was broke and the trip to North Carolina wouldn't be cheap. Between travel and housing and transportation and meals, it was a big cash outlay, a big physical exertion, and a huge risk overall. My prayer to God was a simple one: if this is a mistake, please meet me in my mistake. He met me on take-off.

Your ability to believe will never catch up with God's ability to perform.
Pastor Steven Furtick, Journal #44

"It's ok to be poor and it's ok to be happy," Miss Patty said. We were flying first class.

The irony of me sitting in a first-class seat was an example of not everything being as it seemed. Being homebound for a decade had some advantages in that I had banked a lot of miles. I was excited to be using them. My presence in an airplane seat was a living testimony on its own.

Miss Patty was dripping with diamonds - ears, neck, wrists, fingers, and fingernails - glitz was everywhere. She oozed Southern Charm and we made fast friends. Miss Patty was in transition, too. She and her husband had sold their home in the North and were moving back to the South. They had made their millions, and raised their children, and now Miss Patty was hungry to give back to the community she came from. When she said that, I realized hunger could take a different form.

Miss Patty had grown up in the Ozarks and at seven, delivered her baby sister on her own. Her father had left and her mom "didn't do well in pregnancy." There was no phone or running water or transportation to the hospital, so when the baby started coming, at seven years old - the same age I was when I would fall out a window - Miss Patty would pull a baby from a womb. As people we are so broken, but we are also so incredibly cool.

She asked me what I was excited to see in North Carolina.

"Elevation Church," I said. "And fireflies."

"Oooooo!" Miss Patty exclaimed. "Fireflies!"

For the rest of the trip Miss Patty told me stories of catching fireflies in jars, running in open fields, walking on railroad tracks, dancing in the warm summer rain, and lying lazily on warm rocks in the afternoon sun at the edge of a riverbank. It sounded like heaven.

"I was so happy," she said. "We all were. We had no money but we had each other, and there was so much to do. Sure, there were some people who had big needs, and I want to go there with the money I have and help meet those core needs, but if there is one thing I learned growing up there, it's that it's ok to be poor and it's ok to be happy."

The day after I landed, Kent and I took a tour around Charlotte, picked up canvases for one of his commissions, and in general just tooled around. He had a big truck and we drove with the music on and the windows down. I sat cross legged on the seat bench with my head pitched back, letting the warm southern air melt across my face, and thought about being poor and happy. I was definitely poor in the financial sense. I had almost no money to my name and very few possessions. But I also knew that here, in this moment, I was happy. And that was ok, too.

My time in North Carolina passed in busy days and languid afternoons. I had rented the downstairs mother-in-law apartment below a beautiful farmhouse in Indian Land, South Carolina, just a stone's throw away from North Carolina. Every day, when I was driving around, my car GPS would welcome me to North Carolina or South Carolina, depending on my direction. It was a constant reminder of where I'd been and where I was going.

The downstairs mother-in-law was tucked below a back porch and butted up to the edge of a forest. It was a cool, dark respite from the brutal southern sun but to me - a woman from Seattle with a decade indoors under my belt - I craved anything but.

"Girl, come, you can sit up here," Ginger said, welcoming me to the big veranda in front of the main house where the sun shone in from all angles.

Ginger and Bobby, the Airbnb hosts of the farmhouse I had rented, had been pastors for twenty years. They prayed over me from above, as I lay sleeping down below, and filled my spirit to the brim as I sat on their veranda. The big veranda was home to a huge farmhouse table, a porch swing, two rocking chairs, and several overhead fans. We all weathered one of the hottest Mays on record together, sipping tall glasses of iced tea as warm air whispered down from above. Ginger and I often spent early evenings together, just the two of us. Pushing the pads of our feet into the planks of the wooden porch, we'd bring movement to the rockers, while sharing intimate stories, marveling at the work God had done and sure he was going to do so much more.

During the daytime, I looked for work in Charlotte, and on weekends attended church at Elevation. The mix of interviews and Elevation was a curious one. I had come to North Carolina driven by the alignment of placing faith at the epicenter of my heart and wrapping it in wholeheartedness. I was hoping to get a very clear direction on my commission, and that it would translate into a job of some kind. Since I wasn't totally clear on the difference between commission and assignment, I looked it up to find out: **assignment** is the allocation of a job or a set of tasks, while **commission** is a sending out; a mission to do or accomplish something. I had gotten pretty clear my Assignment was to tell my story through a book, but that still felt very siloed and stagnant. I was looking for the action and direction of a commission and, as always, a person or team that would send me out.

I was working on some interview prep when Ginger's father walked across the lawn on their compound and headed straight in my direction. I knew loosely what to expect.

"Howdy!" he shouted, with still a great expanse left to cross. I stood up and walked over to the stairs and waited at the top to greet him.

"Well, hello there," he said once he reached me and stood at the bottom of the stairs, looking up. "I'm Willie-Jesus. Willie is my first name and Jesus is my brother, so my name is Willie-Jesus."

He was wrapped tight and wiry, skin over bones, and jam-packed with rascal energy. I smiled at his introduction. All of it.

"You saved?" he asked, in a deep southern accent and provocative tone.

"I am," I said, smiling even wider. Lord help the person who ever answered no to that question.

"Well good, good. Hallelujah!" he said jubilantly. "What's your name?"

"Cor," I said.

"Cor, you say?" he asked.

I nodded.

"Well, Cor, God made you sweet and he sure made you purdy. Your presence here is a blessing to us all!" he shouted, over his shoulder. He was already walking away.

At the height of the day, I retreated to my private lower-level porch, but stayed outdoors. I lay my body across the porch swing, slung my feet over the side, and squeezed the chain together with one hand over my head to drive movement into the swing. It didn't rattle me at all when a large, black, seven-foot snake slithered across the back lawn and under my swing on its way to the forest. I was in a time-warp, so far from the erudite chill of the people and place of Seattle. I was in the Bible Belt with Willie-Jesus, evangelical churches on every corner, and snakes in the grass. It was weird and wonderful and weird all over again. Over the course of three weeks, my heart had been stirred up, undone, and laid open. For me, this place held a peace that passed all understanding. For me, this was holy ground.

KENT and I spent Saturday afternoon preparing for Broken Canvas. I had stopped at Trader Joe's for some snacks and laid chips and dips and veggies and nuts and dried fruits across torn sheets of paper. Kent's studio was large and cavernous. Air conditioning fans blew cool air across the paint brushes and chilled my shoulders as I stood at the side wall, carefully pinning up each one of the twenty-six Archetypes of Style boards. Kent sat on a stool and painted a large rendition of the same core graphic I had used during the Starbucks speech. It included WHO you are at the center, HOW it's expressed in the second ring, and WHAT you're going to do about it surrounding it all. It was tried and true brand strategy as I knew it, but also a depiction of the way God had drilled down to the core of who I was and methodically rebuilt my life from the inside out. I now knew who I was in a way I never had before. I had a good understanding of how that was expressed both in how I was uniquely crafted but also the types of behaviors that flowed out of my new identity in Christ. The problem was the last circle. I was still unclear on what I was going to do about all of it. I guessed the Broken Canvas event was as good a place as any to start.

I had no expectations of the event. I was simply thrilled to be in the same room with Kent, after all this time, and excited to share my testimony. I wanted to share it and I wanted to release it from me.

The evening of the event, a small but potent group showed up. Everyone's reason for coming was different. One man was there without his wife. He said it was his birthday and he wanted to learn more about himself so he could bring a fuller expression of himself into his home. Another couple was there that was about to get married. They wanted to do something fun together and get dirty in the process. She also brought along her brother, who was curious and open and expansive and on a journey of his own. One woman was there, trying to find answers around what to do with her retail store. She wanted to discover more about her customers by discovering more about herself. Another was there carrying a deep wound she had done a really good job covering over with a great personality, bawdy laughter, and winning smile. I recognized her immediately.

I stood at the front of the room wearing all white, the trademark I'd adopted when telling this story for the first time at Melody's Urban Campfire: a blank canvas personified. Over the course of ten short minutes, I talked about myths and archetypes, and how companies used universal stories to make brands instantly recognizable and connect emotionally with people. I shared how, as humans, our stories were at once unique and yet archetypal, too. From there, I moved into core alignment, and how all growth had to come from the core, and work its way out. And how WHO a brand is, resides at the very center of the core as its aligning source; its centering force. As such, the WHO alone must be the heart of all decisions made, or the entire brand would get off course. Any small act of mistaken identity could derail an entire brand. It could also derail a life.

It had mine.

Fifty-cent thinking had clouded WHO God made me to be, and altered the journey of my life, causing me to spend forty years in the wilderness, going nowhere. I shared how God met me in brokenness, and how he had been in the process of making me whole and bringing me out. Then I encouraged the group to reflect on any fifty-cent beliefs they might hold of their own, and embrace their re-creation, in the spirit of the night.

With that, Kent came forward and led everyone through quick instructions on how to approach their "broken canvas." In preparation for the event, Kent had laid out a canvas for each person and painted a little on each one. In this way, each person's canvas was no longer clean. It was no longer perfect. He gave the instructions that every person could decide what to do with this brokenness. They could paint over it. They could paint with it. They could paint around it. However, they approached and interacted with their "brokenness" was completely their choice. At the end, he promised, he would co-create the painting with them, adding his unique flair as an artist. He would be their co-creator in the very same way he had been mine. I piled all of that in only ten minutes, but knew God had the power to work through whatever little time I had. If there was a heart that was listening and open, he would meet it. My job was to tell the story; the act of speaking to someone's heart, that work was God's alone.

I had been telling the story in a variety of settings since telling it the first time in August 2015. Over the course of four years, I had seen countless people impacted and transformed by the message of redemption. Young women in business classes who had been told their assertiveness was unseemly or their smarts made them unsexy; seasoned snipers for the US Army carrying burdens of brokenness I was incapable of touching; veterans who were at the mouth of transition into a new world of living as a civilian after decades of service; a young man diagnosed with AIDS who didn't feel he deserved to go on living; a weathered professor at the end of her rope; a woman with chronic fatigue for whom there seemed to be no end in sight, and many, many more. No matter what the venue or the context of the conversation, people were met by God and transformed. While I should have come to expect it, it surprised me every time.

Once the painting had started, I moved around the room. Kent and I floated from person to person checking in with them as they bent over their work. Staring at a blank canvas could be a terrifying thing. It was an invitation to possibility and failure wrapped in one, before the first application of paint slid across the white porous material. I took my time before walking over to Melissa. Her long black hair hung over one shoulder shielding much of her face. I came up alongside her and looked down at her canvas. She had painted what looked to be a black tornado. She laughed and shrugged her shoulders.

"It's a black tornado," she said, in an upbeat tone.

"I see that," I laughed, matching her humor and nonchalance. "Wanna tell me about it?"

"Well, something pretty terrible happened when I was nine-teen years old. I lost a child of my own. This whole time I've been telling myself it was my fault, but then I heard your story and I had this weird thought," she looked up at me for the first time. She leaned forward and whispered, "What if it wasn't?"

A snap of fingers went off in my brain.

What if it wasn't?

What if it wasn't her fault?

What if it wasn't?

The question was an invitation to release all the guilt and shame she had been carrying around all these years. What if it wasn't? Behind the question was a tsunami of grace.

"What's available to you if it wasn't your fault?" I asked.

"I don't know," she said.

Melissa looked at her canvas a long, long time. I stood next to her in silence and held space with her and at some point, slipped away to leave her alone with that thought. What if it wasn't?

Later that night, I went back to check on her. She had covered her black tornado with gold metallic paint. It was hardly detectable anymore. And over the whole canvas, smack-dab in the middle, she had painted a neon pink heart. She smiled and laughed when I walked up.

"I didn't know what else to draw," Melissa said, and shrugged her shoulders once again.

I came around the table and stood beside her, taking her heart on full-frontal.

"It's beautiful," I said. "And tells me so much about you."

"It does?" she asked.

"It does. It tells me something really bad happened to you and you had two choices: you could have chosen bitterness, or you could have chosen love. You chose love."

She smiled with the whole of her face and tipped her chin up. Kent came over to look at the canvas.

"Can I add a little something?" he asked.

When she said sure, Kent uncapped his pen and across the entire canvas wrote the word, "grace."

You basically want to love every part of yourself.
Emily Mitchell, the Ritual Coach, Journal #14

As I stood at the top of the stairs later that night, the image of Melissa's face, and that word grace, returned from deep within my heart. How was it possible to witness moments where the God of the universe stepped in and restored the brokenness in someone's life? How was it possible to visibly see grace?

The air was warm and still and teeming with life. Living in Seattle, I had become accustomed to air that was cold and chilling and distant. The North Carolina humidity delivered an intimacy I was unfamiliar with. It was a living, breathing conversation. And a seductive one. I exchanged breath with the night.

Most of the guests had gone. I had taken down all the Archetypes of Style boards and packaged them up for easy return shipment and left them on the sofa on my way out the door. One guest was still inside the studio cleaning up with Kent when I headed out to my car alone.

I was still standing at the top of the stairs when it hit me that I hadn't painted anything at the event. I wondered why? Kent had prepared a canvas for me. I loved his work, and painting alongside him, in person, would have been a beautiful moment. Maybe it was because it was my event and I spent most of my time walking around to the other painters, looking at their artwork and listening to their stories. Maybe, I thought. Plausible. But I felt like that wasn't really it. It was something else. I put one foot on the stair below the top landing when I heard God say, *"You're not broken anymore, you're whole."*

Humidity rushed up from within and filled my eyes.

I hadn't painted a broken canvas because I had been made whole. A better word had been spoken over my life and my brokenness was now sealed, covered, and drenched in grace. From the moment Kevin dropped off the broken canvas at my front door to the moment I would use the story of my own brokenness to help others find wholeness, God had been at work all along.

Over the course of five years, God had been doing demolition work. There had been a tearing down of old belief systems; a total destruction of old ways of seeing myself as selfish or less-than or unworthy or wrong. There had been the extraction of the rubble of relationships and circumstances that had to go in order for me to move forward. There had been the jarringly loud excavation work and removal of a foundation that couldn't hold a growing, expansive, and maturing life; one where battles were fought to victory and walls separating me from my creator were torn down. It had been a long season of shedding and releasing on a Biblical level. The leanness in all areas of my life was astonishing. As far as possessions were concerned, I was down to what Shellie called, "Me, my Jeep, and Jesus." I had gotten so good at releasing and letting go and holding everything with an open hand to where it seemed like there was nothing more to release or let go.

But then I took one more step down the stairs and heard, *"Are you willing to burn it all down?"*

NOTHING LESS THAN FULL
SURRENDER

June, North Carolina, 2019

Pastor Steven lay on his face, hands flung above his head, forehead pressed into the floor. The entire congregation was on its feet and it felt as though the roof might come down. Worship leaders stood on stage, faces lifted up to the rafters, belting out, *"This is how I fight my battles."* This is it, I thought. This is the calling. Nothing less than full surrender.

This is my goal: that the whole world will know there is a God.
Pastor Steven Furtick, Journal #46

By the time I landed at the bottom of Kent's studio stairs the night of the Broken Canvas event, I knew I would never see the Archetypes of Style boards again. I didn't know how I knew or why I wouldn't see them again, I just knew I was being asked to let it all go, to burn everything down to the ground.

I got back to the farmhouse late and was exhausted. I put myself to bed with clothes and makeup still on. Right before I closed my eyes, I saw a text message from Elevation. They were inviting me to the early service and had saved me a seat. I was to meet Candace at 9 AM.

As I drifted to sleep, I heard the words of Dr. Phil, "You're already on a team. You already belong."

THE THOUGHT WAS STILL in my mind as I made my way across the parking lot toward Elevation Church's Ballantyne campus. I understood the concept of brothers and sisters in Christ but I never felt like I had a good understanding of the application in action. I had been to Elevation several times over the course of three weeks. Walking through the door, I felt a sense of belonging. Every time.

Candace met me at the door and didn't flinch. I was in last night's hair and makeup. My energy was holding on by a thread. If I looked rough, she didn't mention it. Neither did I. She led us to our seats and while she did, I prayed for anywhere but the front row, which is exactly where we sat.

My toes were only a few inches from the stage stairs when Pastor Steven got up to preach a sermon entitled *When The Battle Chooses You*, from 2 Chronicles 20. The room was electrified.

The story of 2 Chronicles 20 is of a battle of three kings against another, three armies against one. King Jehoshaphat, concerned about his ability to defeat three armies at once, gathers all of Judah and Jerusalem in the temple to pray to the Lord. Jehoshaphat reminds God of all the times he went to battle for the Israelites before, and made a way for them when no way seemed clear. He cries to the Lord and reminds God, as well as all the people gathered:

"For we have no power to face this vast army that is attacking us. We do not know what to do, but our eyes are on you."

My body was not doing well. The room was giant and

cavernous, like a concert hall. Worship had been fantastic but the reverberation of the sound and my proximity to the speakers, coupled with my profound preexisting fatigue from weeks of interviewing in Charlotte and the event at Kent's the evening before, was sending shockwaves through my system.

Pastor Steven gripped the mic and held it close to his mouth. *"Remind God of what he's done when you're not sure what he's doing right now. Not so he can remember, but so you can. Come on, you need to remember, this is not your first rodeo, cowboy."*

I popped up to my feet, gravity threatening to pull me right back down. I didn't care. Pastor Steven leaned on the podium, stepped one foot onto its base and pointed his finger into the crowd.

"This is not the first time you cried. This is not the first time you were short of breath. This is not the first time you didn't see a way clear."

People were popping up all over the place, standing and cheering for the battles they were fighting and the victories already won. I was on my tiptoes, leaning forward into his words. The edges were going black but I was not going to let this moment be taken from me. If I was going to pass out in the front row of Elevation Church, so be it. If I was going to go down, I was going to go down praising.

"This is not the first time you were hurt. This is not the first time your heart was broken. This is not the first time you didn't have enough money. This is not the first diagnosis that came up from behind."

No. No, it wasn't. It wasn't the first time. It wasn't. This was not the first time a war raged through my body. It wasn't. The fact that I was standing in Elevation at all was a miracle. I thought back to the times I thought I was going to die and the moment I considered taking my life on my own.

I thought back to the days, weeks, months, and years I lay in bed, no end in sight.

I thought back to the trips to the ER and how many times I said out loud, "I'm going down."

I thought back to the time the cops came and all the nights I cried after leaving him.

I thought about all the doctors who told me there was nothing wrong.

I thought about all the times I couldn't see a way through the wilderness and how I was now standing in clarity in Christ.

I screamed in my mind and it flew out of my mouth, *"You are my provider, Lord! You are my way maker! Make a way!"*

My words were absorbed in the cloud of battlecries all around me. I was not the only one fighting. We were a room full of warriors waging war with our mouths.

In 2 Chronicles 20:15, while King Jehoshaphat and all of Judah were gathered in the temple praying for intercession, the Spirit of the Lord came over a man named Jahaziel. He hears a message from God for the King and when he does, he stands up in front of everyone and says, "This is what the Lord says to you: 'Do not be afraid or discouraged because of this vast army. For the battle is not yours, but Gods.'"

As I sat out back on a park bench behind the church after the service in the blazing North Carolina sun, I thought about the battle not being mine but God's. What did that mean for me and my life if some of the battles I was fighting were not mine to fight? What if my job situation was not my battle? What if my health situation was not my battle? I struggled with the notion.

I had been around people before who, for any of the situations they were facing offered up a pat, "God will provide," usually said with their hands up, palms out, as if to say, "I take my hands off it. Not my problem." It made me irritated and a little angry. It felt like they were wanting God to do all the legwork. I had always been more in the God-helps-those-who-help-themselves camp. If it was not my battle to fight, what was the part I was responsible for?

I left the bench and started off toward my car, but then stopped. I heard the rumble of the music. The next service was starting. I wanted more. I turned around and walked right back inside.

Once through the front lobby doors, I was funneled into the moving crowd and up to the balcony of the church. When I finally got to my seat, it was in the very last row. Those who came in behind me had to sit on the floor, and those behind them, in overflow. To my right, my left, and in front of me were people from every nation and generation. It was something I hadn't necessarily noticed from my previous seat in the front row.

From the very beginning of the second sermon the energy was different. It was lower. Slower. Quieter. Pastor Steven even mentioned it himself, once or twice. I was anxious for him, then curious, then spellbound. What would it feel like, in his position, to have come off such a high and be met with very different energy only an hour later, with the very same content? Speaking in front of people was an energy exchange, not only with the crowd, but with the words you were feeling in your soul. While I had been so viscerally engaged in the previous sermon, this second one I watched in a more detached manner, my attention coming and going.

As the service was coming to an end, Pastor Steven started winding down. He had shared the whole story of how God fought the battle all the way to victory, at which time there was so much plunder, King Jehoshaphat and his men took three full days to collect it all. On the fourth day, they gathered in the Valley of Beracah, which means the Valley of Blessings, where they praised God for the victory, only to go back to the temple in Jerusalem to praise God some more.

In the end, the battle was won, plunder was garnered, praise was given. Everyone heard what God had done and how he fought the battle on Israel's behalf, and because of how King

Jehospaphat fought, God gave his kingdom peace and rest "on every side."

Wait. How King Jehospaphat had fought? He hadn't fought. Wasn't that the point?

Pastor Steven circled back to that part in the story - after Jahaziel had shared what the Lord had told him about not being afraid because the battle was the Lord's - and walked around the pulpit and stood at the front of the stage.

"In the Bible, it says, King Jehoshaphat 'bowed with his face to the ground...and fell down in worship before the Lord.'"

And with that, Pastor Steven lowered himself to his knees, and then his face, until he lay prostrate on the floor.

I stood up from my chair in the very back row. The entire house was standing. In an instant, the energy had shifted and brought us all to our feet, rapt with attention and shouting praises so loud the whole house rumbled. I absorbed the message immediately: there was power in surrender. There was power in putting ones face to the ground. There was power in a mouth full of praise, and a heart of surrender. Surrender was a power pose. Surrender was the stance of the mightiest of warriors. That was how King Jehoshaphat had fought the battle. It'd be the same way I'd fight mine. God required only one thing of me: nothing less than full surrender.

LEAVE EVERYTHING BEHIND

JUNE, NORTH CAROLINA, 2019

I LEFT church and spent the afternoon packing, but I was filled with restless energy. As evening came, I took to the front lawn.

I had taken a leap of faith coming to North Carolina and I was leaving in the morning, unsure what I had to show for it. I had mixed feelings about going back home. I had come here looking for commission and was leaving in full surrender, willing to let everything I had been holding onto burn to the ground, but I couldn't shake the feeling that there was still something more. As the sun was setting and the evening wore on, I put on my headphones and listened to a sermon from Bishop TD Jakes called *Reel It In* and tore back and forth across the front lawn.

"Get after it, Tiger," Willie-Jesus said to me, on his way over to Ginger and Bobby's house for dinner. I was clawing at it with all my might.

I heard nothing during my hours spent on the lawn. I just

listened to the Word preached and opened my heart and mind to God.

I crawled into bed early, intending to rest until Ginger and Bobby's family left. Then I would go upstairs and say goodbye. I awoke the next morning.

I had loaded the car the night before so as not to wake anyone at my departure time of 4:45AM, but as I crept out under the cover of darkness, I felt sad at the goodbyes left undone. I was coming alongside the vehicle, feeling for the handle, when the farmhouse light went on and the side door cracked open. I spun around. Ginger stood under the light in her bathrobe. I dropped my bag in the dirt and ran up the stairs to her, already crying.

"I'm so glad I caught you before you left," she said.

"Me too," I said and pressed her to me. My tears were instantly absorbed in her terry cloth robe.

"God kept me up all night with something to tell you," she said, pulling me away from her and holding me by the shoulders. "He wants me to tell you, *you're not broken anymore, you're whole.*"

Ginger was my Jahaziel. She used the very same words I had heard Saturday night, as I drove away from Kent's studio after the Broken Canvas event. It was as if God wanted me to hear the words again so they would sink in, in just the way he intended. Not broken, but whole.

"You are not your brain injury. You are not the eight years in bed. There is more to your life than trauma," Ginger said emphatically, as if with divine authority. "It's a new day. You are whole. You need to learn how to walk in it."

Therefore, if anyone is in Christ, the new creation has come.
The old has gone, the new is here!
2 Corinthians 5:17

I drove to the airport in silence, North Carolina in my rear view and an expansive future of wholeness before me, and wondered, who would I be without my story of brokenness? What life lay before me?

I dropped myself down into the same airplane seat assignment I'd had on the way to North Carolina. There was no Miss Patty this time. My seat mate had popped on her noise cancelling headphones before I'd even arrived, and papers containing spreadsheets lay spread out before her. There would be no talking on this flight. That was clear. And that was fine.

I got out my computer and made a spreadsheet of my own. I wanted to capture what I had learned in North Carolina before it turned to dust in my mind. I made two columns: *What I Learned About God*, and *What I Leave Knowing*.

What I learned about God was this:

He is present. I felt his Spirit in me, on me, and all around me. I knew if I just opened to this energy field, heaven, the divine, the spirit realm, the fourth dimension, if I would just open my awareness to it, it was palpable. He was palpable and would always be there.

He is faithful. Standing inside Elevation Church after all that had occurred, after all the stunning losses and all the crushing heartbreak, was evidence to me that God brought me through an incredible wilderness not broken and wounded but whole. I had the wilderness at my back, feet rooted on the plane, closer to God than ever before.

A moment from my life with the Landlord flashed across my mind.

"What do you want from life?" I had asked him once, trying to find my way to his heart as he slid like vapor through my hands.

"I want a sense of family," he said. "I want to travel. And to go running or kayaking or biking. Every day."

"What do you want?" he asked in return.

"I want to feel a sense of adventure. I want to be swept away by mystery and awe and wonder. Every day." I said, at the time not really knowing what that meant.

I paused for a moment and looked out of the airplane window. The sun was rising and illuminated the sky in shades of pink from beyond the horizon. The hairs on the back of my neck lifted and stood at attention and I flooded with peace realizing I no longer sent him notes with my mind. I couldn't find him in the air around me anymore and had long stopped looking. But I did wonder if he was running and biking and kayaking every day. I hoped so.

What I learned about God in North Carolina is that he heard me then as much as he hears me now. He wrapped my life in adventure and my desire for mystery, awe, and wonder was completely fulfilled in him. I knew if I lay my life before him and learned to wait on him, he would always be faithful. He would always come.

During the forty years I spent wandering in the wilderness of fifty-cent thinking, I believed God had completely abandoned me and had no interest in my life. Sitting in the airplane seat on my way back to Seattle, it was crystal clear he had been at work all along.

He is at work. God had proven to be the consummate strategist, making moves by meeting me where I was and calling me to himself. He waited until I had given the whole of my life over to Christ, and then he really got to work. Over the last five years he had been working on me at a core level and changed my life from the inside out. I was no longer in the business of proving, defending, striving, yearning, or making compromises. I was a new creation. The old had gone; the new had come.

Contrary to my original thought, I was not leaving North Carolina empty-handed. God had provided me with all the tools I needed to move forward into wholeness by envisioning a new future and following his will.

I advanced to the *What I Leave Knowing* column and wrote the following:

I belong to a global family. I am not alone. I have brothers and sisters in Christ all over the world. That is a real thing.

I have a new identity. It is a new day. I'm pulling from a new core. I don't need to go back to the past anymore. Now is the time to move forward.

I am no longer broken, I am whole. And that's a whole word on its own.

I was at a crossroads and God was asking me to choose. Would I trust him with the whole of my life, or would I still try and fight battles on my own? The first battle he was asking me to fight through a posture of surrender was not the ones that came from without, but the one that came from within. Would I lean into my past or move forward toward my future? Would I have the courage to answer the question, "Who am I outside of my pain?" Or would I let my pain cover the next forty years of my life as it had the last? That's what God was asking of me. He was asking me to forget the past. He was asking me to begin again. The struggle I went through refined who I was, but it was not my destiny. He was asking me to believe his promise that what he has for me is a future and a hope.

The biggest lie I get distracted by is that I was somehow not enough, too much, selfish, or that it's all my fault. It's a lie. It's designed to keep me looking at myself, so I won't look to God, and I won't be available to serve the needs of those around me. It keeps me misidentifying who I am.

I am a servant and a saint.

I am a child of the living God.

I have a new mind that is not hooked by things of the past.

I have a direction and a focus.

I have a mission and a commission.

I have been trained up to possess a character that will not be distracted.

I am a survivor.

I am an overcomer.

I am filled with joy.

I live in the promise of hope.

I am a transformed woman from the core and now there is fire shut up in my bones.

This is what it is to be a Kingdom Fighter, a warrior in the army of the living God. And the defining mark of a Kingdom Fighter is the willingness, and the ability, to leave everything behind.

2 9

HOLDING OUT HOPE

JULY, SEATTLE, 2019

BEING BACK in Seattle was hard. North Carolina had been transformative. In all the ways that mattered, I felt the reality of the promise of God and was a new creation, but I was still surrounded by so much of the old. I was still at my parents' condo. I was still without a job. I still struggled daily with my physicality. I was still in the same city where I could run into my past at any given moment. If energy in motion stays in motion, my life in Seattle was at rest and I felt incapable of bringing movement to life, despite so desperately wanting to move forward. I rearranged the furniture on the deck in an attempt to feel flow. Fresh from the shower, I sat in its new configuration and thought about newness and change, commission and life.

In the shower I had prayed fervently, "Show me, Lord," over and over and over. "Show me what I have to give. Show me where I should live. Show me what step to take. Show me what move to make. Show me, Lord."

When God was actively healing me, my prayer had been,

"God, hold on to me," and my posture had been one of rest and receptivity. I had very little to give and could really only listen and receive. God pulled me to the inner core and held me close and showed me his face like never before.

When he had been training and transforming me, I was pushed to the outer core, one where the flow of molten hot lava burned away all the things that were not serving me anymore. It was painful and necessary and illuminating and humbling as my life churned and tumbled and burned and rumbled. My prayer had been a simple, "Yes, Lord," as I practiced the powerful postures of submission and obedience and learned the weaponry of fighting battles with faith and song.

But I was in a new layer of learning. I knew it. I felt it. A crust had formed. Solid rock was beneath my feet. All I could do was pray, "Show me, Lord," and wait for revelation in a posture of action-preparedness. I was champing at the bit to be released but the gate was still closed.

I thought about the passage in Isaiah 49:2:

"He made my mouth like a sharpened sword, in the shadow of his hand he hid me; he made me into a polished arrow and concealed me in his quiver."

I wondered what target might cause God to pull an arrow named Cor. What target might be mine to strike? And how would I know when it was time?

On a card by my bed I wrote:

Put a hedge around this time in consecration.
Spend time in the presence.
Tend to your body extravagantly.
Prepare yourself for performance.
Whatever God calls you to do, he will need all of you.
He will need everything you have to give.

I looked out over Lake Washington and tucked my legs and

bare feet beneath me. The air still whispered in overtones of Seattle summer, but underneath I smelled the unmistakable scent of fall. There would be a wedding soon. I had been up at Aunt Nancy's earlier in the evening celebrating Jax and his fiancé. They talked about walking through a time of action-preparedness; for merging, for marriage, and the taking on of new names.

Changing a name is a profound outward and inward statement of identity. It says the old had gone; the new has come, and puts the world on notice that there has been a shift. Biblically, before God sent someone out on commission, he often changed their name. Their new name carried both the seed of their future commission and the fulfillment of God's vision.

In the Old Testament, in Genesis 17:5, God changed Abram's name to Abraham. The meaning of his name went from "high father" (Abram) to "father of a multitude" (Abraham). Simultaneously, God changed Abraham's wife's name from Sarai to Sarah. The meaning of her name went from "my princess" (Sarai) to "mother of nations" (Sarah). He didn't change their names drastically, but the meaning of their names changed entirely. And it came to pass that the physical descendants of Abraham and Sarah went on to form many nations, and was the bloodline from which Jesus descended.

In the New Testament, Jesus, when he first called Peter as a disciple, changed his name from Simon to Peter; from "God has heard" to "rock," and said, "On this rock I will build my church." When Jesus asked all of the disciples, "Who do you say I am?" it was Peter who answered, "You are the Christ, the Son of the living God."

And on that Rock of truth the church was formed.

My full name is Cordila. It was made up by my parents and is wholly unique. Although it is unique, it contains both French and Irish origins and means both "heart of the lion" and "jewel of the sea." In this way, it tells me the intention spoken over my life by my parents was that I would be bold and courageous like a lion but willing to mine the depths of the sea and called to sustain intense pressure. My name is beautiful in principal, but in practice, most people call me Cor, which in Latin means "heart." It is the core of my name that contains the seed of my commission. I am to be a home for the heart of God.

Having God infused into the core of my being is what makes me whole, yet it cannot end there. I cannot simply live in wholeness. Wholeness is a state of being. Commission contains a bias for action. God at my core is my identity. Pulling from the core releases my calling.

In the shower I had encountered my tattoo, as I did every time I was stripped naked. When God commissioned Joshua to lead the Israelites into the Promised Land, he did so by leading them right through the Jordan River. When the feet of those carrying the Arc of the Covenant given to Moses touched the water's edge, the water parted and stood up in a heap until the entire nation of Israel crossed the Jordan on dry ground. To mark this astonishing miracle and make sure the descendants of Israel would never forget what God had done for them, Joshua called together twelve men, one from each tribe, and told them to return to the middle of the Jordan, pick up a stone, and place in on the banks of the Jordan as a monument to what God had done. Then, and only then, did the waters cover the riverbed once again.

My tattoo was a monument to what God had done in my life. That was the intention when I got it. But in the same way the mark had settled into my skin, its meaning had settled over my life and I saw it a bit differently. It is a monument to what God had done, but it is also a reminder of what he's asking me to become:

A home for the heart of God.
A conduit for connection; a lumen for light.

To take on this new identity would mean to become a woman rooted so deeply in God that everything about me would display his heart. To fulfill my destiny would mean to become an opening so wide that who I am would disappear, and who God is would consume me fully, and everyone around me would be bathed in his light. This is the promise of God in a new identity: that we are both whole and holy; refined in darkness and filled with light.

The sun dropped behind the Olympic Mountains and although the source of light was hidden, the sky was still bright. The purpose of life, I realized, wasn't to find hope for myself, but to hold hope out to others; to be someone holding out hope for those who need it, for a humanity that's hurting, for a world that lives in darkness to be a source of light.

In the heat of that North Carolina night, walking away from Kent's studio, I answered, "Yes," when I heard the question, *"Are you willing to burn it all down?"* At the very same time, in the very same whisper, God also said, *"It's time to build."*

Since then, there has been an undeniable, and ever-increasing, prompting in my heart that's said, *"Tell this story. Talk about this journey. I cannot do this without you. Not with the gifts I put in you."*

I think about my friend and former co-worker, Miten, who talks about working with me again, wistfully. Decidedly. Purposefully. To him I am a non-negotiable. To God I am a non-negotiable, too.

There are moments when believing in God is comforting. It feels good. Encouraging. Solid. Safe. In other moments, it feels astonishing. The whisper of his still, small voice pulls me into an adventure that feels beyond me and yet, inside me. When we say yes to a life in Christ, we are led moment-to-moment by the Holy Spirit. We are whispered to by the God of the universe. We are pulled into an intimate relationship in another dimension and, truthfully, that can feel overwhelming, and a little strange, and sometimes scares me to death. I wonder if this is what it means to fear the Lord.

When Joshua and the Israelites crossed the Jordan into the Promised Land after forty years in the wilderness - forty years of wandering, just like me - and stepped forward into their new future, three times the Lord said to Joshua:

Be strong and courageous.

Be strong and courageous.

Be strong and courageous.

I look out over the water as the remnants of the day's light slowly erases definition from the contours of my face. Tears of awe and wonder and fear and mystery stream quietly down my cheeks. That is what's required for this journey of faith. Strength and courage. As I step out into the unknown, I pray I'll have enough of both, knowing wherever God leads me, I will go.

A NOTE FROM THE AUTHOR

September, Seattle, 2019

I awake at 2 AM because the ground is shifting. Seattle is in the throes of a magnitude 4.6 earthquake, but I lay quietly, unafraid. I watch as Kent's paintings shift on the walls, sliding on the wire and nails that hold them into place. I listen to the sheetrock groan as it's rigidity aches against the force of flexibility. I feel the sturdiness of the ground beneath me, knowing that at any moment it could open up and swallow me into a fissure I didn't see coming. It reminds me that life is at once fragile and fierce and through it all, I am in God's hand. I am from Middle-earth, a woman who has burned like molten hot lava, formless and soundless and screaming. I have been to the core and know that God is at the very center, made of iron, impenetrable, but proven to exist. I know that from this core my life will flow and eventually become the hardened, firm earth upon which I stand. And I know, at any moment, God can draw me closer to him and into the fire once more. I lean into his prerogative, knowing that through fire there will be rebirth. This is the cycle of a life in Christ, one of healing and transformation. In this I find my hope.

Two years ago I accepted the Assignment to write this book *and then* God broke me down to finish the work. I thought I was going to roll up to the Assignment and write what I already knew. That wasn't the plan.

I fell out of a window when I was seven years old and it changed my life. Forty years later I was met and reclaimed by God and my life changed again. When I thought I was fifty cents on the dollar, God revealed to me my identity and his grace changed the game. And for a very long time I was more evidence of his grace than of a life made new, but it was absolutely essential that God reach all the way down to the broken level and remake me from the core. Only then could I live whole.

I don't know what caused you to read this book, or what happened to you, or what damage occurred in your life to make you believe you were fifty cents on the dollar, but if no one has ever told you that you are a Full Dollar, that ends now.

You are a Full Dollar.

You are a child of God.

There is a better word spoken over you and over your life.

God is willing, and able, to make you whole.

The challenge for every human being on the planet is to be at peace with who God created us to be. God gives us our identity. He gives it to us. He makes us who we are. He calls us into being before we were knit together in our mother's wombs, and all of what he puts inside us, and the circumstances he allows us to experience, are in order for us to fully express the purpose for which we've been created. And we don't get to know what that is until we know God well enough that we are willing to let go of the control over our lives and trust him to take over.

I don't wonder if God will lay out a path of hope before you because this truth I know: *even in your darkest hour, you will have hope.* Grab hold. Hold tight. God can and will do work in your life that will leave you fully transformed. He will drill down to the very heart of you and will rebuild you from the core. The only path forward is to lean into the understanding that Jesus can resurrect a life. He does it all the time. He did it for me. And he can do it for you. But will you let him do it?

Giving your life over to Christ and allowing for transformation isn't an easy process. It most definitely is not. But it is filled with access to grace the likes of which I have never known. God will hold and cover you in the process. I know this because he held and covered me.

On Rattlesnake Ledge, in the blink of an eye, God told me I was beautiful, not only so that I would know I am beautiful to him, but so you might know that you are beautiful to him, too.

This book is about identity. It's about being radically introduced to God and letting him radically introduce himself to you, so you remember who you are. It's about walking through God's restoration framework for healing and transformation, and all of the pain and all of the heartache and all of the unbelievable freedom that comes from shedding the old and embracing the crazy reality that you are new. You are new. *You are new.* Once we take that into our core, all that's left for us to do is move forward.

When Ottavia and I first met, she was going through a very hard transition in life and I was just starting this book. We met at the Starbucks Roastery and I gave her a flip calendar of quotes from the healing box. Over dinner and drinks, just one year later, she asked me something. "Cor," she said, "when I packed up my old house to move into my new house with my new husband, I packed up your flip calendar, too. Every day for a solid year I have looked at that calendar by my bedside. With each page I turned, a new saying met me right where I was, and invited me to go a layer deeper in my healing. When I packed up the calendar, I made sure to pack it on the last page it was open to, so I could pick up right where I left off. But when I unpacked the calendar on the other side, it flipped to the last page, and that page is blank and it sits that way to this day. That calendar got me through my healing journey and to where I am now, but when I look at that blank page, I ask myself..."

She smiled mischievously and I knew exactly where she was going. We raised our glasses together. The clink of the rims and the resonance of our laughter made an incredibly delightful sound as in unison we shouted, "What's next?!"

So I will ask you the very same thing Ottavia asked me as I come to the end of this journey myself: *Now that you know you're a Full Dollar, what's next?*

In two days, I celebrate my 47th birthday. It will mark the end of forty years in the wilderness of fifty-cent thinking and the beginning of a new life where I have never felt more alive. This is the promise of life in Christ. He brings dead bones to life. With this book I leave my past behind me. To the outside eye my situation has not changed, and yet everything is different because I am. I'm not writing esoteric thoughts about the concept of hope, I am sitting in it. The only thing I have going for me is my wholeness. There is nothing in me but Christ and that is more than enough because in him I have life.

"Be with me, Lord."

It is a new prayer I've been praying and I invite you to pray it with me. It is a prayer of action. It is a prayer of resolution. It is the mark of moving forward.

This is your chance to rebuild on a solid foundation. Don't waste another second weeping over the past. Not now. Not this time. You are standing at the edge where faith takes flight. It's time to decide, *now*, what will you do?

ACKNOWLEDGMENTS

Writing acknowledgements for a memoir that spans forty years of one's life is no easy task. I stand as an amalgamation of a million investments made by individuals who infused me with buoyancy and optimism and faith and love, sometimes only in passing. This list of acknowledgements is by no means an exhaustive list of thanks, not even close.

I want to acknowledge my parents, who have traveled this road with me. If I eagerly await the promise of God to restore the years the locusts have eaten, it is also for them. And if I emerged as a warrior, it is because they provided a cave in which I could heal. At a very base level, they provided food, shelter, clothing - a gift that many people who have fallen on difficult times, or have suffered chronic illness that threatened their ability to provide livelihood for themselves - have not had. Not a day goes by where I am not thankful for this gift of provision, from their hand, and heart, and God's.

Writing this book has not been a solo experience, but rather I've surfed the mosh pit of humanity, moved along by one hundred arms. As I sat typing this section at my local Starbucks, Ben, one of my favorite baristas, came over to lay hands on this project and my heart. "I'm so proud of you," he said. And just like that, released tears. Starbucks, you are awesome. As a company and a community you have been so much more than my Third Place. You have been my incubator, keeping me warm, inspired, nurtured, lifted, and laughing (and caffeinated!) through it all. It is impossible to name all of you but, off the top, thanks goes to Andrew, Jessie, Josh, Max, Courtney, Kenny, Yuri, Bear, Sara, and so many more.

I have also been on the recipient end of many first responder calls over the course of my lifetime and each time have been met with compassion and grace. Thank you specifically to 911 dispatchers, NYFD and paramedics, LAFD and paramedics, and Seattle FD and paramedics. In that same vein, huge thanks to Overlake Hospital and ER staff as well as Swedish Ballard ER. To Karen, Julie, Julie, Erin and all of the nurses at Swedish Oncology Infusion Center, you are life. You healed me, body and soul, and for as long as life stretches out before me, you will never be forgotten. And to Dr. Adam Nadelson, founder of The IV Doc. Your service loosed me to be able to fly again, and for that I am incredibly grateful.

We live in an extraordinary time when, through technology, we have access to some of the most influential pastors and spiritual thought leaders of our time. My faith was seeded, stoked, and fanned to flame because of their obedience to the calling on their lives. I not only want to thank them here, but also provide a list of specific sermons that moved my faith along. So often leaders give out of themselves without knowing what seeds took root. These are only a few of the messages that burrowed deep into the fecund soil of my soul and mind:

Pastor Erwin McManus: *Artisan Soul: Who Told You You Were Naked; Baptism of Identity*

Pastor Kim McManus: *Finding God In The Deep*

Pastor Steven Furtick: *Complete The Cross; When The Battle Chooses You*

Pastor Mike Todd: *Marked*

Pastor John Gray: *The End Zone; The Favor Factor*

Pastor Sarah Jakes Roberts: *Wild Woman*

Pastor Jabin Chavez: *What To Do In A Valley*

Bishop TD Jakes: *Night of Expansion Part I, Part II; Reel It In; Don't Settle Part I, Part II, Part III*

I also want to extend a thank you to Sunny Nassim for all the legal guidance and support of both my business(es) and personhood. You are a gift of a friend. To Nidhi Berry, my "publishing sherpa." You instigated this book and it's direction in so many ways. To Selina Petosa, for the gift of the title of this book and for encouraging me to "get the core out." To Tim Barber, half cover designer, half soul excavator. To Sommer and Koreen, and several others for reading the raw and providing detailed feedback. And to all those mentioned in the book by name, for the investment you made in my heart and life.

And to Christ, my Rock and my Redeemer, for claiming me, restoring me, and guiding me back home.

ABOUT THE AUTHOR

Cordila Jochim leads and inspires as an author, motivational speaker, and brand and business strategist. Ignited by those who are hungry for more, Cor's growth agency, CORHOUSE, drives businesses, entrepreneurs, companies, and movements through seasons of inspired and epic growth.

Cor lives in Seattle, Washington, but, as a woman resurrected, she can often be found in her Jeep on adventures on the wide-open road.

Keynote clip from Washington State Governor Jay Inslee and Results Washington's annual *Governor's Conference* available at: cordilajochim.com/about

Cor would love to hear from you! Connect with her directly through: corhouse.com or cordilajochim.com. Or through social media below.

       facebook.com/cordilajochim
       instagram.com/cordila

Made in the USA
Middletown, DE
26 January 2020

83672500R00196